Ernest Mandel

The Meaning of the
Second World War

VERSO

The Imprint of New Left Books

British Library
Cataloguing in Publication Data
Mandel, Ernest
  The meaning of the Second World War.
  1. World War, 1939–1945
  I. Title
  940.53   D743

First published 1986
© Ernest Mandel 1986

Verso 6 Meard Street London W1

Typeset in Imprint by
PRG Graphics Ltd, Surrey

Printed by The Thetford Press
Thetford, Norfolk

ISBN 0 86091 130 6
ISBN 0 86091 842 4 Paperback

Contents

To the memory of all those who gave their lives fighting against fascism and imperialism – in the first place all those who fell in order to transform that fight into the victory of world revolution:

Abram Leon;

León Lesoil;

Marcel Hic;

Hendrik Sneevliet;

Victor Widelin;

Pantelis Pouliopoulos;

Blasco;

Tha-Thu-Tau;

Cher Dou-siou;

Tan Malakka;

and above all to the heroic unknown editors of *Czorwony Sztandard,* who published their Trotskyist underground paper in the Warsaw Ghetto until the last days of the uprising in which they actively participated.

Part One

The Historical Framework

1.

The Stakes

Capitalism implies competition. With the emergence of large corporations and cartels – i.e. the advent of monopoly capitalism – this competition assumed a new dimension. It became qualitatively more politico-economic, and therefore military-economic. What was at stake was no longer the fate of businesses representing some tens of thousands of pounds or hundreds of thousand of dollars. At stake now were industrial and financial giants whose assets ran into tens and hundreds of millions. Accordingly, states and their armies involved themselves more and more directly in that competition – which became imperialist rivalry for outlets for investment in new markets, for access to cheap or rare raw materials. The destructiveness of such competition became increasingly pronounced, amidst a growing trend towards militarization and its ideological reflection: the justification and glorification of war. On the other hand, the development of manufacturing, the growth in productive capacity of the technically most advanced firms, the total output of the main industrial powers, and especially the expansion of finance capital and investment potential, increasingly spilled across the boundaries of nation-states, even the largest ones. This spread of individual national capital outwards inevitably led to breakneck competition for external resources, markets and control of trade-routes, within Europe but also – and most spectacularly – outside the continent: between 1876 and 1914 European powers managed to annex some eleven million square miles of territory, mainly in Asia and Africa.

Yet the creation of colonial empires following the international thrust of capital proved to be only a temporary answer to the problem of the growing disproportion between development of the productive forces and the political form within which this development had taken place: the nation-state.[1] Given the poverty and low growth rates of the colonies, their demand for manufactured goods was inherently limited; they were hardly a substitute for the lucrative markets to be found in the industrial countries themselves, whose systematic closure – via the high tariffs on imported goods and capital increasingly imposed by the end of the nineteenth century – accelerated the colonial drive. At the same time the fact that the world had become divided relatively early on, to the especial advantage of the Western rim of the European continent, meant that later industrial powers (USA, Germany, Russia, Japan) had little space to expand overseas. Their prodigious development issued in a powerful challenge to the existing territorial arrangements. It upset the concomitant balance of political and economic power. The growing conflict between the burgeoning productive forces and the prevailing political structures could less and less be contained by conventional diplomacy or local military skirmishes. The power coalitions which this conflict fostered merely exacerbated it, ensuring that it would reach exploding-point. The explosion occurred with the First World War.[1]

It is not surprising that the first move in questioning the status quo should have been made by Germany, which had assumed the industrial leadership of Europe and hence was in a position to challenge a colonial share-out favourable to Britain and France by force of arms. The prospect of the continent's unification under German domination, with all its implications for the future of the colonies and other dependent states, was a matter of concern not only to those most immediately affected, like Britain, France or Russia, but also for the non-European powers: Japan and the United States. In the event, US intervention on the side of the Entente proved decisive in the defeat of Germany.

Yet World War One in no way 'solved' the growing contradiction between economy and politics within the capitalist world. True, Germany was defeated, but not so decisively as to eliminate her from the race for world leadership. And the war had opened the door for a new arrival: socialist revolution. The victory and consolidation of Bolshevik power in Russia; the revolutionary ferment leading to the appearance of Soviet power in the other defeated countries and Italy; the generalized revulsion against the war which produced a massive shift to the left in the victor countries themselves at its close – these changed the whole meaning of international warfare for the bourgeoisie. From the outset the new arrangement between victors and vanquished was overshadowed by the desire of the ruling classes to prevent the spread of revolution, especially to Germany. American, British and even French imperialists did not dare completely to disarm their German competitors, lest the German working class take power. Indeed, between November 1918 and October 1923, the *Reichswehr* was the only real force defending the weakened capitalist order in Germany. The contradiction of Versailles was that the victors wanted to weaken German capitalism without really disarming it and while keeping its industrial power intact. This made its military comeback inevitable.

The point has been made many times that the Second World War was a logical and inevitable outcome of World War One. But the link between the two is commonly reduced to the anti-German clauses of the Versailles Treaty, and especially the foolish policy of reparations on which the French bourgeoisie was particularly insistent. In truth, although the terms of the peace settlement certainly helped to exacerbate the political, military and above all economic conflicts that dominated the twenties and thirties and paved the way to WWII, they did not *create* these problems – any more than 'reckless' planning by the Austrian, Russian, German or French general staffs caused WWI.

In this respect it is instructive to look beyond strictly European politics to the peculiar relationship developing between China, Japan and the USA, which would eventually lead to the Pacific War. In 1900 Japan and the USA collaborated in the suppression of the Boxer Rebellion in China. In 1905 the Russo-Japanese peace treaty was signed under US auspices. In the First World War Japan intervened as an ally of the United States and the other two powers with economic interests in the Far East: Britain and France. She was not badly treated by the Paris Peace Conference nor by the Washington Naval Agreement of 1922. Hence the fact that Japanese foreign policy gradually embarked upon a course of violent agression hardly different from that of German imperialism cannot be explained by any 'humiliation' imposed on her by her future enemies. On the contrary, the target of the Japanese war drive was China, the most populous country in the world. Japan's occupation of Manchuria in 1931, and the all-out war it unleashed against China in 1937, made armed conflict with the USA inevit-

able, since the latter was resolved at all costs to prevent the transformation of China into a Japanese colony or dependency. At a
deeper level, the American-Japanese conflict was fuelled by the
grave economic crisis of 1929-32 in both countries. It flowed from
the perception that a long-term solution involved a decisive break
with economic isolationism (a shift from growth centered on the
home market), and hence the need to achieve for oneself (or deny
others) strategic insertion in the world market via hegemony over a
substantial part of the world, as a necessary step on the path to
world dominance.[2]

So the second act of the imperialist drama unfolded according to
the inner logic of the world capitalist system. Once again the stake
was the international hegemony of one imperialist power, to be
won and maintained by an active combination of military conquest
or pressure and economic domination or plunder – the exact mix
depending on the relative strength or weakness of the individual
contestants, deriving from such inner constraints as the level of
economic development and the character of political institutions.
On the eve of the Second World War these powers were the USA,
Germany, Japan and Britain, with France and Italy playing the
role of secondary allies, lacking the strength to be real contenders.

It might be objected that the above characterization of the stakes
of WWII is too sweeping and does not correspond to the real course
of events, which reveal much more limited ambitions on the part of
the warring powers; that one ought to distinguish more sharply
between causes and effects, and differentiate the aggressors from
those states which entered the war in self-defence. Was not the
Second World War simply a concatenation of regional conflicts
whose origin lay in the peculiarities of German and Japanese
politics, inducing a rupture in what otherwise would have been a
peaceful evolution of the world economy towards what Kautsky
had termed 'ultra-imperialism'? In this view, Japan's drive was
limited to the creation of an East-Asian and Pacific zone of
influence and German expansionism to parts of Europe, North
Africa and the Middle East. The British bourgeoisie's desire to
retain its imperial possessions can then be cleared of responsibility
for Japanese or German militarism, and US goals vis-a-vis Asia
and Africa, not to speak of Europe, can be seen as more modest and
benign in essence than the policy of armed conquest sprouted by
German and Japanese fascism.

However, this objection misunderstands the role which inter-
imperialist wars have played in the internationalization of the

capitalist economy and reduces them to the pursuit of – or a reaction to – violent conquest. But the most violent and murderous cases of imperialist aggression are expressions of relative weakness rather than strength. The imperialist conquest of the world is not only, or even mainly, a drive to occupy huge territories permanently with millions of soldiers. On the contrary, the motor of the Second World War was the major capitalist states' need to dominate the economy of whole continents through capital investment, preferential trade agreements, currency regulations and political hegemony. The aim of the war was the subordination not only of the less developed world, but also of other industrial states, whether enemies or allies, to one hegemonic power's priorities of capital accumulation. In this perspective US domination of the countries of Latin America, achieved largely by economic warfare and with relatively marginal military involvement, was not a feasible paradigm for establishing world rule – any more than Tojo's or Hitler's military machines were sufficient in themselves for that purpose. For the USA, an economic power par excellence, this meant building up a powerful navy and forcing Britain soon after the end of the First World War to accept parity on the seas – just as Japan would insist on parity with Britain and USA and thereby torpedo the Washington agreement a decade and a half later. World hegemony, in other words, can be exercised only through a *combination* of military strength and economic superiority. Naturally, it cannot be known what precise combination Germany or Japan would have adopted in the event of ultimate victory; but it would certainly have been some such combination rather than a reliance on sheer brute force. In occupied Europe even the Nazis knew how to deal quite differently with, for instance, the French, Belgian, Dutch or Danish bourgeoisies from the way they treated the Jewish people or the people of Poland or the Soviet Union, exceptional circumstances of the unfolding war notwithstanding.[3]

Equally, there is not the slightest proof of any limitation on the war aims of Japan, Germany or the USA, the real challengers of the status quo in the Second World War. Very early on the Tanaka Memorandum established that for the Japanese army, the conquest of China was only a stepping-stone to the conquest of world hegemony, which would be achieved after crushing US resistance.[4] Indeed, Japan's alliance with Germany could be only temporary, and remained fragile and ineffectual throught the war, for it was seen as a provisional truce with a future enemy.[5] Hitler's understanding of the meaning of the coming war was equally clear: 'The struggle for hegemony in the world will be decided for Europe by possession of the Russian space. Any idea of world politics is ridiculous (for Germany) as long as it does not dominate the continent . . . If we are masters of Europe, then we shall have the dominant position in the world. If the (British) Empire were to collapse today through our arms, we would not be its heirs, since Russia would take India, Japan East Asia and America Canada.'[6]

American imperialism was also conscious of its 'destiny' to become the world leader. 'The decision he (Roosevelt) made in 1940, on his own authority and without clarion calls, involved the commitment of the United States to the assumption of responsibility for nothing less than the leadership of the world.'[7] The breakdown of the world economy in the late 1920s, to which the United States had itself generously contributed, and the creation of exclusive trading blocs (the largest of which centered on the British sterling area) imperilled not only America's markets but also its supply of raw materials. For the United States the war was to be the lever which would open the whole of the world market and world resources to American exploitation.[8] Cordell Hull, the US Secretary of State, put it quite bluntly in 1942: 'Leadership towards a new system of international relationships in trade and other economic affairs will devolve largely upon the United States because of our great economic strength. We should assume this leadership, and the responsibility that goes with it, primarily for reasons of pure national self-interest.'[9]

As for British imperialism, even if it indeed had already chewed off more than it could digest, it by no means ceased jockeying for more positions. Its intervention in East Africa, mopping up of the Italian colonial empire, liquidation of the French enclaves in the Near East, heavy hand laid upon Iran, preparation of a Balkan invasion with the evident purpose of making Greece a stepping stone for the creation of British client states in Eastern Europe replacing the French satellites which had emerged in 1918, various attempts at power politics in Latin America (such as the backstairs encouragement given to Peron against US imperialism)—indicate that the dream of hegemony was still being dreamt in the City too, albeit under conditions where the disproportion between end and means became increasingly pathetic.

In the era of imperialism, even a quest for regional zones of influence presupposes a readiness to fight on a world scale. The logic of this emerges in the military directives and decisions of the

Second World War's opening stages. Already in November 1940, Hitler's Directive No.18 mentions the need to capture the Canary and Cape Verde islands, the Azores and West Africa, because of their strategic importance vis-a-vis the USA. Iraq and Iran were mentioned as further goals of the Caucasion operations, and Directive No.24 of 5 March 1941 extends German war plans as far as Australia.[10] Echoing these concerns, Iceland, the Azores, the Cape Verde Islands and the port of Dakar were all seen by US strategists as necessary for the reconquest of Europe and a line of defence to be held against possible German attack.[11] Roosevelt was convinced in 1940 that 'if Britain fell, a disastrous war for the United States would be inevitable, (for) Germany would attack the Western hemisphere, probably at first in Latin America, as soon as she assembled a sufficient naval force and transport and cargo fleet (not too long a process with all the shipbuilding facilities of Europe at Germany's disposal) and Japan would go on the rampage in the Pacific.'[12]

To be sure, geographical constraints and military requirements partially dictated these lines of expansion.[13] But underlying these constraints and considerations was the inner logic of imperialism, which can be seen quite clearly in the planning councils of the warring states. Oil, rubber, copper, nickel, tin, manganese, iron ore, cotton, etc. had to be secured; sea-lanes had to be kept open to ship these home; workers and forced labour had to be mobilized, housed and fed; exports had to be expanded and foisted upon reluctant clients; foreign competitors had to be dragooned into partnerships or simply absorbed; opponents' exports had to be cut and their populations starved. The war indeed showed itself to be nothing but the continuation of politics by other means.[14]

But if the meaning of the Second World War, like that of its predecessor, can be grasped only in the context of the imperialist drive for world domination, its significance lies in the fact that it was the ultimate test of the relative strength of the competing imperialist states. Its outcome determined the particular pattern of the world accumulation of capital for a whole period. In the world organised by capital based on nation-states, war is *the* mechanism for the final resolution of differences. For although military power is not the only kind of pressure which a capitalist state can bring to bear upon its rivals, nevertheless it is the highest form of power: the potential or actual use of armed might to impose its will is the decisive proof of an imperialist state's superiority. Therefore, what we are dealing with here is the capacity of each of the belligerents to use military force in a sustained way and more successfully than its opponents, which in turn depends on the ability of each state to mobilize all necessary resources, human as well as material, for victory. Consequently, wars on this scale are the supreme test of the solidity of the social order and its economic health, as they are of the political stamina of the ruling classes and their leaderships.

So far as the latter are concerned, the central issue is the ability of the bourgeoisie to reign in its own back yard, above all over its native working class. In the final analysis, imperialist expansion expresses an insatiable thirst for surplus value, its production and realization – the snowball dynamic of capital accumulation. But qualitatively increased surplus-value production is possible only through a specific relationship with wage labour, a subordination of the working class to capital. Hence a strategic integration of the working class in the metropolitan centres is a necessary component of the imperialist countries' ability to pursue the struggle for world dominance. The world that emerged from the 1914-1918 war was at least partially shaped by the unprecendented rise in working-class self-organization and self-confidence, especially in Europe but also in the USA, during the quarter century that preceded it. The attitude of the working class to imperialist wars was therefore of importance not only to the ruling classes, but also to the future of the working class itself. The historic debate which took place among the parties of the Second International between 1907 and 1917 – a debate which started before the war (though at a time when the warring alliances were already in place) and continued right through it – linked the question of the forthcoming war to a wider discussion on whether the workers' organizations should be instruments of reform of the bourgeois order or its grave-diggers. [15] When the war started, and after initial nationalist euphoria had evaporated amidst hunger, death and destruction, the social truce broke under its impact right across the continent.

Mutinies in the French, German, Austrian and Russian armies; hunger marches and strikes in factories; the overthrow of Tsarism in Russia; the dissolution of Austria-Hungary; the overthrow of the Ottoman sultanate; the abdication of the German Kaiser; the advent of revolution in the cities of Central, East and Southeastern Europe; and finally the success of the Bolshevik-led revolution in Russia – these represent the many varied attempts by the exploited populations of this part of Europe and Asia to find alternative solutions to captalism's intensifying structural crisis and to the war-prone anarchy of the international order established by the bourgeoisie. The abdication of the Second International majority before the *raison d'état* of the national ruling classes in 1914 found its response in the organization of the minority into a Third International and in the formation of Communist parties throughout the world to challenge the discredited social-democratic formations.

Labour's resistance to the hegemonic drive of the bourgeoisie, and the young Soviet republic, which survived despite the concentrated efforts of the imperialist powers to destroy it, constituted formidable obstacles to the pursuit of imperialist designs, especially for European capital. Both had to be, if not eliminated, then at least neutralized before any imperialist power could seriously contemplate starting another international war. The history of the preparation and unleashing of WWII is, therefore, not just the history of an increasingly explosive differentiation of sectional (national) interests of the world bourgeoisie, but also of its sustained and more or less successful efforts to remove these obstacles. In other words, it is also a history of counter-revolution. By 1939 the record of this counter-revolutionary consolidation was promising but uneven. The fate and evolution of the Soviet Union was particularly crucial. The revolutionary upheavals following WWI had been strong enough to prevent the restoration of capitalism in erstwhile Imperial Russia. But the fact that they produced no new victories gravely weakened the Soviet working class: the Soviet republic had survived, but in a greatly distorted form. This in turn contributed to the impotence of the European working class in the inter-war period. A downturn of revolution gave the green light for a new onslaught against the labour movement as soon as the crisis demanded this. The stepping-stones towards World War Two were Chiang Kai-Shek's massacre of Communist and other labour militants in Shanghai in 1927; the rise of fascism in Italy and Germany in the 1920s and 1930s; the defeat of the Spanish republic; the collapse of the Popular Front in France. The failure of the British General Strike and the stranglehold imposed by the CIO bureaucracy upon the rising militancy of the American working class likewise played far from marginal roles in preparing the new conflict.

The assertion here that the real stake of WWII was the establishment of the world hegemony of one imperialist power, and that the war was also the culmination of a process of counter-revolution, should not, of course, be taken to refer solely to the particularly abhorrent role played by Hitler and German Nazism in bringing about a new world war. On the contrary, it represents a general judgement upon imperialism, as a specific form of capitalism generated by the fundamental contradiction between the internationalization and socialization of the productive process, on the one hand, and its continued organization by private and national interests, on the other. Those revolutionary Marxists, beginning with Trotsky, who clearly understood this and said so repeatedly from the early 1930s on, showed more foresight than those who waited for the Cold War and the Korean conflict to rediscover the structurally barbaric nature of imperialism *as a system*, not limited to any particular political form of the bourgeois state or any particular national ruling class.

In addition, because ever since the mid-nineteenth century wars between great powers have led to revolution or at least drastic reform on the losing side, the ruling class of the imperialist states, individually and collectively, of necessity also learned to manage counterrevolution. Here the historic turning-point was 1914. The abdication of large parts of the labour movement's leading strata, and of key sectors of the liberal intelligentsia, in the face of colonialism, imperialism and war signified an acceptance of violence, mass slaughter, nationalism and racism, as well as the restriction of civil and working-class rights (i.e. an acceptance of the impermanence of the civilizational gains of many generations) for reasons of *Realpolitik* dictated by national bourgeoisies.

Those who refused to pay any possible price for overthrowing the bourgeois order in 1918-23 and then again in 1932-37, and accepted the very real and horrible price of imperialism and war, [16] bear the historic responsibility for allowing a second attempt at an imperialist solution to the world crisis of capitalism – this time, at a price far greater in human life and suffering than that paid in 1914-18. Nobody who soberly examines the history of 1918-45 can seriously question the conclusion that Nazism and World War Two were the price which humanity paid for what even Léon Blum called the refusal, or failure, of German Social Democracy to overthrow the bourgeois order in November-December 1918. [22] Stalin and his followers share this responsibility, because of the contribution of their policy to the establishment of the Nazi regime in Germany, the defeat of the Spanish revolution and the strengthening of bourgeois rule in France.

The 1914 war opened with a shot fired by a Bosnian youth at a future Emperor of Austria, seen as personifying national oppression and social injustice. It closed with an unsuccessful intervention by Western liberal states on the side of counterrevolution in the civil war in Russia. This was no mere accident: the two events symbolized the close relationship between imperialist wars and wars of national liberation and revolution. The issue of national self-determination was forced onto the agenda at Versailles by revolutionary Russia; unlike Wilson and Clemenceau, who limited this right to the peoples of Eastern Europe and the Balkans, the Soviet Union under Lenin extended its support to the emergent national liberation movements in colonial and semi-colonial countries (it should be recalled that the Amritsar massacre and the emergence of the May 4 Movement in China occurred during the peace deliberations at Versailles). As the centre of world politics shifted away from Europe, the anti-colonial struggles in turn became crucial allies of the proletariat in the advanced capitalist countries.

2.

The Immediate Causes

If imperialist expansion and its contradictions were the under-lying historical causes of World War II, it was a specific imperialist power – Germany – and a specific sector of the German ruling class, those groups most directly tied to arms production and most responsible for assisting Hitler in the creation of the Third Reich, which deliberately set off that war.

As early as 1931, Trotsky had predicted: if Hitler takes power, he will unleash a war against the Soviet Union.[1] With hindsight, the British historian Trevor-Roper wrote in 1964: 'In order to realise his ultimate aim, the restoration and extension of the lost German empire in the East, Hitler had always recognised that diplomacy could not be enough. Ultimately there must be war: war against Russia'.[2]

A large mass of historical evidence confirms that judgement. Practically from the moment of becoming Chancellor, Hitler started to rearm Germany. From the beginning, his programme had a double objective: to make possible the immediate pump-priming of a crisis-ridden German industry, under conditions of a sharp upward push of profits (both of the mass of profit and of the rate of profit); and to prepare at some point in the future – not later than within ten years – an onslaught against the Soviet Union, in order to conquer for German imperialism in Eastern Europe the equivalent of Britain's Indian empire.

The *Lebensraum* in question was by and large already mapped out by the Brest-Litovsk Treaty and the general annexationist trends of radical German imperialists and big business interests at the time of World War One. The greater knowledge which the German bourgeoisie had acquired since then about Russia's natural resources, and the very progress of industrialization of the USSR, could only make these objectives both broader and more tantalising. Of course, a war of imperialist conquest and plunder against the USSR did not automatically imply a full-scale European war, let alone a world war, at least not from the point of view of the particular economic logic of German imperialism, or even within the framework of the particular political logic of the Nazis. The latter would certainly have preferred to maintain their various adversaries divided, and knock them out or neutralise them one by one. To coax Czechoslovakia and Poland into becoming reluctant allies of the Hungarian type in a war against Russia, would have been less costly for German imperialism than to have to subdue them militarily first. But that was only possible if important changes of bourgeois leading personnel occurred in these countries, and if they ceased to be client states of French (and to a lesser extent British) imperialism. This in turn was possible only through the consent or passive resignation of Paris or London to German hegemony on the continent.

Hitler tried to achieve that objective step by step between 1935 and 1939, through a pragmatic combination of threats and enticements, of blackmail and military pressure. These manoeuvres scored a series of successes between 1934 and 1938 (remilitarisation of the Rhineland, *Anschluss* with Austria, annexation of the Sudetenland). But their failure was ensured once the German army occupied Prague in March 1939. From that point onwards British imperialism (taking a reluctant French ally into tow) was determined to resist by force any further German expansion in Eastern Europe. Hitler knew this. But he did not want to forego the advance in modern weapons he still enjoyed for a couple of years. He deliberately risked war with Britain by attacking Poland on 1 September 1939. From 3 September 1939 onwards, he found himself at war with Britain and France, as a result of that conscious decision.

There was a half-hearted attempt to end the war after the conquest of Poland – in exchange for a recognition by London of the international status quo as it existed at that point in time, – i.e. without the restoration of Polish or Czechoslovak independence.

Stalin gave diplomatic support to that manoeuvre. But Hitler knew that he had little chance of getting Britain to accept such a political capitulation.

British imperialism was committed to the long-term objective of preventing a hostile power from completely dominating the continent of Europe, because it understood – and correctly so from the point of view of its own interests – that such a domination would only be an interlude before an all-out onslaught by German imperialism against the British Empire as such. Had not Hitler claimed that he would guarantee Czechoslovak independence, once the question of the German minority was resolved? London knew what had become of that pledge. Any promise Hitler made to respect the British Empire was not worth the paper it was written on.

A second, even less serious attempt to avoid a full-scale world war was made by Hitler after the defeat of France in May-June 1940. Once again what was required from British imperialism was recognition of the accomplished fact. But to acquiesce in a European continent dominated by Berlin without the existence of a powerful independent French army (the situation in June 1940) made even less sense for the City than did the earlier prospect of September 1939, when that army was still around. In either case it meant certain disaster for Britain as a world power, not to speak of the risk of being militarily crushed and occupied in a few years' time. Although, as we know today, inside the war cabinet Halifax supported an attempt at mediation by Mussolini, the overwhelming majority of the British ruling class rallied around Churchill's resolve to fight matters out there and then, without letting Hitler consolidate, digest and organize his gains. Hitler knew that, and did not halt for a single day his military, economic and political plans for extending the war, either after the conquest of Poland or after the rout of France.

Likewise, Hitler quite deliberately chose to launch an attack on the USSR even before Britain was eliminated, i.e. to spread the war geographically and militarily on a qualitatively new scale. This decision was taken as early as July 1940. It was his. No outside force was accountable for it, although other powers influenced and facilitated these decisions through their own actions and reactions. The responsibility of German imperialism in the outbreak and extension of the Second World War was overwhelming – in contrast to the situation in July-August 1914, when all the major powers more or less blundered into a world war without really knowing what they were doing.[3]

German imperialism's option in favour of open and large-scale aggression can only be understood against the background of the profound economic, social, political and moral crisis which shook German bourgeois society from 1914 on. There is no need to recount that history here. For our purposes, it is sufficient to recall that the upturn of the German economy engineered by the Nazi-led cabinet was from the start decisively weighted in favour of heavy industry, machine-tools, and road-building. All available foreign exchange was used to amass stocks of raw material for the eventuality of war. At the same time chemical industries were developed with the aim of substituting man-made for war materials. Such measures unambiguously pointed to the growing probability, if not inevitability of war. As early as 1935 they were combined with a step-by-step liquidation of the provisions of the Versailles Treaty – in a build-up of military power technically much in advance of that of the Western powers (although less ahead of the USSR than Hitler could realize).

Various forces of a more conservative and cautious inclination within the German ruling class, including among the military, periodically questioned the wisdom of the reckless course embarked upon not only by the Nazis but by their main backers inside the bourgeoisie. Their timid protest remained completely ineffectual, at least as long as Hitler's path seemed strewn with success. Only after the defeats of El Alamein, Algiers and Sta-lingrad, did such opposition become more widespread, for obvious reasons of self-preservation – obviously the German ruling class did not want to be extinguished, above all not by the Soviet army. But even then its reservations remained pitifully weak.

The way in which the structure of German industry and finance capital evolved during the first years of the Third Reich is a telling indicator of these basic options by the German ruling class.

But the race towards an all-out rearmament was not only reckless from a diplomatic and military point of view. It also represented a desperate gamble with the German economy itself. In 1938-39, the economy slid into a grave financial crisis. A huge budgetary deficit emerged: public expenditure of 55 billion RM in 1939-39 (which was to become 63 billion in 1939-40) was offset by tax and customs receipts of only 18 billion RM that year and 25 billion the next. A colossal build-up of public debt ensued. Inflation could less and less be contained. Timothy Mason suggests that there was a direct link between this crisis and the option in favour of Blitzkrieg in

Production Index (1913 = 100)

	Total industrial output	Metalworking	Chemical industry
1929	121.4	170.3	186.1
1932	72.8	84.2	138.4
1936	137.2	202.6	234.8

Investments in industry

		of which, means of production
1928	2.6 billion RM	66%
1933	0.3	55%
1934	1.1	66%
1935	1.6	75%
1936	2.2	76%
1937	2.8	77%
1938	3.7	80%
1939	4.4	81%[4]

1938-39.[5] For as interest payments on the national debt became a grave problem, and exports stagnated in spite of increased recourse to barter, the laws of reproduction of capital asserted themselves. A severe contraction of the economy threatened unless a new and massive stream of material goods was brought into circulation. But German output capacities were already stretched to the utmost. No more could easily be extorted from the working class, the lower middle classes or the Jews within the Third Reich. The only solution was to extend the scale of physical production through massive plunder outside of Germany's frontiers. That meant war of conquest. And that type of war was unleashed.

In his *Origins of the Second World War*,[6] the British historian A.J.P. Taylor has questioned the particular responsibility of the Nazi regime for unleashing World War Two. Despite the many interesting insights he offers, his overall thesis is indefensible. He argues that Hitler was basically an opportunist who had no clear time-table for wars or conquests, but seized the chance to act only when favourable circumstances presented themselves. Yet surely one does not need to have a precise schedule for establishing hegemony in Europe, any more than one need prepare for hostilities to commence at a precise date for war preparation to be very real indeed. Hitler, or better still German imperialism, did intend to create a new order in Europe – and this in turn made war inevitable. Taylor's book abounds in examples of statements unsubstantiated by facts. There is the assertion, for example, that 'Until 1936, rearmament was largely a myth.'[6] This is disproved by the many memoranda drawn up by the *Reichswehr* and sectors of German big business which prompted a tripling of military expenditure between 1932 and 1934.[7] Taylor also writes: 'Rearmament cost about forty thousand million marks in the six fiscal years ending 31 March 1939 and about fifty thousand million marks up to the outbreak of the war.'[8] But this figure is much too low: the actual sum was more like seventy or eighty billion RM.[9] Then again, 'On 15 March 1939, Bohemia became a German protectorate. . . . It was the unforeseen byproduct of developments in Slovakia.'[10] Yet developments in Slovakia were far from unforeseen; indeed, they had been deliberately planned and executed in order to break up an already truncated Czechoslovakia.[11] He further writes: 'Nor was there anything sinister or premeditated in the protectorate over Bohemia . . . Bohemia had always been part of the Holy Roman Empire.'[12] But was there nothing 'sinister' in breaking a solemn promise publicly made a few months before (*'Wir wollen ja keine Tschechen! Meinetwegen werden wir ihnen garantieren'*)? Would there likewise have been nothing 'sinister' in claiming Alsace, Lorraine and Artois for Germany because they had also once been part of the Holy Roman Empire? And what of yet again splitting Italy or Germany into dozens of independent principalities, on the grounds that they had existed in that form for centuries? Once you start redrawing the frontiers of Europe, where do you stop? Taylor's argument is clearly inconsistent here. Either you stand by the logic of realpolitik and moral judgements about what is 'sinister' are irrelevant – but then the British reaction to the *Wehrmacht*'s occupation of Bohemia was as much a 'fact' as the occupation itself and a realpolitik which failed to foresee it was inefficient and bungling. Or, if the historian may legitimately pass judgement on the reaction – 'exaggerated', 'misplaced', etc. – then the occupation which provoked it should likewise be judged: was it 'reasonable', 'unavoidable', 'justified' – or was it not? Taylor writes: 'He (Hitler) had no idea he would knock France out of the war when he invaded Belgium and Holland on 10 May 1940. This was a defensive move: to secure the Ruhr from Allied invasion. The conquest of France was an unforeseen bonus.'[13] But surely the whole of the Manstein-Guderian plan had as its specific aim to knock out France, not Holland and Belgium. [14]

In Taylor's conception of history, foreign policy is determined by realpolitik reacting to contingent international situations. The actors are not anchored in internal political and economic forces, articulated by parties, states and movements, but float in a space constrained ultimately only by individual character and motivations. In this way Hitler is seen as a 'prisoner' of his own timetable, [15] and the success of his project (New Order in Europe) appears endangered solely by his own irrationality: 'The European struggle which began in 1918, when the German armistice delegate presented himself before Foch . . . ended in 1940. . . . There was a 'new order' in Europe: it was dominated by Germany. . . . Hitler's success depended on the isolation of Europe from the rest of the world. He gratuitously destroyed the source of this success. In 1941 he attacked Soviet Russia and declared war on the United States.'[16]

This is wrong on all counts. The Second World War was inescapably a war for world hegemony. There was no possibility of 'isolating' Europe from the rest of the world, not only for military and strategic but also for evident economic reasons. Hitler, Roosevelt and eventually even Stalin understood this well. No 'European struggle' ended in June 1940: operational studies for a campaign against the Soviet Union began in July, even before the Battle of Britain had really started. In any case, the New Order in Europe could not be stabilized so long as it was not recognized by *all* the major powers and at least passively acquiesced in by the peoples involved – and that was no more the case in the summer of 1940 than in the spring of 1941. [17]

What is basically correct in Taylor's approach is his understanding that German imperialism was not intrinsically different from other imperialisms: all are stained by blood, treachery and odious crimes against humanity. But to recognize the fact that you live in a gangsters' world does not imply the conclusion that a specific crime is not committed by a particular gangster at a given moment. There cannot be the slightest doubt that German imperialism deliberately and brazenly unleashed the war against Poland, and therewith the Second World War, on 1 September 1939. Whatever the responsibilities of the world capitalist system as a whole, and of the other imperialist powers, that particular act was the work of the German ruling class led by the Führer and his military henchmen.

Was the demoralisation and growing defeatism of the French

ruling class a contributory factor in Hitler's reckless course towards a new world war? Undoubtedly. But that demoralisation corresponded to a material reality and to specific social interests. France enjoyed political-military predominance on the European continent at the end of World War I. But that status in no way corresponded to the real economic balance of forces on that continent, let alone on a world scale. Neither French capital nor French industry could sustain armies in Western and Eastern Europe ready to crush any German attempt at regaining the upper hand. If anything, the disastrous financial and diplomatic consequences of Poincaré's occupation of the Ruhr in 1923 only confirmed the total discrepancy between French diplomatic ambitions and economic power. Subsequent absence of political will was a result – and not a cause – of material weakness.

Furthermore, large sectors of the French ruling class were terrified by the potential strength of the French working class, exemplified by the general strike of June 1936. To eliminate the 'Communist danger' became an obsession with many of them, taking precedence over any international design. They increasingly viewed parliamentary democracy as an intolerable burden that prevented any effective elimination of trade-union strength. Laval was the embodiment of this outlook, which enjoyed large-scale support inside parliament. Pétain was widely deemed the ideal figure for a new order, even before the war had started. In a report sent to Rome by the Duce's main agent in Paris – Lavoni – and recently discovered in the Italian archives, Laval is reported as saying on 17 March 1938 that he was about to form a national government under Pétain. When asked what would be the reaction of the Communists, he answered by making a gesture which could mean either putting the screws on them or breaking their necks.[18]

Because of his tiny parliamentary majority, Paul Reynaud, when he became Prime Minister on 23 Mary 1940, included several conservative sympathisers with such projects in his Cabinet.[19] Fear of a workers' uprising in Paris, even after the defeat of the September 1938 general strike, remained intense. 'Weygand and the others were afraid of a Commune in Paris', Admiral Auphan told Raymond Tournoux. This was the main motivation behind Weygand's desire to end the war at any price – one fully shared by Pétain and Laval. 'If the morale of the Army was to be preserved and a revolutionary movement in Paris avoided, the government has to assert its will to remain in the capital at all costs, to keep control of the situation, even at the risk of being taken by the enemy. "The issue is one of internal order and dignity" declared Weygand.'[20]

So far as England was concerned, throughout the period from 1929 to 1938 British policies were unfavourable to French hegemony in Europe. But they never implied any acceptance of a substitution of German hegemony for it. Chamberlain's 'appeasement' was essentially a function of London's judgement of the time necessary to overcome Germany's lead in rearmament – Hitler having started in 1933, while British imperialism seriously began to rearm only three to four years later. In other words, it was an illusory and foolhardy attempt to outmanoeuvre Hitler, not an acceptance of a Europe dominated by Berlin. By contrast with the French bourgeoisie, the British ruling class was in no way demoralized or defeatist where the defence of Britain's world position – in the first place that of the British Empire itself – was at stake. The difference between its Chamberlain and Churchill wings was not one between those ready to capitulate before German imperialism and those who were not. It was a conflict over the most effective way to preserve the Empire and to oppose Hitler: now or later. Given Hitler's course, Churchill's wing was bound to win that argument. For a short time, some of the 'appeasers' played with the idea of diverting the aggressive dynamic of German imperialism against the USSR, but after the occupation of Prague it became clear to them that the conquest of Eastern Europe by Hitler would give him formidable strength to strike against the British Empire. So further concessions would be suicidal for British imperialism.

On the other side of the globe, Japanese imperialism was likewise engaged in a step-by-step conquest of China – while aiming at South East Asia as the next prize. From the point of view of the more radical imperialist circles in and around the Imperial Army, such a course did not necessarily imply an open conflict with Britain and certainly not with the USA. Indeed, the conquest of China increasingly appeared as a formidable undertaking – much more complicated, protracted and costly than the Japanese warlords had calculated. Here again the preferred variant was to have *faits accomplis* recognised by London and Washington, rather than to embark upon a simultaneous confrontation with China, Britain, the USA and possibly the USSR too.

But whatever may have been the temptation of such a prospect for London — not to speak of the lesser French and Dutch colonial powers in the region – Washington was as hard set against such an acceptance of Japanese conquests in Asia as was London against acceptance of Germany's conquests in Europe. The reason was the same in both cases.

American imperialism considered a future conflict with Japan for hegemony over the Pacific-East Asia area (including China) as in the long run unavoidable. Under these circumstances, it would be foolish to let a future enemy first consolidate formidable conquests, allowing him to double, triple or quadruple his industrial, financial and military strength, and thus to enable him to unleash the final confrontation under conditions much worse for the USA than the current relationship of forces. Hence the Roosevelt administration embarked upon a policy of informal embargo of vital raw materials for Japan, and of growing help to Chiang Kai-Shek's China. In face of stiffening resistance from Washington, Tokyo had the choice of either retreating from China or pressing ahead towards a confrontation with the USA. It deliberately opted for the second course by the occupation of Indo-china on 23 July 1941, with the help of Vichy France (an occupation, incidentally, which was later to permit the Imperial Army to take Malaya and Singapore from the rear). Roosevelt responded by making the US blockade official.

Tokyo's course was largely determined by overwhelming economic necessity. Before the war, Japan imported 66% of its oil from the USA. Ten million tons of the coke needed for its steel-plants in China, all of the bauxite it needed for aircraft production, all the nickel for its weapons programme, all its tin and its rubber, 60% of its copper and nearly all its industrial salts came to Japan from the outside. Virtually all these goods could be supplied from the Dutch East Indies, Indochina, Malaya, the Philippines or China.

In the beginning, the war in Europe and the war in the Far East seemed separate and self-contained. Inevitably, however, the sheer momentum of the initial Nazi victories made the two conflicts interlock. Unable to decide at first between a 'northern' and a 'southern' option, the Japanese military leaders were now encouraged to move against the exposed European colonies in South East Asia. The final argument was supplied by the United States, intent after July 1941 on denying Japan the raw materials essential for prosecution of the war against China.

But even after the decision was taken to strike at the United States on 5 November 1941, Tokyo did not necessarily expect a fight to the finish. Rather, it was hoped that Japan's initial successes, coupled with those of her ally Germany, would influence

Washington to seek a compromise peace that would give her a stable and secure sphere of influence in East and South Asia. Washington, however, was dead set against any recognition of something that might lead to Japanese hegemony in Asia, as is shown by the State Department's intransigence in the US-Japanese negotiations of November 1941.

Japan's attack on Pearl Harbor on 7 December 1941 supplied the United States with an immediate and unambiguous *casus belli*, capable of capturing American popular imagination and harnessing it to a war of revenge. But whatever the degree of US interest in the promises and opportunities of the East, it was the future of Europe, its wealth and its control over large tracts of the world, that primarily preoccupied US strategists from 1939 onwards. At the beginning of 1941 the American and British chiefs of staff had agreed to fight the war on the basis of 'Europe first' (the plan ABC-1), and this strategy was re-affirmed after Pearl Harbor provoked war between Tokyo and Washington.

American imperialism's determination to involve itself decisively in the redrafting of the international political order has to be considered as the third immediate cause of World War Two (the other two being Germany's and Japan's thrusts beyond their national borders). It reflected a deliberate policy of the Roosevelt administration (challenged, it is true, by the so-called isolationists as late as 1940 – but they never represented more than a provincial splinter group in the US ruling class).[21] This resolution was the product of the wholescale transformation undergone by the US economy after 1929. US imperialism had at its disposal tremendous reserves of unemployed capital, productive capacity and manpower. The attempt to mobilize them via the New Deal (i.e. an orientation towards the internal market), while lifting economy and society out of their worst crisis, was to a large extent a failure. In 1938, there were again twelve million unemployed. The turn towards the world market became imperative. Capital had to be invested and lent abroad. Goods had to be sold abroad, to a qualitatively larger extent than before 1929 or between 1933 and 1939 (as indeed they would be after 1945).[22] But first the world had to be made safe for such giant capital and commodity exports. That was the material content of the formula: 'making the world safe for democracy' and the meaning of the decisive and final break with American isolationism. Gabriel and Joyce Kolko summarize the situation and the intent of US imperialism admirably: 'The deeply etched memory of the decade-long depression of 1929 hung over all

American plans for the post-war era. The war had ended the crisis in American society, but the question remained whether peace would restore it. . . . At the end of World War II the leadership of the United States determined on a policy intended to prevent the return of an economic and social crisis in American society – a policy which explicitly demanded that they resolve America's dilemma in the world arena.'[23]

Roosevelt had to manoeuvre in a more cautious way than Hitler or the Tokyo warlords, for inside the USA democracy still prevailed. The American people could not be forced into the war; they had to coaxed into it. The prospect was not very popular in the USA (nor was it in any major country). Japan's surprise attack at Pearl Harbor made things easier for Roosevelt. But the intention to intervene at virtually any cost was not his personal choice. It was the American ruling class's option, as deliberate as those of its German or Japanese counterparts.

The attack on the Soviet Union did not come, as many had expected, by the united efforts of world capitalism. The very isolation of the Soviet Republic, and the internal convulsions which it generated had given free rein to inter-imperialist struggles, so that the opening of the Eastern Front primarily derived from the desire of German imperialism to strengthen its hand vis à vis its Western competitors. Within the USSR itself an explosive contradiction appeared between the strengthening of the USSR's industrial and military infrastructure under the Five Year Plan on the one hand, and the grave political crisis into which Stalin's purges and his reckless diplomatic game plunged the country, on the other. The second process decapitated the Red Army, disorganised the defences of the country, delivered Poland and Europe to Hitler, and facilitated the Nazi attack on the USSR. The first enabled the Soviet Union to survive in the end.

The Red Army's complete lack of readiness in 1941 was the direct result of Stalin's disastrous misunderstanding of the political situation in Europe and of Hitler's – i.e. German imperialism's – intentions in the coming war. Only a few years earlier Tukhachevsky, then First Deputy Commissar for Defence, had argued that the French army would offer no active opposition to Germany and that in any case the latter's aggressive intentions lay in the East. In contrast, Stalin was convinced that if the Soviet Union behaved 'correctly' Hitler would not attack: the Nazi-Soviet Pact of August 1939 appeared increasingly as a strategic orientation rather than a tactical move.[25] The idea that Germany was a potential enemy was firmly suppressed at the important chiefs of staff war study conference of December 1940, as was any notion of the possibility of war in the near future. The training plans released after the conference were therefore not the product of any in-depth study of the state and needs of the army, nor did they form part of any coherent war plan. The 'State Frontier Defence Plan 1941', which the General Staff released in April 1941, and with which the Soviet Union entered the war two months later, committed the Red Army to defend the forward frontiers of the Soviet Union and paid minimal attention to strategic defence.

Considering the wavering (to say the least) of the French and British governments over military collaboration in the event of a German aggression against Poland, the Soviet government had every right to ensure its immediate safety in case of a German conquest of that country. But the Hitler-Stalin pact contained a secret protocol which, even before that conquest had commenced, implemented a fourth partition of Poland. Therewith Stalin gave the green light to Hitler's aggression, temporarily saving the Third Reich from the nightmare of a prolonged war on two fronts. Russian historiography continues to deny this – by keeping silent about the secret protocol of 27 August 1939. Likewise, it draws a veil over Stalin's formal opposition to the survival of any Polish state. The consequences of this cynical realpolitik for the Polish people's attitude towards the USSR remain disastrous to this day. It was certainly a concomitant cause of the unleashing of World War II.

3.

The Social Forces

World War II witnessed a conjunction of action by a broad spectrum of nations, social classes, fractions of social classes, political parties and narrower cliques (financial, industrial, military and political) over the whole globe. Increasingly, its course became determined by this interaction, which reached a climax in the years 1943-45, when literally millions of men and women were engaged in conflict across a geographical area from France to Bengal, from Chad to Leningrad, from the Philippines to Birmingham, from Detroit to Bosnia, from the North Manchurian plain to Egypt, from Avellaneda to Milan. Never before had so many people, on all continents, participated directly or indirectly in political and armed combat. The contradictory nature of contemporary capitalism was expressed in the fact that the war at one and the same time saw centralized, progressively brutal control by military hierarchies over millions of soldiers, whilst other millions rose and intervened in it outside the control of any established hierarchy. The contradiction, was visible, moreover, from the very start of the conflict.

The great powers succeeded in surmounting all the major obstacles on the road to war; the progress of counter-revolution was marked by their successive removal. The lights of civilization seemed to go out one by one – in Europe, in Asia, in the USSR. Barbarism seemed on the move everywhere. The years 1940, 1941 and 1942 were the blackest of our epoch. Victor Serge gave one of his novels the apt title: *Midnight in the Century*.

But what the powers were unable to do was to whip up enthusiasm for the slaughter. In sharp contrast to August 1914, no trains or convoys of soldiers in these years went to the front bedecked with flowers and followed by cheering crowds. War-weariness was present from the beginning. Hitler received his first shock neither at the airports of The Hague nor from the Brest Litovsk Red Army Cadets, nor even at the gates of Moscow. He got it on 27 September 1938 when, after his speech at the Sports Palace announcing his ultimatum on Czechoslovakia, he waited avidly at the window of the *Reichskanzlerei* for cheering crowds to wave at the crack division he ordered to parade for that purpose through the streets of Berlin: the crowd never cheered.[1] Granted, people were resigned to the war, accepting it as a fatality they could not prevent. But passive resignation was a far cry from enthusiastic support. And that was something largely absent from any country at the war's outset.

The situation gradually changed in the later phases of the war, in a manner which differed widely from country to country. In Britain, a combination of fear of German invasion, traditional nationalism and class hatred of fascism rallied the overwhelming majority of the working class behind the National Government headed by the arch-reactionary Churchill.[2] In consequence, the prosecution of the war became linked after May 1940 with a wide-ranging programme of social reform, which a significant section of the middle class – critical of the high conservatism of the Tory leadership in the inter-war period – could and did endorse. The British war effort, despite its dependence on the USA, commanded a degree of national unity exceptional among the Allies. Churchill, as head of a government which actively incorporated the reformist Labour party, was therefore able to get away with inroads on British workers' standard of living which Hitler did not initially dare to impose upon the German working class. Obsessed by his memories of hunger revolts and workers' insurgency at the end of World War I, Hitler was ready to sacrifice even some war industry priorities to ensure a regular minimum diet to German workers at the start of the conflict.[3]

After Pearl Harbor, acceptance of the war as one of revenge against the Axis powers – with accompanying chauvinistic and racist overtones directed especially against the Japanese – also became widespread in the USA, though the war there never enjoyed popular support of the kind witnessed in Britain. After all, its theatres were very far removed from the North American continent. Indeed, the unwillingness of the US leadership to send sufficient troops to fight the Japanese in Asia – because it would have meant escalation of casualties – was crucially important in determining American war policy towards the USSR and China. Throughout the war, class tensions grew more in the USA than in Britain.[4] Moreover, they were increasingly combined with racial tensions, as the influx of black people into the great industrial centres of the Mid-West and the East accelerated, and as the new workers started to react against the generally racist atmosphere prevalent throughout the industrial establishment and in the neighbourhoods. Workers in the United States were more prone to rebel against no-strike pledges than in Britain. Similarly, officers' control over soldiers was more readily questioned in the US forces than in any other regular army. War weariness, which spread only gradually in Britain in the last two years of the war, by contrast erupted on a large scale in the US services, with soldiers' strikes and mutinies in 1945 expressing the men's desire to return home as soon as the war was over in Europe and the Far East.

While the situation in the USSR was far more complex – and is still an object of debate among historians – a similar pattern emerges there too. Despite identifying with the Revolution – a phenomenon much more widespread in 1939-41 than today – the mass of the Soviet people was hostile to Stalin's dictatorship. In certain areas like the Baltic republics and the Ukraine, where national oppression had been combined with the large-scale terror and famine of the collectivization period, hostility to Stalin among large sectors of the peasantry, the professional classes and layers of the working class had turned into outright hatred – and was intensified by the experience of being abandoned to the German invaders in 1941. Yet whatever potential this might have created for a significant degree of collaboration between invaders and local population was soon negated by the monstrous crimes perpetrated by the Nazi occupation forces. The systematic destruction of the infrastructure of civic life; the mass enslavement of tens of millions of people under inhuman conditions; execution and maltreatment on a scale in excess of anything Stalin and his supporters had conducted – these soon turned the tide. The Soviet masses – in the first place the working class and the soldiers of the Red Army, but by no means them alone – displayed the indomitable resolve in resistance of which the defence of Leningrad, in many ways even more than Stalingrad, became a symbol.[5]

No amount of exhortation by the state, party or military leadership would have succeeded without this determination of the Soviet masses to fight and win the war. Tested to the utmost, the achievements of October now revealed their historic superiority amidst the death and violence of war. The offensives of the Red Army found a vital complement in the partisan movement emerging behind German lines, which in Hitler's own words created an intolerable situation. Its strength was rooted in the same obstinate will to fight to the death against Nazi terror that would also be encountered in the heroic combatants of the Warsaw ghetto. Hitler became a victim of his own demented myth of racial superiority. His *Ostpolitik* never foresaw that 'inferior races' such as Slavs or Jews could fight with greater energy, courage, intelligence and dedication than the *Herrenvolk*. The inhabitants of Eastern Europe and the Soviet Union – who were supposed to be expelled, exterminated or turned into slave labour in the forging of the new German Empire – chose instead to resist at any cost. They rose in their millions, forced dozens of German divisions to withdraw from the front, and by their admirable struggle became one of the key factors which tipped the scales against German imperialist plans.[6]

Under the military push of German revanchism the rotten foundations of the bourgeois order created in large parts of Europe at the end of World War One gave way. Its successor grew out of actions from below, as workers and poor peasants formed alliances for the goals of national liberation and radical social reform: goals which the local bourgeoisies and landowning classes were neither able nor willing to endorse. The ruling strata waited for the Allied armies to defeat the Nazis and restore them to power, in the meantime actively collaborating with, or showing passivity in the face of, the invading troops. But the bulk of the population of the occupied countries chose instead to fight – and thus to take an active part in the reshaping of Europe after the war. As the anti-fascist resistance grew in strength, so did the propensity of the local ruling class for collaboration with the Nazis. By 1943 the social rather than the national divide became permanent and the war acquired a revolutionary dynamic directed not only against the return of the old order but also against any more reform of it.

The case of Yugoslavia demonstrates this most clearly. The monarchy, the bourgeois establishment, the regular army all collapsed miserably within weeks if not days of the invasion. What awaited the population was heralded by the large-scale bombing of the open city of Belgrade, even before the war was officially declared. This was a measure – and many others were to follow, starting with the effacement of the country from the map of Europe – designed to punish and intimidate the population for its 'crime' of opposing Yugoslavia's adherence to the Axis. But the reaction was totally unforeseen. The Yugoslav masses rose in their thousands to resist the occupying armies and their domestic collaborators. What began as a war of national liberation soon acquired the character of a social revolution, whose unfolding would be ensured by the creation of a partisan army numbering some half a million men and women by the end of 1945. Seven successive concentrated offensives by one of the most powerful armies in the world could not break that resistance.

Initially, the resistance in Greece was also a spontaneous reaction to fascist occupation. The organized form it soon took – the National Liberation Front (EAM), initiated but not controlled by the Greek Communist Party – was politically more broadly based than in Yugoslavia, and for much of the war numerically larger. Its original aim was a radical reform of the Greek political order (including abolition of the pro-fascist monarchy). But as the struggle developed, EAM shifted steadily to the left. As in Yugoslavia, this resulted in a sharp social polarization which the Greek CP, consciously reformist and largely obedient to Soviet diktat, refused to recognize and confront. The decision not to resist by force of arms – until it was too late – the British expeditionary forces sent (with US backing) to restore the prewar order, and the belief, founded on nothing but faith, that the Allies would respect the democratic rights of the Greek people, meant that the massive and heroic struggle of hundreds of thousands of Greek workers and peasants organised into the People's Liberation Army (ELAS) would be crushed by the white terror unleashed against them by the Western Allies.

A similar radical ferment from below was to be found, in varying degrees, not only in the occupied countries but also in those which had joined the war on Germany's side. Italy, the first Axis power to surrender to the Allies, provided a notable example of the energy with which the masses threw themselves into the struggle to destroy the fascist state and of Allied determination to resist any revolutionary impulse.

What the Allies feared above all else was the spectacular growth of resistance in the North, still under German occupation, where the main industrial centres of the country were located.[7] The reconstitution of the labour movement from the end of 1943 on led to a whole series of strikes in northern cities, involving some one million workers and lasting, in the case of Turin, for eight days. As in Austria between 1934 and 1938, the success of this working-class militancy proved that when the class regains self-confidence and a medium-term political perspective, it is quite capable of organizing illegally on a mass scale.

Would a development similar to those which occurred in occupied Southern Europe and Italy – large-scale uprisings under left-wing leadership – have been possible in Germany itself, if massive terror had not decimated an important part of the surviving cadre of the German labour movement after the 20 July 1944 attempt on Hitler's life, and if heavy bombing had not destroyed much of the tissue of industrial civil society in the second part of that year?[8] There is every reason to believe that this would indeed have been the case. After all, the German workers had retained an elementary class consciousness on economic issues at least throughout the war. The SS secret intelligence reports quoted in note 4 below *(Meldungen aus dem Reich)* record frequent working-class protests whenever wage-cuts occurred. When Goebbels's 'total war' mobilization of 1943 led to widespread replacement of male by female labour in industry, the employers used the occasion to cut wages by twenty per cent: both men and women protested vigorously. According to Ludolf Herbst: 'Towards the end of 1943, class-specific differentiation appeared inside the population. It became clear that the upper and middle classes put their hopes especially in the Americans and the British, while the workers had at least less fear of the Soviets.'[9]

The extent of resistance to the Nazis in Germany itself has been systematically underestimated by virtually every historian. Yet between February 1933 and September 1939, 225,000 men and women were condemned by Nazi courts for political reasons. To this figure we must add those imprisoned without trial in concentration camps, who on a given day – 10 April 1939 – were estimated by a secret Gestapo report to outnumber political convicts by fifty per cent: 162,734 as against 112,432. There were a further 27,369 prisoners who had been officially charged with political crimes but not yet convicted.[10] So it would not seem exaggerated to estimate the number of Germans arrested as political opponents by the Nazis from the day they took power until the start of the war as between 400,000 and 600,000 (depending on the turnover of concentration camp inmates). During the war itself, the figures increased. By the spring of 1943 the concentration

camps held some 200,000 Germans, many of them dying. Between
1 January and 30 June 1944 alone (and thus prior to the massive
terror unleashed as a result of the attempt on Hitler's life) nearly
30,000 Germans were arrested for political reasons, plus a further
6,000 for political reasons classified as 'criminal'.[11] (These figures
do not include foreigners – deportee workers, 'free' foreign
workers, slave labourers, prisoners of war, etc. – also arrested for
political reasons, whose number is twice the figure for German
nationals: in total, more than 100,000 prisoners were arrested
during that half year in Germany as opponents of the Third
Reich.) According to an American estimate, in toto 1,663,550
people were imprisoned in concentration camps in Germany
during the time of the Third Reich, roughly one million of whom
were German nationals.[12]

It was a fear of Germany going revolutionary, as much as the
growing power of the Soviet Union in Europe, which stimulated
the desire of the Western Allies to have their troops in France and
Germany at the time of the latter's military collapse. As in the case
of Greece, Italy and Yugoslavia, so also in the case of Germany, the
Soviet Union's influence over the Communist Parties was seen as a
potential bulwark against the 'anarchy' – indeed 'Communism' –
lurking behind the power of the resistance movements, which
emerged in full strength in March 1943.

In that month, following a conversation between the American
and British leaders on the subject of the left in Europe, Harry
Hopkins (Roosevelt's closest adviser) wrote in his memo: 'I said
that I thought there was no understanding between Great Britain,
Russia and ourselves as to which armies would be where and what
kind of administration should be developed [in the occupied areas].
I said that unless we acted promptly and surely, I believed one of
two things would happen – either Germany will go Communist or
an out and out anarchic state would set in; that, indeed, the same
kind of thing might happen in any of the countries in Europe and
Italy as well. . . . It will obviously, be a much simpler matter [i.e.
simpler than a formal agreement with the Russians] if the British
and American armies are heavily in France and Germany at the
time of collapse, but we should work out a plan (with the British
and the Russians) in case Germany collapses before we get to
France.'[13]

Stalin too considered Western Allied occupation a weapon
against 'anarchy', as emerges from Eden's report to Churchill of his
conversations with him in March 1943. Stalin, Eden noted, also

desired a Second Front in Europe for political reasons, since: 'If Germany collapsed, he had no desire to take full responsibility for what would happen in Germany or the rest of Europe, and he believed it was a fixed matter of Russian foreign policy to have both British and United States troops heavily in Europe when the collapse came. Eden expressed this purely as his private opinion and said that he was sure that in Russia a different view was held in some quarters but, nevertheless, he thought he had stated Stalin's positions.'[14]

A fusion of social and anti-imperialist struggle – this time directed as much against invading armies as against West European colonial powers – emerged as a dominant trend in the wartime politics of Asia as well, especially in China and in the South East. Here too uncontrollable and unpredictable social forces increasingly came to upset imperialist calculations for the region.

Key to the future of Asia was the growing resistance to the Japanese onslaught of millions of poor peasants, uprooted villagers and starved city inhabitants in North and Central China.[15] The Japanese Imperial Army occupied the Chinese ports, controlled all railway centres, took over most of the big cities, installed a stable administration in the occupied areas and cowed the Chiang Kai-Shek regime into passive acceptance of Tokyo's rule over a large part of the country. To all intents and purposes, the war should have been over. That is certainly what the Army High Command and the government in Tokyo eagerly expected to happen, month after month, year after year. But the war did not fade away with Chiang's armies. On the contrary. Intolerable exploitation and humiliations at the hands of foreign imperialists had roused the 'sleeping giant' of Asia: the Chinese people. Spontaneous resistance developed, and the brutal Japanese response only succeeded in transforming it into a vast guerrilla army.[16] Leadership of this resurgence was not forthcoming from the Chinese bourgeoisie, which increasingly feared it. Instead, the Communist Party of China became the leader of the national struggle for survival.

Chiang and his cohorts viewed the mushrooming strength of this Communist-led alliance with growing concern. The Japanese, by comparison, were seen as a secondary problem, which would in any case be solved by an American military victory. For its part, the United States found itself spending vast sums of money on an ally which had no intention of fighting but was at the same time – from the standpoint of longer-term American interests in China – increasingly difficult to replace by a suitable right-wing alternative. The US policy in China thus stumbled over the same basic contradiction faced by the British in the Balkans, brought about by an increased intertwining of national-liberation and class wars. The more the masses organized, the more the pressure for revolutionary change grew and the less, in consequence, was the ruling class prepared to fight the invaders. The Kuomintang forces were instead kept in reserve for the final test of strength with the People's Liberation Army. On the other hand, the less Chiang fought the Japanese, the more the PLA became the centre of the national liberation struggle and the more the tide turned in favour of revolution. [17]

Such an acceleration of social and political contradictions by the war was not limited to China. Similar reactions and upheavals, completely unforeseen by Washington, London or Vichy (later Paris), occurred among the populations who had previously endured the inhuman conditions imposed by Western imperialism. In the Philippines, the hostilities of World War II became interlocked with a civil war dating back to the 1930s. The resistance to Japanese occupation, primarily Communist-led, grew to a 100,000-strong force controlling large sections of the archipelago. The return of American troops signalled the start of a counter-revolution, since when the civil war has continued with uneven tempo right up to the present day. [18]

Whereas the Filipino masses by and large fought the Japanese armies, those of Indonesia, for centuries exploited and crushed by Dutch imperialism, greeting the invading troops in 1942 as liberators – to the surprise of many, including the Japanese themselves. An anti-imperialist mobilization began which, in the years that followed Japan's defeat, was (with tacit US support) to end the Dutch empire. Meanwhile the Indochinese resistance movement fought obstinately against all the various post-war projects of colonial 'normalization' attempted, in combination with the native ruling class, by British, Chinese Nationalist, French and, much later, American forces. For the Indochinese people, the war did not end in 1945 but continued until the middle of the 1970s: their struggle, lasting nearly thirty-five years, conducted against Japan, France and the United States in succession, is without parallel in contemporary history. Given its relative isolation, the tremendous sacrifices it imposed on the population and the material and human destruction it entailed, the outcome of their heroic fight has been more painful for these courageous people (calamitous in Kampuchea) than one had expected or wished for. The vicious policy of

44

economic and political blockade orchestrated against Vietnam in particular since 1975 by the United States has done much to sour the fruits of victory. Yet the stubborn and magnificent struggle of the Vietnamese masses continues to stand as a monument to the strength of popular aspirations and military resistance, capable of rudely upsetting imperial arrogance and conceit. In Vietnam as in China, the tempestuous intrusion of class war into inter-imperialist conflict was confirmed as a trans-continental phenomenon in WWII.

In India, too, resistance by the masses to the British colonial presence persisted throughout the war, despite all the blandishments of 'anti-fascist' ideology eagerly employed against the autonomous mass struggles by the British Labour Party and the Communist Party of India (a party notable, unlike that of China or Vietnam, for its slavish obedience to Moscow). Outside the Japanese war-zone the war likewise gave a powerful impetus to anti-imperialist sentiments and organized resistance, for instance, among growing sectors of the Arab masses, especially in Egypt and Algeria. On 8 May 1945, there were huge demonstrations in Setif in favour of Algerian independence. A massacre by the colonial army followed: according to nationalist sources, the repression cost some 40,000 dead. The French Communist Party, fully engaged in its class collaborationist honeymoon, with Maurice Thorez serving as vice-president in De Gaulle's cabinet, behaved scandalously, going to the lengths of covering up for the repression by calling the Algerian nationalist leadership Nazis! Colonial repression of a similar kind was launched by the De Gaulle-Thorez-Ramadier government against the Syrian and Lebanese national movements in the May-June 1945 period. Although the French and British imperialists were temporarily successful in reimposing their rule, the political radicalization of the urban petty bourgeoisie (in Egypt, the young officers) was to lead a decade later to the phenomenon of Nasserism, and to the burgeoning of the Algerian revolution.

Imperialist bourgeoisies; bourgeoisies in independent, colonial and semi-colonial countries; professional classes and the intelligentsia; urban and rural petty bourgeoisies; the working class; the landowning class; poor and dispossessed peasantry – all these major and minor classes and fractions of classes, organized by states and armies, parties, professional organizations and movements, entered voluntarily or under compulsion into the cataclysm of a war that began as an inter-imperialist struggle for world power.

Given the participation of this multitude of mutually antagonistic social forces, how are we to characterize the Second World War?

By the end of 1945 the war had become not only a transcontinental but also a multifarious affair involving: revolutionary class struggle from below; revolution from above; national liberation movements under bourgeois and working-class leaderships; reform of the old order; and violent counter-revolution. The exact outcome in each instance depended on the strength and maturity of the class leaderships, the degree of importance the victors attached to a given area or country, and their ability to impose a political settlement.

Bearing this in mind, the overall character of the Second World War must be grasped as a combination of five different conflicts:

1. An inter-imperialist war fought for world hegemony and won by the United States (though its rule would be territorially truncated by the extension of the non-capitalist sector in Europe and Asia).

2. A just war of self-defence by the Soviet Union against an imperialist attempt to colonize the country and destroy the achievements of the 1917 Revolution.

3. A just war of the Chinese people against imperialism which would develop into a socialist revolution.

4. A just war of Asian colonial peoples against the various military powers and for national liberation and sovereignty, which in some cases (e.g. Indochina) spilled over into socialist revolution.

5. A just war of national liberation fought by populations of the occupied countries of Europe, which would grow into socialist revolution (Yugoslavia and Albania) or open civil war (Greece, North Italy). In the European East, the old order collapsed under the dual, uneven pressure of popular aspirations and Soviet military-bureaucratic action, whereas in the West and South bourgeois order was restored – often against the wishes of the masses – by Western Allied troops.

By 'just wars' are meant wars which *should* have been fought, and which revolutionaries supported then as they do now. This categorization avoids the political ambiguity of the formula according to which the forces active in the war are divided into 'fascist' or 'anti-fascist', the division being based on the notion that – because of their specific nature – the German, Italian and Japanese forms of imperialism should have been fought in alliance with the ruling classes of Britain, the United States, France, etc. The politics of 'anti-fascist alliance', whatever the semantic meaning of the words involved, amounts in reality to systematic class collaboration: the political parties, and especially the Communist parties which maintained that the Western imperialist states were waging a just war against Nazism, ended by forming coalition governments after 1945 wherein they actively participated in the reconstruction of the bourgeois state and the capitalist economy. In addition, this incorrect understanding of the character of Western states' intervention in the war led to a systematic betrayal of the colonial populations' anti-imperialist struggles, not to speak of the counter-revolution in Greece.

4.

Resources

World wars result from imperialism's general tendency towards aggressive expansionism. But they also have a more specific cause. They result from the operation of the law of uneven development, that is, from the contradiction between the tendency of the industrial-financial balance of imperialist forces to undergo periodic modification (through the upsurge of specific bourgeois classes previously retarded in their development) and the tendency for the division of the world into spheres of influence to remain frozen for a longer period. This last division is reflected in military-naval build-up, in international alliances and preferential trade, custom and monetary systems which change much more slowly than the industrial-financial relationship of forces in and of themselves.

Hillman estimates the share in percentage terms of the different great powers in worldwide manufacturing output on the eve of the Second World War as follows.[1]

	1937	1938
USA	35.1	28.7*
USSR	14.1	17.6
Great Britain	9.4	9.2
France	4.5	4.5
Germany	11.4	13.2
Italy	2.7	2.9
Japan	3.5	3.8

*(This decline in percentage is due to the economic crisis which broke out in 1938.)

He calculates the participation of these powers in what he calls the 'potential of world armaments economy' in 1937.

USA	41.7
USSR	14.0
Great Britain	10.2
France	4.2
Germany	14.4
Italy	2.5
Japan	3.5

If one compares these percentages with the map of the world, the incongruity is striking. In the final anlysis it is the industrial-financial balance of forces, in conjunction with the weight of political-social factors, which decides the outcome of any conflict for a redivision of the world into colonial empires and/or imperialist spheres of influence. Wars are precisely a mechanism for adjusting or adapting the military and political balance of forces to the new industrial-financial one, through the victory (or partial victory) of some, and the defeat (or partial defeat) of other, powers.

It must be established from the outset that what is relevant in the calculation of the various powers' economic resources is not only their industry's productive capacities and available manpower (the number of men and women capable of being pressed into production) in a purely quantitative sense. We use the expression 'industrial-financial strength' rather than 'industrial strength' because it is important, in particular, to include the gold and currency reserves through which national resources can be supplemented with those imported from foreign countries. The expression therefore implies a degree of 'soundness' of the national currency, i.e. its convertibility into gold or 'solid' foreign currencies. It also involves the physical capacity to transport goods bought in other countries to a place desired by a given warring power.[2]

At the same time, the formula 'industrial-financial strength' includes the degree of training, skill and culture of a given workforce. Together with gold and currency holdings, this is one of the key reserve funds of a contemporary industrial power, and cannot be bombed out of existence – as Germany, Britain and the USA successively discovered, to their dismay. It is as hard to destroy a great country's skilled manpower as it is to destroy gold. It can only be eliminated as a source of the competitor's strength through sheer physical destruction or direct seizure.

As to vital raw materials, again, it is important to distinguish between those that can be found or produced on the territory controlled by a given power and those which that power is able to buy or otherwise physically integrate into its own industrial production. Germany was poor in output, and access to such vital raw materials as oil, rubber, iron ore, aluminium, nickel and several rare metals necessary for the production of key alloys in weapon production. But in and of itself this dearth did not limit her industrial potential, even in arms output, for the duration of the war, contrary to what many strategists both in the West and the USSR believed.

In the first place, the German military-industrial establishment had embarked systematically on a huge programme of stockpiling vital raw materials before the start of the war. Indeed, this had become one of the essential aspects of war preparations.[3] Once war had begun, and after the signing of the Molotov-Ribbentrop pact, important additions came from, or via, the Soviet Union itself.[4] In the second place, the same establishment had systematically organized the substitution of chemical raw materials (above all synthetic rubber and oil), generally drawn from coal, for natural ones, which it knew it would lack in case of a prolonged war. These preparations were quite successful, although they made the resources vulnerable to concentrated aerial attack. In the third place, military conquest and long-term occupation of specific territories gave the German war machine access to riches it could neither produce nor afford to buy. To mention one example: by occupying France, Germany acquired a stock of natural gasoline larger than the whole annual production of synthetic oil in German factories. The German High Command, and Hitler personally, were absolutely obsessed with this aspect of direct physical plunder, and on several occasions modified basic military priorities in line with that objective.[5] In the fourth place, military strength enabled Germany to blackmail neutral powers into 'selling' raw materials either against increasingly valueless paper currency or by exchange in the form of barter. The outstanding example of this was Swedish iron ore, but Turkish chrome and Portuguese wolfram also featured.[6] Henri Michel has summarised Sweden's collaboration with the Third Reich thus: 'From 1940 onwards, and thoughout the war, Sweden supplied Germany with virtually all the iron-ore that it did not process itself, or some 9 million tons a year. After initial objections, it allowed the *Wehrmacht* to dispatch or withdraw troops and equipment across its territory by rail, or through its coastal waters. Between July and December 1940, 130,000 moved across Sweden in this fashion, in both directions, and more than 500 waggons. By the time that a whole German division, with guns and baggage, travelled through Sweden to the Finnish lines against the Soviet Union in June 1941, Swedish neutrality was scarcely more than a fiction, as Nazi aircraft flew freely through its air-space. Yet Sweden did draw a line it was determined not to cross: it refused to sign a political treaty with Germany, and rejected German proposals to integrate it not merely de facto but formally too, into the economic order of Nazi-dominated Europe. 'Sweden enjoyed benefits from its policy that were far from negligible: it was allowed to buy German coal three times more cheaply than Switzerland; and if it suffered economic losses to the Third Reich, as did the rest of Europe, in its case these were quite mild.'[7]

By means of conquest Germany imposed the same 'clearing system' on large factory owners in France, Belgium, Holland, Denmark, Norway and later Italy, where factories worked full-time for the German war industry, while the occupied countries received less and less 'real value' in exchange for their deliveries.[8] In Czechoslovakia, Yugoslavia and Poland, industrial plant was in most cases directly appropriated, as it was in the occupied terri-tories of the Soviet Union.

As for Japan, the 1941-2 offensive had the single important goal of reaching Indonesian oil and bauxite, Malaysian rubber and tin, and Indochinese, Thai and Burmese rice, so as to create the large and stable pool of raw-material resources required for a long war against China, the USA and Britain. Thereafter, the transpor-tation of these materials to the homeland, hence the need to keep the sea-lanes between Singapore and Yokohama/Kobe open, became the key medium-term military objective of Japanese imperialism.

Whilst all these considerations have to be taken into account in judging the overall industrial-financial balance of forces, it is nevertheless the basic productive capacity of a country – its industry, agriculture and transport – which remains the surest index of economic power. And here the laws of reproduction come into their own. There is no way in which tanks can be produced with guns, or airplanes with ammunition dumps. To produce tanks and airplanes you need machine-tools, steel and aluminium; and to produce these you need other machine-tools, iron ore, coke, bauxite, oil or coal. Once you are forced – in the final analysis through lack of sufficient overall industrial capacity and/or raw materials – to produce less machine-tools, less steel or less coal, you will inevitably end up producing fewer and fewer guns and airplanes.

The iron rules of reproduction do not apply only to the realm of the means of production. They also apply to the field of consumer goods. Wage goods are material preconditions for reproducing human labour power, i.e. they are indirect means of production. Without a normal calorie input, labour's output of tanks, guns and airplanes steadily declines. Goering's formula of 'guns instead of butter' makes sense only in the short run. In the long run, you cannot produce enough guns without enough butter. Without a given (and steadily increasing) *overall* productive capacity, any industrial power embarking upon large-scale war production will end up by cutting civilian production, which will in turn curtail the material basis for any further expansion of war production itself.

Attempts by academic science to determine more precisely the concept of 'war potential' generally suffer from an insufficient understanding of this dynamic of the laws of reproduction. Nicholas Kaldor, for example, writes: 'The war potential of any country must be determined by at least one of the following four factors: the capital equipment of its industry, its available manpower, its supply of raw materials, and finally, the ability and skill of its industrial organisers, engineers and technicians . . . the ultimate limits to a country's war potential are set simply by the quantity and skill of its manpower, and by the richness of ores and minerals of the areas under its control or with which it is trading.'[9] Milward's formulae suffer from the same weakness. He produces a formula according to which war potential is equal to $p + r + S + e^* - f$, in which p represents the Gross National Product, r the reserve of the economy, S savings from a reduction of replacement investments compared to the peacetime ones, e^* and f reduced efficiency as a result of less competent administration. The reduction in productivity of labour is not even considered, and the precise proportions in which the GNP has to be divided in order to make expansion of war production possible in a given timespan are not taken into account.[10]

The problem of the manpower needed both for a monstrous growth in the armed forces, and for the industry capable of supplying them with a steady flow of more and more sophisticated weapons, became a growing source of crisis and a subject of agonizing choices for all major powers during WWII – with the exception of the USA. (And even in that country, partly due to the massive influx of Southern black sharecroppers into the industrial cities of the North, it caused deep and lasting upheavals in the social structure.) Between May 1939 and September 1944, the male and female labour force engaged in the German economy declined from 39 to 28 million, with women accounting for more than fifty per cent of the final total. Simultaneously, the number of foreign labourers and prisoners engaged in the economy rose from 300,000 to 7.5 million. Thus the Nazis, who had proclaimed their wish to 'cleanse' Germany of 'lower races', imported ten times more so-called *Untermenschen* than the number of Jews and Gypsies they killed outright or in the concentration camps: economic necessities superseded racist obsession with implacable logic.

The balance-sheet of the interplay of all enumerated material and human resources (including the so-called social and moral ones) required to conduct a long war is summarized in the following figures produced by the German author Dieter Petzina:[11]

Arms Production in Billions of 1944 Dollars

	1939	1940	1941	1942
Germany	3.4	6.0	6.0	13.8
Britain	1.0	3.5	6.5	11.1
USSR	3.3	5.0	8.5	13.9
USA	0.6	1.5	4.5	37.5
Japan	0.6	2.0	3.4	4.5

These figures are in part misleading. They leave out the direct French and Italian contributions to the German war industry (the indirect contributions are included in Germany's output figures). They abstract from the differential quality of weapons. In particular, they underestimate the industrial advance of the USA, which shifted into top gear in 1944 (the 1944 figure would be at least double those of Germany, France and Japan put together). They obscure the decline of Soviet arms production in the second half of 1941.[12] But they do reflect the basic relationship of forces in unambiguous fashion. In this light it can be seen that there was no way in which Germany and Japan could have beaten the US-led alliance either in mechanical warfare or in the wherewithal to conduct such warfare.

Some additional conclusions can be deduced. Germany's

advance in rearmament at the start of the Second World War is graphically recorded in the 1939-40 figure, as is the US's delay in converting to a war economy. Britain's tremendous productive effort after Dunkirk is likewise strikingly portrayed; she actually surpassed German arms production in 1941. And the enormous German effort to catch up with the rapidly expanding output of its enemies yielded better results than are generally assumed. But what is especially striking is the enormous increase in Soviet war production between 1941 and 1943 (the 1944 figures are even higher) – in spite of the Nazis' capture of more than forty per cent of Soviet industrial resources through the occupation of Belorussia, the Ukraine, the Donetz basin, as well as the destruction of the factories of Leningrad and Stalingrad. So although overall Soviet industrial output fell dramatically in the summer and autumn of 1941, reaching its lowest point that December, it picked up with a rapidity no foreign observer thought possible, demonstrating the economic and social superiority of a planned economy. This amazing resilience was due to four basic factors: the systematic development of the industrial base in the Urals and other eastern regions during the second and third Five-Year Plans (by June 1941, 39% of Soviet steel, 35% of its coal and 25% of its electricity came from the East); the successful attempt in the last two months of 1941 to dismantle industrial plant in the Western USSR and transport it further east, involving some 1,360 large factories; the building of 2,250 new factories in the eastern part of the country in 1942-4; and the tremendous individual commitment of the Soviet working class and peasant women to keep production going under terrible, sometimes inhuman, conditions of deprivation and destruction.[13]

By 1942, the balance of material resources had already shifted decisively against Germany and Japan, America's entry being the crucial factor though by no means the only one. By mid-1944 Germany's and Japan's material and human resources were severely depleted. In Japan, reproduction contracted to the point where functioning machinery was converted into scrap metal for arms production. In Germany, key sectors of the war economy were paralysed by bottlenecks due to shortages, affecting in particular the production of synthetic oil production (at a time when Romania's oilfields were no longer available) and of ball-bearings.[14] In addition, it became increasingly impossible to maintain the existing level of armed forces and industrial manpower. The influx of prisoners and slave labour dried up with successive military defeats and the loss of occupied territories. The pathetic effort of the *Volkssturm*, i.e. the conscription of young boys and old pensioners, indicates the absolute decline in human resources available to German imperialism. From this moment on, the Axis war effort no longer had a material basis to sustain it. It was no longer a question of avoiding defeat: it was only a question of how long the agony would last.

5.

Strategy

The question of strategy in the Second World War has to be viewed in the light of Clausewitz's famous dictum, often quoted but equally often misunderstood: war is a continuation of politics by other means. The point lies in the term *continuation*. In a war, specifically military means are used to advance a given political (more precisely socio-political, economic-political and class-political) goal. It follows that the subsequent peace settlement should be measured not so much against the damage or defeat inflicted upon the enemy, but against the extent to which the political goal is realized.

General David Fraser's more detailed definition of strategy is therefore quite useful: 'The art of strategy is to determine the aim which is, or should be, inherently political; to derive from that aim a series of military objectives to be achieved; to assess these objectives as to the military requirements they create, and the preconditions which the achievements of each is likely to necessitate; to measure available and potential resources against the requirements; and to chart from this process a coherent pattern of priorities and a rational course of action.'[1]

But while this definition is useful inasmuch as it concentrates on the need to determine priorities in the light of available or potential resources, in order to achieve a central political goal (i.e. it sets out the dialectical relationship between politics and war correctly), it is nevertheless crucially flawed since it neglects the decisive determinants and constraints governing the choice of priorities and, with it, the use of available resources: the class nature of the state which wages the war and hence the class interests which ultimately shape military and geopolitical considerations. The freedom of choice of a given national ruling class is decisively limited by the social and material correlation of forces.

Regarding the *social* correlation of forces, Franz Mehring, writing at the start of WW1, added new insights to the Clausewitz formula: 'War is an explosion (*Entladung*) of historical contradictions which have sharpened to the point where no other means are available for their solution since there are no judges in a class society who can decide by juridical or moral means those conflicts which will be solved by weapons in war. War is therefore a political phenomenon, and not a juridical, moral or even a penal one. War is not conducted in order to punish an enemy for supposed or real sins, but in order to break his resistance to the pursuit of one's own interests. War is not a thing in itself, possessing its own goal: it is an organic part of a policy to whose presuppositions it remains attached and to whose needs it has to adapt its own successes. There has been much debate on whether it is foreign policy which determines internal policy or vice versa. But whatever one's opinion on this subject, the two are indissolubly tied to each other: one cannot act in the one field without provoking a reaction in the other. It is possible to misunderstand this inter-relation, but such miscomprehension does not eliminate it. One may try to suspend class and party struggles during a war, gladly or reluctantly, deliberately or under compulsion, but whatever one does, these struggles will continue, albeit latently. For under the influence of war, the correlation of forces between different classes and parties is considerably modified.'[2]

Lenin accepted Mehring's interpretation of Clausewitz and, characteristically, gave it greater precision. The First World War was 'a continuation of the politics of Great Powers and of the principal classes within them'. The social character of the war was thus determined by the politics the war was designed to continue, by the class which conducted the war and decided its goals. In approaching the strategies adopted by the warring states in WWII, one should therefore bear in mind that they reflected not only 'foreign policy' intentions of nation states but also 'internal' class and party struggles – i.e. one should understand them in their global class determination.[3]

As for the *material* correlation of forces, what the enemy can and intends to do weighs heavily upon any government's rational choice of its own priorities in the utilization of resources.[4] Most of the powers engaged in World War II underestimated this aspect of strategy, paying a heavy price for their mistakes.

The history of modern warfare reveals a habitual succession of predominantly offensive and defensive weapons. A major conflict dominated by mobile warfare is generally succeeded by one in which military thinking is based on defense. The American Civil War and the Franco-German War of 1870-1 were wars of movement; they were succeeded by the trench warfare of WWI. The invention of the machine gun, able to mow down thousands of soldiers per hour from an entrenched position, made offensive war virtually impossible in 1914-18. In WWII, by contrast, the use of tanks, armoured cars or artillery mounted on lorries, coupled with aircraft attacks on weak spots along defense lines, meant that offensive strategies once again dominated military thinking. After WWII, in conventional warfare too the development of a whole family of guided missiles for use in air, on land and sea, signals the return of the strategy of defence. Naturally, there is a constant incentive to conduct research in order to counter the effects of any efficient offensive or defensive weapon. Since the First World War, scientific-technological research and development (R and D) has become an integral part of big business; being highly concentrated, it can easily be state-funded for military purposes. The integration of the industrial and military needs of a given nation-state in turn considerably boosts industrial development.

Imaginative military experts before World War II – Tukhachevsky, Guderian, Fuller, Liddell Hart, de Gaulle, Martell, Swinton, Doumenc – all basically understood the implications of the trench warfare of WWI.[5] For some, the lessons of that war dictated the establishment of a chain of impregnable forts based on heavy artillery: the *Maginot* line, the so-called Stalin line,[6] and the Eben-Emael/Liege system of fortification along the northern part of the Belgian-German frontier[7] were the prototypes. Against them, the new strategists of mobile warfare asserted that heavy fire-power, based on the combination of field artillery, aerial bombardment, and heavy armoured guns enabled concentrated tank units to break through almost any defensive line, and encircle and destroy large enemy forces. Such an offensive strategy would focus its efforts on those weaker points of the enemy's fortified positions which any front of hundreds or thousands of kilometres could not avoid. The emphasis was now on *initiative in the offensive*, reinforced by surprise attack.[8]

This military strategy triggered off a qualitative increase in the importance of secret services, engaged by both sides to discover the enemy's plans and to hide one's own. Deliberate deception of the enemy developed into an art. At each of the war's turning-points, the techniques of camouflage and deception played such a role as they never had before and probably never will again.[9]

What the combination of armoured cars and fighter bombers were for land battles, aircraft carriers and torpedoes were for battles on the sea. Dreadnoughts became hopelessly obsolete with the development of these weapons. Torpedoes launched from airplanes catapulted from aircraft carriers could inflict heavy damage upon any battleship or heavy cruiser. The British Navy used them successfully against the Italian fleet in the Mediterranean in the battle of Matapan in November 1940, only itself to become a victim of Japanese superiority in aircraft carriers: a large part of its Far Eastern fleet was destroyed by the Japanese navy in the South China Sea in January 1942 due to inadequate air cover. And the fact that the Japanese air force did not destroy all the US aircraft carriers moored in Pearl Harbor turned their success into a Pyrrhic victory.

German imperialism, preoccupied in the first half of the war (1939-42) with the development and employment of offensive weaponry, was thereafter forced – thanks to increasing enemy superiority in offensive weapons – to turn its attention to design and manufacture of defensive weapons, especially anti-tank guns and anti-aircraft artillery. The famous *Panzerfaust* then developed was far superior to the American bazooka. Nevertheless, neither the anti-aircraft gun nor the *Panzerfaust* could counteract the superior fire power of the fighter bomber and the armoured car on the battlefield. Offensive weapons dominated WWII till the end and decided its key battles.

But if military strategy is largely determined by the superiority of a given type of weaponry, amenable to mass production at any given moment, it does not exclusively depend upon it. The decision to adopt an offensive or defensive strategy flows from the overall relation of forces in which a warring state finds itself enmeshed. It is generally recognized that, given its particular position, German imperialism had to opt for a *Blitzkrieg* strategy in 1939-41: time was against the Third Reich. The two-year advantage in rearmament with which the *Wehrmacht* entered the war[10] risked being lost if the war became a protracted one. Both its enemies in Europe, Britain and the Soviet Union, could draw on much larger reserves of raw materials and manpower than Germany possessed, and after the American entry into the war, on the practically inexaustible resources of US industry as well. It was therefore imperative for Germany to achieve decisive victory in Europe before the USA became involved on the other side. For Hitler at least, the war against the Soviet Union was the key: 'Britain's hope is in Russia and the United States. If the hope in Russia disappears, America is also lost, because elimination of Russia would tremendously increase Japan's power in the Far East', he told his political and military chiefs in July 1940.[11] Once the war on the Eastern Front turned against Germany after the battle of Stalingrad, Germany's overall position changed as well. She could no longer win the war, so her military strategy became one of defence, meanwhile hoping that a political compromise could be reached with the Western Allies on the basis of common hostility to the Red Army's advance beyond the Soviet border. Germany's defensive strategy was highly effective, as her enemies learnt to their great cost in the East and West alike. In the end, however, it was the German bourgeoisie which paid an even heavier price because its new military strategy became increasingly divorced from any feasible positive political goal after 1943.

Japan's military strategy was dictated by a position quite different from that of Germany. Its interest lay in the pursuit of war against China and the attack on Pearl Harbor was designed to secure raw materials with which to continue its engagement on the Asian mainland. Thereafter, it was a matter of keeping an outside defence perimeter for these conquests. Part of its success was based on brilliant strategic concepts such as the Malay campaign conceived by Akira and executed by Yamashita. As a result, Japan's strategy became defensive after less than six months. But Japan committed the decisive strategic blunder of attempting to combine defence of this vital perimeter with unnecessary offensive forays into the South Pacific and even into the Indian Ocean. They thereby overextended themselves and lost, through attrition, such vital forces as their main aircraft carriers and crack infantry divisions in battles around Guadalcanal, Midway and upper Burma.

British imperialism initially opted for a defensive strategy, aimed at keeping open the two lifelines of its economy: the Atlantic and the Mediterranean. At the beginning of 1943, when a shift onto the offensive became possible, British political interests dictated its military priorities. With the defeat of Germany in sight, the British bourgeoisie wanted above all to avoid Soviet military superiority in Central and Southeastern Europe. It therefore favoured the Western Allies' entry into Europe from the South (via Italy or the Balkans) so as to prevent the Red Army from occupying the heartland of Europe. Furthermore, British financial and manpower resources were in a parlous state in 1943-4. Its foreign holdings were draining fast.[12] The number of soldiers committed to Operation Overlord made steady replacement or reinforcement practically impossible. Montgomery's sudden and uncharacteristic commitment to Blitzkrieg on the Western front reveals that a rapid victory became as important to Churchill in the autumn of 1944 as it had been to Hitler in 1940-1.

Only American imperialism could face the war with total confidence, enjoying as it did a huge reservoir of manpower, raw materials and productive capacity. Given sufficient time, its military force could increase well beyond the bounds of the current war's requirements – provided, however, that the USSR and China would fight major continental battles. The USA fought a war on two continents, its forces divided in the ratio of two to one between theatres separated by more than fifteen thousand miles. The USA could fight a long war in the knowledge that time worked against the other participants, 'friends' and foes alike; the longer the war lasted the more economically and financially weakened by it they would be. A long war was indeed the shortest route to the 'American century'. Consequently, US strategy became a matter of slow, plodding, steady advance, particularly in Europe, based on overwhelming air superiority and a considerable presence on the ground – a strategy devoid of any real initiatives, breakthroughs or daring surprises. When events took an unexpected turn – e.g. the capture of the Remagen bridge – it came as a jolt to the American warlords too.

The distance of Washington from the theatres of war gave the US military commanders a degree of autonomy others did not possess, and hence the capacity to exploit opportunities uninhibited by rigid war plans and chains of command. In the Pacific theatre, Admiral Nimitz displayed considerable talent as a strategist: the leap-frog advance in a straight line from Guadalcanal and New Guinea to Okinawa, avoiding the superior Japanese forces entrenched in Indonesia, Malaya and on the continental rim, is evidence enough. After having achieved naval and air superiority in the Pacific at Midway, Saipan and Truk islands, the

US high command could pursue this course, knowing that since the Japanese could not adequately supply their forces in South-East Asia, they posed no threat to the flanks of the American thrust towards the Japanese homeland.

The Soviet bureaucracy entered the war with its military forces wholly unprepared for what was to come. The disastrous Finnish campaign of 1939-40 confirmed the terrible state of the Soviet armed forces and encouraged some rethinking and reorganization. This had been brought about largely by Stalin's criminal purge of the Red Army, which compounded the effects of the bureaucratic mismanagement of the economy and society.[13] Totally surprised by Operation Barbarossa, the Soviet leadership did not recover the initiative until the autumn of 1942.[14] It was able to do so because the tremendous increase in its industrial potential and productive reserve created by the October Revolution and the planned economy – in sharp contrast to the military débâcle of Tsarism in WWI. A new echelon of field commanders soon emerged from the tough school of battle and Stalin's instinct for self-preservation was sufficiently strong to allow them considerable scope for independent strategic initiative. This led to the victories at Stalingrad, Kursk, Minsk, of the Pruth and Vistula which broke the backbone of the Germany army.[15]

At the end of the war crude attempts were made to present the Red Army's defeats of 1941-42 as the products of a strategy of calculated retreat, deliberately drawing the *Wehrmacht* into the Russian interior only to destroy it in a series of counteroffensives. There is no substance whatsoever in such claims. Indeed, Stalin himself vigorously denounced such rumours at the time; they were militarily counterproductive since they encouraged the troops to go on the defensive and fostered defeatism in the ranks.[16] Once the battle for sheer survival was won, however, and the war had switched from the defensive to the offensive, military strategy began to be influenced by the Kremlin's plans for a post-war settlement, themselves a reflection of the bureaucracy's fundamentally contradictory political objectives. Torn between the desire to maintain the 'great anti-fascist alliance' and the need for national security, its policy remained in the traditional mould of European power politics – a combination of diplomacy and military strength in pursuit of clearly defined spheres of influence to which it was ready to subordinate the revolutionary upheavals in Europe and Asia. However, this strategy foundered upon the bedrock of a significant development to which the war gave rise: the emergence of the United States as the dominant imperialist power.

Unable to provide for its security via an enduring alliance with Britain and the United States, the Soviet leadership chose instead to transform the East European border states into a strategic *glacis* designed to protect the country's western flank against possible future German revanchism. Given the revolutionary possibilities present in the last phase of the war and the immense sacrifice of the Soviet people themselves, this was a modest enough aim. But it encountered increasing hostility from the erstwhile allies, leading directly to the Cold War. Given the American bourgeoisie's enhanced perception of its own economic and military might, especially after the use of the atomic bomb against Japanese cities, this was in the last instance inevitable, yet it still came as a surprise to Stalin and his administrators.

The fate of Chiang Kai-Shek's regime affords a good illustration of the over-determination of purely military strategy by political or, more fundamentally, socio-political interests. It was perfectly feasible for the Kuomintang command to develop an offensive strategy against the Japanese invaders.[17] Chiang's army had been trained by *Reichswehr* officers in the thirties who were partisans of mobile warfare. Indeed, Chiang hastened his defeat in the civil war by frequently reckless offensive thrusts of his main forces deep into the quagmire of Manchuria and the North China plain in 1945-6. What made him reluctant to commit his growing reserves of American weaponry and American-trained soldiers against the Japanese army – to the great despair of US General Stillwell as well as other American officers and diplomats – was not any military incapacity but basic political priorities. For Chiang (as ultimately also for the USA), the future of capitalism in China was ten times more important than the war against Japan. The main trial of strength was to come after Japan's defeat, with Chu Teh's, Peng Te-Huai's, Lin Piao's and Ten Hsiao-Ping's armies – i.e. with China's peasants and workers in uniform.

The Chinese case exemplifies a fundamental truth of any major war: although the outcome is heavily influenced by a given material and human balance of forces, military strategies are not solely a function of these. They are ultimately a function of the *relations of forces* between the main classes involved in the war, and hence of political and economic goals. Class prejudice, self-perception, inhibitions and self-deception, as well as inadequate information and outright errors of judgement, can therefore all play important roles in determining military strategy. A whole series of errors of an essentially political nature influencing the outcome of WWII can be cited:

1. Hitler's belief that his enemies would not unite and that he could therefore take them on one by one;
2. Stalin's illusion that the USSR could avoid war with Germany;
3. the French, British and Soviet leaders' underestimation of the likely success of the German *Blitzkrieg* in 1939-41 in Europe and a similar underestimation by the British and Americans of Japan's 'first strike' capacity and the scope of its victories in South-East Asia in 1941-2;
4. Hitler's underestimation of British imperialism's resilience at the start of the war and the Allies' of Germany's after the tide had turned in 1943;
5. general underestimation of US war potential and its bourgeoisie's determination to go for unconditional surrender;
6. the capitalist powers' underestimation of the anti-imperialist and revolutionary dynamic unleashed by the war in Europe and Asia, one largely shared by Stalin;
7. the capitalist powers' underestimation of the USSR's industrial and social strength.

Of all these it was the last three which more than any others determined the final shape of the post-war settlement. The underestimation of the class struggle and of the Soviet state's ability not only to survive the onslaught of Europe's most powerful capitalist state but also to go on to defeat it, was shared by all the capitalist powers and led to the now familiar landmarks of contemporary history: the division of Europe; the victory of the revolution in China, Yugoslavia and Albania; the rise of revolutionary and anti-colonial struggles in the Third World.

Errors of judgement in the conduct of the war were closely linked to an obstinate refusal to accept information which conflicted with both political and military-strategic prejudices. Stalin's refusal to treat seriously news of impending German attack was a classic example of this tendency. On the eve of the German invasion in May 1940, Gamelin, the French commander-in-chief, was convinced that the main thrust would be delivered at the Louvain-Namur sector and not through the Ardennes, despite information to the contrary.[18] On receiving news that a strong

Anglo-American convoy had crossed the Straits of Gibraltar on 8 November 1942, Hitler rushed to strengthen Crete and Tripoli and refused to consider the possibility that the landing would take place in French North Africa. He likewise refused to believe in the concentration of huge Soviet reserves north of the River Don and Stalingrad in the autumn of the same year. In December 1941, when Roosevelt and his chiefs of staff learnt that Tokyo was recalling its negotiating team from Washington, they knew that this meant war but would not entertain the possibility of a Japanese attack on Pearl Harbor.[19]

Such errors were not just questions of personal idiosyncracies but referred to an important problem confronting war leaders: the problem of initiative. As Mehring noted in 1914, they are faced with the terrifying choice between inertia and daring, between *Wägen* and *wagen* (in the words of von Moltke, the architect of the German victory over France in 1871), 'lucidity' and 'audacity' (as Napoleon put it).[20] This problem is inherent in the very nature of action, be it military or political. Striking a correct balance between lucidity and audacity, caution and initiative, reality and desire is what the art of war is all about.

Moreover, if war is a specific form of politics, then a precondition for its successful outcome (achieving the desired goals) lies in grasping all the possibilities offered by war. By the same token, it also resides in understanding the limitations inherent in the use of armed violence. A fundamental failure of German imperialism during its Nazi phase lay in its overestimation of the instrument of force in the pursuit of European hegemony. Having crushed its domestic class opponent, the German bourgeoisie offered the peoples of Europe nothing but subjugation. The dire urgency of Trotsky's warnings on what the Nazi victory in Germany portended for the European labour movement was confirmed with a vengeance in the enormous death-toll and in the destruction of the very foundations of civilized existence entailed by the war.

The American and British ruling classes fought the war not in order to defeat fascism, but to break the resistance of the German and Japanese bourgeoisies to the maintenance or extension of their own particular interests. Those sections of the labour movement in Europe and Asia who entered the war supporting their national bourgeoisies in this enterprise, and without elaborating their own independent class goals, necessarily also ended up by supporting the denial or restriction of democratic and national liberties for millions of workers and peasants in large parts of Europe and Asia, whenever these latter rose to assert interests that ran counter to those of the Western bourgeoisie. In other words, this lack of clarity regarding the social character of the war waged by the capitalist states was to lead – as confirmed by practical experience, especially after 1943 – directly to class collaboration and the strangling of the revolutionary possibilities which emerged during it. There is a striking parallel here between the ends of the First and Second World Wars, with the important difference that the ability of the European working class to formulate independent war aims was considerably greater in 1917-8 than in 1943-5.

When all is said and done, moral and political forces have their autonomous weight in determining the success of any given strategy. Tukhachevsky expressed this most clearly in a talk given six months before his execution, to the Soviet General Staff Academy on the nature of military operations in the initial period of the forthcoming war, which he was convinced would be fought against Germany. 'As for the *Blitzkrieg* which is so propagandized by the Germans, this is directed towards an enemy who doesn't want to and won't fight it out. If the Germans met an opponent who stands up and fights and takes the offensive himself, this would give a different aspect to things. The struggle would be bitter and protracted; by its very nature it would induce great fluctuations in the front on this side and that, and in great depth. In the final resort, all would depend on who had the greater moral fibre and who at the close of operations disposed of operational reserves in depth.'[21]

6.

Weapons

The Second World War appears above all as a war of mass-produced mechanical weapons. It was a conveyor-belt war, the war of military Fordism. (There is some irony in this, as Henry Ford himself was an early supporter of Hitler and personally opposed to the US entry into the war.[1]) Mass production of airplanes, tanks, artillery, machine-guns, mines, ammunition, took place either in factories specially created for that purpose or in reconverted textile, automobile or tractor plants. Oddly enough, neither the USA nor the USSR tried to standardize and mass produce spare parts – wheels, axels, etc. – for the weapons requiring them. It was Hitler's architect, Albert Speer, who took this step forward in weapons production in the framework of the post-Stalingrad 'total war' launched by the Nazi regime. The results were impressive.

The capacity for mass production of weapons was a function of the general industrial resources of the warring powers analysed in a previous chapter. In this respect Germany and Japan were over-whelmed by the sheer superiority of America's industrial capacity. The *Wehrmacht* had used 2,700 tanks on the Western front in May 1940, 3,350 in its invasion of the USSR in June 1941. The US government decided to produce 45,000 tanks in 1942 and 75,000 in 1943. Germany's annual airplane production amounted to around 11,000 in 1940 and 1941. The US government decided to build 43,000 airplanes in 1942 and 100,000 in 1942. Its output of merchant ships rose from 1 million BRT in 1941 to 7 million in 1943 and 10 million in 1944. The German and Japanese governments made desperate efforts to overcome this handicap after Stalingrad and Midway respectively. General Thomas, the real boss of the German armaments industry, wanted to quadruple weapons output compared to the 1941 level. He did not succeed in this goal in 1943, but came near to it in 1944, as is shown by the following figures:[2]

German Arms Production during World War II

	1940	1941	1942	1943	1944
Airplanes	10,826	11,776	15,556	25,527	39,807
Armoured vehicles	2,154	5,138	9,278	19,824	27,340
Automatic infantry weapons	170,880	324,850	316,724	435,384	787,081
Grenade throwers	4,380	4,230	9,780	22,955	30,898
Guns equal to or bigger than 7.5 cm	5,964	8,124	14,316	35,796	55,936

Japan's warlords undertook a similar programme from 1943 onwards. In the middle of 1943 the Tojo government decided to build up to 40,000 airplanes (the navy and army had together called for 70,000, which Tojo considered unattainable).[3] In order to achieve this, virtually the whole of the Japanese textile industry was reconverted into airplane factories. New factories were built alongside the Tokkaido railway line, especially in Nagoya and Shimatsu, while Mitsubishi trust undertook a similar effort in Manchuria. Terrible labour conditions were imposed upon the working class. More than one and a half million handicraftsmen and small shopkeepers were forcibly pressed into wage labour for arms and munition factories, working more than twelve hours a day at starvation wages. Fourteen-year-old girls were sent into coalmines. Infant mortality rose to a level three times that of Britain or France.

But despite these efforts, the quantity of weapons produced in Germany and Japan could not catch up with the American conveyor belt, let alone the combined output of the USA, the USSR and Britain. Under the guidance of Albert Speer and in a context of increased war effort from the second half of 1942, Germany concentrated instead on trying to beat the enemy with qualitatively superior weapons rather than to overwhelm him through sheer quantity.

As a result of specialist research conducted on a strictly military-professional basis, the Third Reich came up with several trump cards in the field of weaponry; two tanks, *Tiger I* and the *Panther,* qualitatively superior to their American and British rivals, though less so vis-à-vis the Soviet heavy tanks (especially where the efficiency of the gun and the thickness of the plate was concerned); the 88 mm anti-aircraft gun of superior accuracy, which was also efficient as anti-tank weapon (as the Western Allies discovered in Normandy[4]); turbo-jet planes, especially the *Messerschmidt* 262 and 163 (only 1,000 of which were used in 1944-5); and guided missiles, among them the famous V1 and V2 rockets, which briefly came into their own at the end of the war.

Japan's attempt at producing qualitatively superior weapons largely failed, although the navy maintained its advance in the field of sea and air torpedoes, probably the most efficient used on either side throughout the war. In spite of the quality of Mitsubishi 00 and 01, the 40,000 airplanes produced from 1943 onwards were often of inferior quality, as a result of production errors due to the lack of skilled labour and sufficient quality control. Many of them crashed on their carriers before even being used against the enemy.[5]

Japanese 'secret weapons' took the pathetic form of explosive charges mounted inside paper baloons, which the wind was supposed to carry across the Pacific. Of the 9,000 balloons launched between November 1944 and March 1945, only 900 reached the American continent, generally exploding over fields and forests far from any factory or city. Only six inhabitants of the USA were victims of these war toys.[6]

Artillery and explosives played a key role during the war. According to some estimates, over thirty per cent of the soldiers who died in battle were killed by artillery. The hollow charge and the proximity fuse were the two big innovations in this field introduced by the German and American army respectively. But the perfection of mobile artillery – howitzers for tanks, half-track vehicles towing guns and self-propelled guns – was the key factor making the *Blitzkrieg* and generally mobile warfare of the World War Two variety possible.[7] Whilst at the beginning of the war the *Wehrmacht* also enjoyed some superiority in light artillery, mines (the famous magnetic underwater mines which the British Navy so feared turned out to be largely a flop), fog- and flame- throwers and hand grenades, as well as in the use of dive bombers, these advantages were progressively lost as weapons production advanced in

Britain, USA and USSR. In the field of light artillery, the Soviet *Katyushka*, mounted on trucks, was superior to any German weapon, as were American flame-throwers and hand grenades. The 'crabs' and the 'crocodiles', special British tanks, played an important role in Normandy in 1944.[8] American skill and ingenuity produced them in record time, just as it provided the armies invading Western Europe with a steady flow of oil delivered via pipelines first under the Channel and then across France. The superiority of the Soviet T-34, already mentioned above, meant that half of the German tanks engaged in the invasion of the Soviet Union were destroyed after three weeks of war.[9]

In general, Soviet efforts in weapons production during the war were tremendous, as can be seen from the following figures (which slightly underestimate German output):

Weapons Output during the German-Soviet War
(1000s)

	USSR (from July 1941 till August 1945)	Germany (from January 1941 till April 1945)
Tanks and armoured gun carriers	102.8	43.4
Military aircraft	112.1	80.6
Guns of all calibres	482.2	311.5
Grenade throwers	351.8	73.0
Machine-guns	1,515.9	1,096.6
Machine-pistols	6,173.9	1,097.9

These figures are all the more impressive as the total industrial potential of German imperialism was greater than the Soviet Union's after the conquest of a large proportion of Soviet Western provinces. Soviet success suggests the superiority of a planned economy in centralizing and mobilizing resources as well as the existence of considerable morale among the workforce and the fighting men and women. To be sure, one should not forget that valuable military aid was extended to the Soviet Union by its allies. (The relative and absolute value of this aid has always been in dispute). However, one should bear two factors in mind. Firstly, that Soviet military successes were based primarily and unmistakably on the efforts and sacrifices of the Soviet people themselves, and not on the external aid given to them by the United States. Secondly, that the amount of aid extended by the USA through Lend Lease and otherwise to all its allies was relatively small: some fifteen per cent of its military output and an even smaller percentage of its food production.[10]

Soviet military aircraft design, largely obsolete before the war, advanced steadily, especially under the impact of talented designers like Tupolev, Ilyshin, Yakovlev and Lavochkin; several of these specialists had to be brought out of the Gulag to work in the war industry. Soviet air defence was very successful in defending the capital; whereas the Allies, and especially the Western Allies, could inflict heavy damage on the German cities, the *Luftwaffe* never succeeded in overcoming Moscow's air defence.[11]

After some initial muddle, and despite ongoing quarrels among air commanders, Anglo-American fighter-bombers, especially the Mustang, achieved decisive superiority and wiped the German airforce from the West European sky – something important to the outcome of the battle of Normandy and for France in the summer of 1944.

In the realm of naval warfare, Germany's feeble attempts to defeat the British Navy with pocket cruisers and destroyers of superior design yielded no significant fruits. Neither did Italy's attempt to employ fast small seacraft (*Schnellboote*) in the Mediterranean, nor the Japanese Navy's attempts to use pocket submarines against the US Navy in the Pacific. Under the guidance of Doenitz, a fanatical believer in offensive submarine warfare, the German Navy concentrated all its efforts on developing U-Boat technology and tactics. The end-products were the *Schnorkel* and the 'pack' tactics – attacks on convoys by many submarines. But while inflicting a lot of damage, in the end they did not stop the transatlantic flow of goods thanks to the massive use of anti-submarine aircraft, sonar and other sophisticated means of submarine detection, and especially the amazing achievements of the US naval yards, which built new ships considerably faster than Doenitz could sink the old ones.[12]

Mass-produced landing crafts and amphibious vehicles in the USA were one of the most important innovations of WWII, one which Japan and Germany never seriously tried to match. The simplicity of the design made them – like trucks, tanks and merchant ships – into typical conveyor-belt products, in which the US proved insurpassable. They created the material preconditions for the invasion of Europe in the West, and for the American

Navy's 'island hopping' strategy in the Pacific.[13] In contrast, the Japanese Navy concentrated on the design and production of superior battleships and aircraft carriers. Given the relative weakness of Japan's heavy industry, it achieved startling success. But as the war dragged on, the increasing lack of resources caused proportional loss of momentum, with results such as the suicide attacks by Japanese pilots against the American fleet, the *Kamikaze* using planes partially built with wood.[14]

In the mass production of standard weapons, accelerating scientific research and industrial innovation increasingly came into their own. In that sense, the Second World War was also the war of late capitalism for which that acceleration was a landmark.[15] At the same time it acted as a detonator of the third technological revolution, three of whose main components – the electronic calculating machine (out of which grew the computer), nuclear energy and automation, – actually originated in weapons production. A much underestimated component of WWII weaponry was a revolutionary improvement in communications systems, in the first place in the use of two-way radio transmission and radiotelephony, which enabled tank, division and even army commanders to be in instant contact on the ground. It played a decisive role in the breakthrough battles of the war: the Meuse battle of 1940; the *Wehrmacht* victories in June-August 1941; the Red Army victories at Stalingrad and at Jassy on the Pruth; and the Western Allied advance in France in the summer of 1944.

The most revolutionary advance in weapons production was of course the development of the atomic bomb at the end of the war, after Japan had already been defeated. It is the main, and most gruesome, legacy of this war – a symbol of bourgeois readiness to use ultimate aggression if and when it feels threatened in its global economic and political interests.

7.

Logistics

Logistics in the strict sense of the word – transporting and quartering armies and keeping them supplied with food, clothing and weapons – acquired a new dimension during World War Two, parallel to that of the arms industry. This was primarily due to changes in the transport industry before the war, above all the impact of the motor car. America's top strategist, General Marshall, was to call the Second World War the automobile war.

The use of Paris taxis during the battle of the Marne notwithstanding, World War One had largely been a railway war. Indeed, there are historians who defend the somewhat mechanistic thesis that the constraints of the railway time-tables imposed such a rigid framework on the mechanics of general military mobilization that they made war inevitable at the end of July 1914 – at least as far as the Russian, German and French general staffs were concerned.

Be that as it may, flexibility in the transport of large numbers of men and arms increased dramatically with the massive use of automobiles and trucks by the armed forces. Indeed, WWII became the first motorized war in history. The Third Reich illustrated this basic logistical switch when it centered its war preparation not on the construction of new strategically important railways, but on the construction of an up-to-date network of motorways, the *Autobahnen*.

As the war operations neared Central and Western Europe, the railway network again played a key role in German logistics. The *Reichsbahn* administration became a vital cog in the war machine, a fact reflected in increased salaries for the railway employees.[1]

The extent of motorization of the great powers' armies varied. In fact, only the American and British armed forces became thoroughly motorized from 1942 onwards, to such an extent that the landing of one million soldiers in Normandy was accompanied by no less than 140,000 motorized vehicles (100,000 in the first eleven days alone). The German army still employed horses widely, and increasingly so as the war dragged on. The German infantry literally walked into the Soviet Union and walked back home, its supplies driven by horse-carts. The Soviet and Japanese armies were even less motorized. Japan's war in China was largely a railway war. The importance to the Japanese high command of instituting direct railway links between Singapore and Manchuria, especially the Singapore-Burma-Thailand link, is well known.[2] As to the USSR, the car and tractor factories almost completely switched over to tank production for much of the war. Its armed forces were consequently heavily deficient in trucks and this was one area where deliveries from the USA did play an important role.

The movement and supply of troops are vital complements to the elaboration of strategy and tactics; the outcome of battles often depends on their proper coordination.[3] Quite distinct problems arose for the five main warring states, reflecting their differential economic power and different social structures.

The Japanese armed forces, spread over an enormous area and disposing of a much more limited material base than the other belligerents, suffered after 1942 from a scarcity of food and clothing. In the occupied territories they largely lived on local supplies, causing increasing want among the local population and ultimately among the soldiers themselves. Wholesale starvation of prisoners of war and other such phenomena in response to the ever more desperate state of food supply characterized the last years of the war in the areas under Japanese occupation. The crucial battle of Guadalcanal was lost mainly as a result of insufficient food; the Japanese troops had to survive for weeks on a diet of wild berries and herbs. The Imperial Navy, unable to bring enough ships to its outposts, tried to have supplies transported in cylinders towed across the sea. These efforts bore meagre fruit: of the 1,500 cylinders launched in this way, only some 300 actually reached the beaches. In Japan itself, food rations began to shrink in 1943 and by 1944 were largely inadequate, notwithstanding the great frugality of the Japanese people.[4] This contributed to a growing war weariness in the country and the spread of the black market.[5]

The Soviet Union entered WWII with its agriculture in deep crisis, caused by Stalin's reckless policies of forced collectivization. But whereas the *kolkhoz* structure for the most part withstood the test of war and no basic structural changes ensued in the organization of Soviet agriculture, food shortages remained acute for the duration of the conflict. They were exacerbated by the loss of the rich agricultural lands of the Ukraine in the summer of 1941 and the massive conscription of the adult peasant population (a large proportion of agricultural output had to be shouldered by women). The terms of trade between industry and agriculture now changed in the peasants' favour, but the increased paper money revenue of the village brought no significant increase in agricultural production. The soldiers of the Red Army were inadequately fed, and tended to compensate by procuring food en route. The possibility of living off the land was itself severely restricted, however, by the devastation wreaked by Hitler's scorched earth policy and the Soviet desire to deny the enemy food. The alimentary situation of the Red Army only improved after it had moved further West, in the concluding stages of the 1943-44 counter-offensive.

Further to the East, when the survival of Chiang Kai-Shek's rump China was seriously threatened, the supply of government and armies at Chungking became one of the key objectives of the Japanese-Allied test of strength in Burma. The Imperial Army had succeeded in cutting the Burma road, but the USA managed to build the Ledo road – at great expense and with limited logistical capacity – via which it was able to supply US troops in China (not to speak of the black market consequent upon its presence and the largesse extended to Chiang and his family by the US).

German imperialism went to the war with a strict system of rationing, intended to ensure all the basic needs of the armed forces as well as a certain minimum to all German citizens. Such rigid priorities determined the treatment of the population in the occupied countries and of prisoners of war. Extreme cruelty resulted: the progressive plundering of local resources caused near-starvation, especially in the food-deficient areas of the Balkans; inmates of the concentration camps and the Jewish ghettoes were literally starved to death; hundreds of thousands of Soviet prisoners of war met with the same fate. The Italian rationing system started to break down in 1942, inflicting terrible hardship on the working-class and poorer strata of the population. At the end of 1943, the cost of living was seven times higher than in 1939, while money wages had hardly doubled. Per capita meat consumption had fallen to an annual level of 11 kilos, against 63 kilos in Britain, 51 in Germany and 39 in France.[6]

The supply of the British armed forces emerged as a problem in the summer of 1940 following the opening of the war in the Atlantic. Strict rationing was applied both to the civilian population and the armed forces. Transportation was the weak link and remained so until the war against the German submarines was won. The British units in the Middle East, on the other hand, received adequate provisions – far better than the Italian and German – initially coming through the South Atlantic via the Cape, thereby tying up an enormous amount of shipping. This is why control over the Mediterranean became a strategic objective for British imperialism. The Axis lost the war in Egypt essentially because of the unresolved logistical problems, above all the inability to cut the supply lines of the British Eighth Army in the Mediterranean and their own acute shortage of oil, ammunition and spare parts for tanks.[7]

In contrast to its allies and enemies, American armed forces enjoyed nearly unlimited supplies. Roosevelt deliberately opted in favour of conducting a 'rich man's war'. German and Soviet commentators, but also British officers and men – especially in the Far East – mocked the GIs as 'soldiers of comfort', thereby making a virtue of necessity. Each American division consumed 720 tons of supplies a day, against barely 200 for its German counterpart.[8] While the enormous logistical infrastructure of the US army, navy and air force tended to clog up supply lines, often interfering with the actual conduct of the war itself, it nevertheless brought about a steady increase in the armed forces' efficiency and preserved morale among soldiers fighting far from a home never threatened by invasion. Indeed, this 'policy of comfort' was socially indispensible and paid off for the American ruling class.

For the most part Japan was able to keep its sea lanes between the homeland and its far-flung conquests open in 1942 and 1943, albeit with increasing difficulty. In the North, the supply lines between Manchuria – which had become the main industrial base of the Japanese war industry – and the homeland were adequately protected until the very end of the war. But in the south, the majority were cut from the second half of 1943 onward. Loss of merchant ships as a result of US submarine action was staggering: 139 cargoes or half a million BRT in 1942 and 300 cargoes or more than one million BRT in 1943 (one should bear in mind that the whole Japanese merchant navy amounted to only five million BRT before the war, and that many of its ships were turned into troop transports after hostilities commenced). It would not be an exaggeration to say that Japan's merchant navy had suffered a fifty per cent reduction by the end of 1943.[9]

Japan started the Pacific war in order to attain the rich raw materials of South East Asia required for the maintenance of its war machine in China. Although it controlled them until August 1945, it could not deliver them to its war industry after 1942. The battle of the Pacific turned out to be a key battle of the war, reflecting its global character. As in the Atlantic, another key theatre, the sea battles were essentially fought between submarines and military vessels protecting the merchant convoys – though mines, airplanes and surface combat ships also played a role. The offensive element started with a large advantage, enhanced by the changes in submarine construction and tactics referred to in the previous chapter. Protection of submarine bases also became increasingly important, being more successfully prosecuted on the Atlantic coast than in the Pacific. Gradually, however, defence caught up with offense in the Atlantic, thanks especially to the *sonar* and other submarine detection devices, and to the massive use of longer and longer range aircraft against the submarines. The broadening of the perimeters of British and particularly American aero-naval bases in the Atlantic during 1940-41 proved of great importance, as did the construction of special airplanes geared to anti-submarine war. After the spring of 1943, following terrible losses, Doenitz had to withdraw his forces; so demoralized were they by the Western Allies' technical superiority that he did not dare use the still considerable number of submarines at his disposal against the landing crafts during the Normandy invasion and after.[10]

In war, keeping one's own supply lines open is a task complemented by simultaneously trying to cut off the enemy's. Blockade, a deliberate attempt to starve a country of raw materials, ammunition and food has been a permanent feature of modern warfare since the Napoleonic era. Indeed, the importance of economic warfare was well understood by the British government, which established a special ministry to deal with it in its defensive and offensive aspects. In Japan, another island power, economic warfare assumed an essentially defensive character from the outset. The same was true of the Soviet Union. As long as the Third Reich was strong, Hitler calmly contemplated starving the British population as a way of winning the war against Britain, but took moral exception to the Western Allies' economic blockade of Germany.[11]

The importance of food during the war transformed the position of at least one country: the formally neutral Argentina. The longer the war dragged on, the higher food prices rose on the world market and the stronger became Argentina's position as a main source of wheat and meat. The Argentinian bourgeoisie was able to build up a reservoir of foreign currency with these windfall profits, thereby achieving a prerequisite for the industrialization and capital accumulation relatively independent of imperialist control which became the basis for the Peronist regime. The millions of victims of the great Bengali famine and Argentina's sudden enrichment graphically confirm the link between world war and world market, irrespective of whether those who benefited or suffered from it were formally involved in the hostilities.

8.

Science and Administration

World War One had already witnessed the novel impact of science on the actual conduct of military operations – especially through the development of poison gas and Germany's production of synthetic oil, both linked to the second technological revolution based on the chemical industry. In the inter-war period the importance of scientific research for technological innovation steadily increased, thereby laying the basis for further military-scientific research and invention.

Four radical innovations during WWII were directly stimulated by scientific research for military purposes: radar; sonar; the proximity fuse; and the atomic bomb.[1] In all four areas the Western Allies enjoyed a decisive advantage. In the case of harnessing atomic energy, the advantage was gained with the help of scientists fleeing the continent of Europe under the onslaught of the fascist regimes.[2] Germany had been ahead in the use of radio beams for offensive purposes (especially guidance of bomber aircraft towards their targets), but the British RAF was the first to realize the decisive role that radar, linked to ground control networks, could play in protecting airfields and guiding fighter aircraft.[3] This was probably the decisive factor in the Battle of Britain in the summer and autumn of 1940.

The use of radar was, however, much more extensive than the widely-publicised role it performed for RAF Fighter Command. For example, it played an important part in protecting the *Luftwaffe's* airfields in Russia in 1942-3, thereby foiling the Red Army's attempt to destroy the German airforce on the ground shortly before the *Wehrmacht's* assault on the Kursk salient on 5 July 1942 (Operation Citadel).[4]

Radar was used for guiding naval artillery towards their target, bombers or missiles towards their objectives, anti-aircraft batteries towards incoming aircraft, and for defending aircraft carriers against enemy attack. The combination of micro-wave radar and computer-type mechanical calculators made anti-aircraft guns into deadly weapons against bombers towards the end of the war. Radar also became a powerful means of detecting surfacing submarines, thus severly impeding their chances of survival during the lengthy process of charging their batteries. (Its impact was reduced when the German navy developed the *Schnorkel*-type submarine.)

For a considerable time sonar remained a British secret weapon. The German answer to sonar, and to the combination of sonar and rocket-armed aircraft equipped with radar for attacking submarines, was the high-speed submarine and the long-range torpedo, which made it possible for a submarine to attack a convoy from a distance and escape before being detected.

Special mention should be made here of advances in the science of cryptography just prior to and then during the war, which were intimately linked to the enhanced importance of secrecy, surprise, deception and espionage in contemporary mobile offensive warfare. Operation *Ultra*, the successful decoding by the Western Allies of the majority of German military codes, unquestionably influenced the outcome of many battles, though its overall effect upon Germany's defeat has been exaggerated.[5] A similar judgement applies to the American decoding of the Japanese Navy's codes.

In the three cases of radar, sonar and the proximity fuse, the collaboration between scientists and military planners was very close. Indeed, it is difficult to pinpoint the particular person or group of people actually responsible for their use in military operations. This is even more true of the atomic bomb; one hundred and fifty thousand people were involved in making the Manhattan Project operational – a huge scientific/military/industrial complex in order to produce and deliver just two nuclear devices. A systematic gearing of scientific research for military purposes was essential to the success of all these projects: 'the universities transformed themselves into vast weapons development laboratories. Theoretical physicists became engineers, and engineers forced solutions at the frontiers of knowledge'.[6]

But given the nature of contemporary armies, their size and complexity, the actual utilization of scientific-technological inventions in the war depended as much, if not more, on planning and production than on scientific discovery per se – or even on the recognition of the importance and potential use of the discovery. That is why World War Two was not so much a 'wizard's war' (as Churchill claimed), as a war of administrators and planners, therewith reflecting the organizational implications of its being a conveyor-belt war. Keitel, Eisenhower, and also, to a large extent, Stalin were not so much strategists as administrators, and something similar can be claimed for Tojo (who started his career in the Japanese Army's secret police [*Kempetei*] in occupied China and played a relatively small role in determining military operations). Of the military leaders who made their mark in WWII, Zhukov and Montgomery were notable exceptions, being primarily soldier-strategists.

The correlation between scientific discovery and its large-scale application varied from country to country. A country might be the first to make a scientific discovery, but then be unable or unwilling to apply it on a mass scale, either because of its leaders' inadequate foresight or incompetence in planning, or through a lack of productive resources. In contrast, another country might be able to imitate a discovery made elsewhere and develop it, because military planners understood its importance and could fit it into their offensive or defensive concepts in a way the original inventors themselves might never have foreseen. A given army could make a real breakthrough in weapons efficiency by correctly exploiting a new invention, but remain hamstrung by lack of the wherewithal to utilize it on a large scale. (The *Luftwaffe,* for example, was forced to keep half of its deadly ME163s on the ground in the final phase of the war because of fuel shortages.) Even premature employment of a revolutionary new weapon could be self-defeating if it was not properly tested and improved before being mass-produced. The German V1 and V2 rockets are examples of this applicability of the law of uneven and combined development to military-scientific innovation and production.

The planning and administration of the utilization of scientific breakthroughs thus become a matter of synthetic judgement, of determining priorities, and weighing advantages and disadvantages before taking certain decisions. Once the decision has been made, however, it changes the overall situation – and for some considerable time. Before a given invention can be employed on a mass scale in actual warfare, the decision to build (or reconvert) the factories in which it is to be mass-produced must be taken; the resources to build the plants and devices have to be made available; personnel must be trained both for the production and the use of the new device; military staffs have to be prepared for integrating these devices into their planning, etc. While all this is going on, some new revolutionary invention might occur, which renders the original invention either partially or totally obselete even before it has been widely introduced.

The parallel with civilian technological innovation, and the way it operates in the framework of great corporations intent upon maximising profits through competition for larger shares of the world market, is striking – and confirms that contemporary warfare is far more of a product of contemporary capitalism than is generally recognised. And just as the key finance groups in control of the large corporations and their chiefs, and not the managers, bankers or technologists, are the masters of the economy under monopoly capitalism, so the top layers of the bourgeoisie (and their key political representatives) are the masters of military-scientific decisions – not the scientists or generals themselves.

In this respect, the differences between countries under bourgeois democracy and those under various types of dictatorship largely disappear in war conditions. It could be argued that Roosevelt and Churchill – but especially Churchill – actually enjoyed more power to impose such decisions than did Hitler, Tojo, Mussolini, or even Stalin. Centralised decision-taking is unavoidable given centralisation of economic and political power, it is not possible to delegate the authority to build a new type of airplane (say, a jet plane) to ten different authorities covering one hundred different factories.

Whether the administrative character of World War II produced the optimum military result is another question altogether.[7] It arose from the very nature of late monopoly capitalism. It displayed the same contradiction as does the system in its totality: false choices made by a handful of people led to disasters from which millions suffered.[8] The top decision-makers, confronted with a growing number of urgent choices, more and more depended on information and advice given by committees, and became overwhelmed by papers to be read.[9] Thus they in turn were forced to delegate authority on matters seemingly of secondary importance, but which could decisively impede progress or even cause major setbacks. As with the modern corporation, the

end-result was a complex – and over-complicated – structure com-
bining overcentralization and overdecentralization. On balance, it
was probably less efficient than smaller units and collective leadership.[10]

Something that needs to be stressed is the lack of realism of those
who argue that oppressive regimes are, by their very nature, unable
to develop increasingly sophisticated weapons or seriously participate in the technological race. There is nothing in the record of the
armaments industry during World War Two to warrant such an
optimistic conclusion. On the contrary, qualitative breakthroughs
in weapons' 'progress' occurred in all countries which had passed a
certain threshold of industrial/scientific infrastructure. Those who
establish alleged causal links between 'modern arms and free men',
to quote the title of a once famous book by Vannevar Bush,[11]
seriously underestimate the capacity of any government, state,
ruling class or stratum to mobilise over-specialised partial knowledge in pursuit of specific projects – independently of its overall
nature or of the 'immoral' global goals it pursues. Even the most
inept of Second World War dictatorships, France's Vichy regime,
developed a revolutionary grenade launcher – and in secret, under
the very nose of *Gestapo* and *Abwehr* agents.[12]

The point is not so much the servility of scientists and technologists, or their capacity to become corrupted by hubris, money,
honour, power or false values (albeit that all these factors come into
play). The point is that the very nature of contemporary production, geared as it is to generalised (capitalist) or partial (post-
capitalist) commodity production, puts a premium on achieving
specific partial goals, irrespective of their global long-term impact on
society or humankind as a whole. 'Ours not to reason why' has,
since the sorry days of the Crimean War, become the standard
apologia of the overwhelming majority of scientists and technologists.

The case of the atomic bomb built in the USA proves the precise
opposite of what defenders of the thesis of 'modern arms and free
men' claimed to demonstrate. For not only was the Bomb conceived and built by 'experts' who, for the most part, did not know
whether it would be used, how it would be used, against whom it
would be used, under what conditions and with what side-effects
(the long-term effects of radiation were generally ignored, to take
just one example); in the debates leading up to its use, the 'free
men' were conspicuous by their absence. The vast majority of
those concerned were not allowed to participate. Nobody was

given a vote – neither the population, nor Congress, nor the scientific establishment itself.[13] A tiny handful of people, probably no more than a dozen, were instrumental in taking the final decision to drop the bomb on Hiroshima and Nagasaki, with all the frightening consequences for the the future course of human history and human destiny that entailed. It was not 'science gone mad' which led to the use of the atomic bomb in contemporary warfare. It was militarism and aggressive imperialism outside the control of any form of popular sovereignty that led to such disasters – and can lead to similar or graver disasters in the future.

No more than contemporary science should contemporary weapons be reified. They possess no independent social momentum blindly imposing its 'will' on people. The atomic bomb or the computer have no 'will' of their own. The people who control them and are ready to use them have wills; and these wills are determined by powerful social interests. Their power over machines and weapons is a function of their power over other people. That is the message to be drawn from the Third Reich's relative success in developing sophisticated weapons, from Stalin's breakthrough in having Katyushkas put on the conveyor belt, from American imperialism's success in producing the atom bomb. A monopoly of decision-making by human 'experts' or attempts to stop scientific progress cannot prevent disastrous developments. The mass of the people genuinely in control of the means of production, in contrast, can. There is no 'inevitable sequence of events'.[14]

If nevertheless there is a positive lesson to be drawn from the increasingly inhuman implications of the subordination of science to war, it is that the human spirit and human praxis will never submit to state-terrorist blackmail and threats – something partially confirmed even by the story of the atomic bomb. Robert Sherwood recalls that the first initiative to set up the National Defence Research Council 'for the mobilization of American scientists to work on new weapons to meet and overcome the awful challenge that Nazi technology had presented', came in response to Charles Lindbergh's attempts to 'scare the living daylights of his listeners' after the fall of France, by telling them stories about Germany's supposedly insuperable strength.'[15] Likewise, the terror of nuclear weapons has unleashed an international spirit of resistance to the madness of nuclear war. The struggle between those ready to unleash it and those ready to oppose it by all means necessary is not decided in advance in favour of the madmen. It will be decided politically by a clash of basic social forces, motivated not only by interest, but by conviction and moral stamina as well.

9.

Ideology

If World War II was the conveyor-belt and motorised war, it was also the radio war. In no previous conflict had warring governments enjoyed the possibility of directly reaching so many millions of men and women with their attempts at indoctrination and ideological manipulation.

The radio had already played an important role in the rise of the Nazi Party in Germany as a mass party of the petty-bourgeoisie and *déclassé* elements of other social classes. It played a similar role in maintaining an iron grip over the Germans and Japanese populations during the war, drenching them with propaganda more and more based upon the complete suppression of 'unpleasant' facts of life. Churchill and Roosevelt likewise exploited the radio in a masterly way to induce the British and American people to sustain the imperialist war and the requisite war effort. The BBC (and later, to a lesser extent, Radio Moscow) were crucial in neutralising Nazi propaganda in the occupied territories and motivating the inhabitants to support the Allies.

At the same time, however, the limits of state-run war propaganda became visible. In less developed countries, the low standard of living meant that the average Chinese, Indian or Indonesian villager, and even a significant part of the urban population, did not possess a radio set. Timid efforts to substitute loudspeaker transmission destined for collective consumption were largely ineffectual. Amongst populations generally hostile to the powers-that-be, the existence of a large number of radio sets made it possible to diffuse 'enemy propaganda' on a scale unheard of in World War I or even during the Russian Civil War, (the Spanish Civil War, however, had already foreshadowed this development).

Having lost their illusions with regard to the efficacity of their propaganda, the rulers had no other recourse than to confiscate all radio sets, thereby recognising their basic ideological failure successfully to manipulate a given population. The Nazis did this in occupied Poland, Yugoslavia and Greece virtually from the start, and later, in all occupied territories. It is interesting to note that according to Ilya Ehrenburg's *Memoirs*, Stalin and the NKVD took a similar measure in autumn 1941 in Moscow.[1]

These examples clearly indicate that the weight of ideology in warfare is not a purely mechanical question of mass production, mass distribution and the availability of adequate means of communication. The contents of propaganda – which involve both the nature of the ideas to be spread and skill in facilitating their reception—is a co-determinant of the results. And here a subtle interplay between objective class interest, social (self-)consciousness (i.e. such interests as refracted by prevailing ideologies), and deliberate attempts on the part of governments and those charged with propaganda to exploit or transform that consciousness, has to be analysed.

For British imperialism and its allies in the minor European imperialist countries, the main ideological weapon was antifascism. By playing upon the British and European masses' justified hatred of Hitler's and other fascist regimes' suppression of the labour movement – encroachments upon vital workers' rights and freedoms and crimes against humanity – such propaganda by and large succeeded in subordinating basic class antagonisms between capital and wage labour to the priority of defeating the Nazis. The imperialist character of the British, French and American states, their continuing exploitation and oppression of hundreds of millions of human beings in the colonial empires, the wholesale denial of elementary human rights therein, was successfully effaced by that propaganda – or at least pushed into the background. The complicity of social-democracy, the trade-union bureaucracy and the international Communist apparatus was vital to the effectiveness of that campaign. With the exception of the CPs during the interlude of the Hitler-Stalin pact (when ugly concessions were made to German imperialist ideology), it was forthcoming.

In the occupied territory of Europe, the phenomena of super-exploitation and national oppression added a nationalist dimension to anti-fascist ideology, making it even more acceptable to the broad masses.[2] In Britain, traditional nationalism and even chauvinism formed an element of the ideological campaign, but with minor effects on the working class (as the failure of Churchill's election campaign in 1945 would demonstrate).

In the United States, where, in contrast to Europe, the absence of political class consciousness in the working class is an enduring characteristic of the political situation, the interplay of ideological motifs in government propaganda was less complex than in Britain or the rest of Europe. Militant anti-fascism, and a cruder version of the 'war-for-freedom' theme than Churchill's or de Gaulle's, were indeed prevalent. But they were hamstrung by such palpable realities as anti-Black racism in the South and, increasingly, in the North too. Moreover, traditional populist 'anti-colonialism' made it difficult for the Roosevelt administration to cover up wholesale for the continuous denial of political rights and self-determination in the British and French colonies. So straightforward nationalism, in the first place anti-Japanese nationalism fuelled by popular indignation against Tokyo's 'day of infamy' at Pearl Harbor, became the main ingredient in Washington's war propaganda. The world would learn that it was not possible to step on the toes of Innocent Virtuous Red-blooded White Americans without unleashing a mighty boomerang effect – the world, and not only the *Tempei*, the Führer and the comic-opera *Duce*. The message was received loud and clear, and largely accepted, – at least inside the USA. It was rather more difficult to get it through overseas, although it was quite successful there too.

Compared to English, French, German or Italian chauvinism, this American nationalism was a relatively recent ideological concoction. President McKinley had issued its first instalment, not surprisingly to coincide with the emergence of US imperialist expansion in the Philippines and the Caribbean.[3] A second coincided with America's entry into World War I and 'primitive' expeditions against the Mexican Revolution. Both had rather limited popular impact, as the USA's subsequent return to 'isolationism' illustrated. Pearl Harbor and America's entry into the Second World War initiated the conclusive internationalization of America's bourgeois society. Precisely because the upsurge of American nationalism was functional not only for maximizing the war effort, but also for the broader project of underpinning US imperialism's thrust for world hegemony, it had a nasty racialist undertone to it. This turned above all on an anti-Japanese axis,[4] of which the Japanese-American population, the *Nissei*, became the first victims. But it was by no means restricted to a single target.

At the beginning of World War II, the Soviet bureaucracy tried to stick to the peculiar ideology that had emerged from the Thermidor: a mixture of crude, dogmatised and simplified 'Marxism-Leninism', doctored and deformed to suit the bureaucracy's specific interests; a no less crudely byzantine cult of Stalin (the soldiers and workers were literally called to fight and die 'for the Fatherland, for Stalin'); and a growing Great-Russian nationalism. Following German imperialist agression, the Communist and pseudo-communist themes rapidly receded into the background, as, incidentally, did the Stalin cult – at least until 1943. Russian nationalism more and more came to the fore, together with pan-slavism. This culminated in Stalin's Victory Manifesto of May 1945, which defined the victory as that of the Slav peoples in 'their century-old struggle against the Germanic peoples'. So much for the counter-revolutionary (Trotskyist?) formula of the *Communist Manifesto*, according to which the history of all societies is the history of class struggles, not the history of ethnic struggles.

Oppressed peoples' national consciousness emerged as a powerful mass phenomenon, partially channeled into the interests of the national bourgeoisie in the world's two main underdeveloped countries, China and India. Contrary to the nationalism of oppressor nations, this consciousness contains a progressive ingredient. It can unleash a progressive political dynamic. But when it takes the form of nationalism it also carries the seeds of reactionary class collaboration, potentially stifling the struggle of the workers and the poor peasants for political class independence and the defence of their material interests against their 'national' exploiters.[5]

This was especially clear in the case of China, where the war of national liberation increasingly became combined with civil war. But it was also obvious in the case of India. The dismal failure of the Indian Communist Party to stimulate the national liberation struggle against British colonialism, coupled with its open betrayal of the July 1942 national uprising, gave the bourgeois Gandhi-Nehru Congress Party a near-monopoly of that struggle – which in turn gave it absolute political hegemony over the Indian masses for three decades.

World War II also witnessed the slow emergence of mass

nationalism in the Arab countries and the first example since the Mexican revolution of organised mass nationalism in Latin America, above all in Argentina with Peronism.

The dominant ideology of Japanese imperialism was extreme chauvinist nationalism, with a growing ingredient of 'pro-Asian anti-white-power' demagogy. Demagogy, because the Japanese imperialists, if and when victorious, treated 'their' colonies' Asian peoples, if anything, worse than did the British, French, American or Dutch colonialists. Many elements of the ideology, of both semi-feudal and imperialist-racist origin, were based upon the myth of the ethnic superiority and exceptional status of the Japanese people, not only in opposition to the 'Caucasian race' but also to other Asian people. Yet this demagogy, which had little immediate impact outside of Indonesia and Burma, undoubtedly set off an ideological time-bomb which would explode after the Japanese defeat in 1945.

While the limits of the impact of Japanese chauvinism outside the homeland are obvious, it is harder to judge the degree of thought control it achieved in the archipelago itself. Nobody can doubt its effects in fanaticising middle- and upper-class, as well as (partially) petty-bourgeois, youth; the motivation of the *Kamikazes* was ample testimony. But to what extent were they simply cowed, intimidated, terrorised and paralysed by atomisation into passive submission? It is difficult to answer without studying original sources, which we are unfortunately unable to do. But some translated material – as well as a source like Shigemitsu's *Memoirs* – bear witness to the latter interpretation.[6]

Nazi ideology, with its specific mixture of extreme chauvinism, anti-Communism, pseudo-socialist demagogy and racism (culminating in mass murderers' anti-semitism) successfully welded together the bulk of the middle and upper class (including the officer corps), the traditionally non-organised (non-class conscious) minority of the working class and the *déclassé* elements of all social classes. This was never more, and probably less, than half of the German people. The other half, CP and SPD members and sympathisers, the bulk of the Catholic workers and intelligentsia, and a minority liberal sector of the upper classes (including the 'liberal-conservatives') never backed Hitler and his crimes. But they were for the most part condemned to passivity through sheer physical repression, terror and – especially – the lack of a political alternative. The effects of massive carpet bombing did the rest.

The pseudo-'socialist' demagogy was just that: demagogy.

German workers lived a hard life during the war. Their wages and standard of living were low. An increase in the price of margarine was considered a big blow; butter and meat they hardly ate at all. On the other hand, Hitler frequently went out of his way to assure the capitalists that he would protect private property.[7]

Nearly all commentators have treated Hitler's fanatic anti-semitism leading to the Holocaust as beyond rational explanation – something totally different from all other ideologies of the twentieth century (i.e. the imperialist era). We do not think that such drastic historical exceptionalism can be empirically or logically sustained.

In its extreme form racism is congenitally linked to institutionalised colonialism and imperialism. Indeed, the one cannot function without the ideological protection of the other. It is impossible for thinking human beings – and colonialists, imperialists and defenders of their specific 'order' *are* thinking human beings – to deny millions of men, women and children elementary human rights without attempting to rationalise and justify these indignities and oppressions by a specific ideological sophism – to wit, that of their 'racial' or 'ethnic' or 'intellectual/moral' inferiority, or a combination of these – i.e. by an attempt to 'dehumanize' them ideologically. But once large groups of human beings are considered as intrinsically inferior – as 'sub-human', as *Untermenschen*, as some species of animal[8] – then it only takes one more ideological-political step to deny them, not only the right to liberty and the pursuit of happiness, but the right to life itself. In the peculiar – and increasingly destructive – suicidal combination of 'perfect' local rationality and extreme global irrationality which characterises international capitalism, this step is frequently taken.

In other words, the seeds of the Holocaust are not to be found in traditional semi-feudal and petty-bourgeois anti-semitism – although, naturally, such anti-semitism among sectors of the Polish, Ukranian, Baltic, Hungarian, and Russian petty bourgeoisie offered fertile ground for tolerating and aiding the Holocaust. This type of anti-semitism led to pogroms, which were to the Nazi murderers what knives are to the atom bomb. The seeds of the gas chambers resided in the mass enslavement and killing of Blacks via the slave trade, in the wholesale extermination of the Central and South American Indians by the *conquistadors*.[9] In such cases, the term genocide is fully justified: *millions* of men, women and children were killed just because they belonged to a supposedly 'inferior', 'subhuman' or 'wicked' collective group.[10] It is true that these crimes of colonialism/imperialism occurred outside Europe. But it was precisely German imperialism's 'manifest destiny' to colonise Eastern Europe. The Nazis and the most extreme proponents of the imperialist doctrine of racial superiority by no means intended the enslavement and extermination only of the Jews; gypsies and sections of the Slav people figure on the same list.[11] Most historians and other commentators conveniently forget that the first group of *Untermenschen* to be slaughtered in the gas chambers during the war were not Jews but ethnic Germans certified 'mentally insane': two hundred thousand of these (again, men, women and children) were exterminated in 1940-41 in *Aktion T 4*.[12]

One should add that the Japanese atrocities in 'unit 731' in Manchuria are only one rung below Auschwitz, and can only be explained by a mentality and motivation basically similar to that of *Herrenvolk*. As for the callous killing of two hundred and fifty thousand Japanese civilians (again, men, women and children) by dropping the atom bomb on Hiroshima and Nagasaki, even if it is not exactly comparable to the Holocaust in the scope of its inhumanity, it certainly reflected a contempt for human beings of a 'special kind' which is not at all that far removed from extreme racism.

When we say that the *germ* of the Holocaust is to be found in colonialism's and imperialism's extreme racism, we do not mean that the germ inevitably and automatically produces the disease in its worst form. For that eventuality, racist madness has to be combined with the deadly partial rationality of the modern industrial system. Its efficiency must be supported by a servile civil service, by a consistent disregard of individual critical judgement as basically 'subversive' *(Befehl ist Befehl)* by thousand of passive executive agents (in fact: passive accomplices of crime); by the conquest of power by desperado-type political personnel of a specific bourgeoisie, and that class's readiness to let them exercise political power; by a frenzy of a *va banque* aggression unleashed, not only by these desperadoes, but also by significant sectors of big business itself; by cynical realpolitik leading to the worst blackmail and systematic state terrorism (Goering, Hitler and co. threatening to eradicate, successively, Prague, Rotterdam, London, Coventry – *'wir werden ihre Stadte ausradieren!'*: something which became credible only if such threats were occasionally implemented); by the gradual implementation of that state terrorism unleashing an implacable logic of its own;[13] by a fetid substratum of unconscious guilt and shame, which had to be rationalised in spite (or better: in function) of monstrous crimes. The Holocaust only comes at the end of this long causal chain. But it can and must be explained through it. Indeed, those who understood the chain were able to foresee it.[14]

Himmler told the assembled *Gauleiter* and *Reichsleiter* of all Germany on October 6, 1943: 'The following question has been posed to us [in relation to the extermination of the Jews]: "What to do about the women and children?" – I reflected, and here too I found an obvious solution. I didn't think I had the right to exterminate the men . . . and let the children who would eventually take vengeance on our children and their descendants grow up. The grave decision had to be taken to have this people disappear from the face of the earth.'[15] Two days earlier, Himmler had developed the same theme more extensively at Poznan, before an assembly of leading SS officers.

How easily such rationalisation emerges is strikingly confirmed by the following quotation from the United States: 'One man from the audience asked Major Lessner: "Would not the punishment of all Germans inflict needless hardship on millions of German children who can in no way be held responsible for the crimes of their elders?" Major Lessner answered: "Of course it would. These innocent German children are the potential soldiers of World War III, just as the innocent German children who had been fed after 1918 later served in Hitler's army and did remarkably well" '.[16]

One should not forget that anti-semitism was widespread among most nationalist-conservative circles in France and Russia as well as in Germany, before and during World War I. It reached a paroxysm at the end of the war, during the revolutionary period. Extreme sentiments were expressed which Hitler had only to pick up and systematise. Many examples could be given. For instance, the Kaiser wrote in his *Diaries* in December 1918 the following ominous sentence: 'Let no German rest until these parasites [the Jews] have been wiped out from German soil and exterminated.'[17]

Explaining and understanding a crime does not imply any apology for it: the Holocaust – the deliberate and systematic killing of six million men, women and children simply because of their ethnic origin – stands as a unique crime in mankind's sad criminal history. But what explaining and understanding *does* imply is that similar causes can have similar effects; analogous crimes could be repeated against other peoples if capitalism survives long enough to unleash the totality of its barbaric potential once again.

The question has been asked: was not this wanton killing of potential labourers, including highly-skilled ones increasingly scarce in German war industry, totally irrational? In general systems of super-exploitation and slavery are largely irrational. But they have existed in many places for long periods of time. Whilst not constituting the basis of capitalism (free wage labour), they are often integrated into the capitalist mode of production, different as it is from the slave mode of production per se. They have a partial rationality: the costs of such labour can be reduced to almost nothing, a miserable pittance which rapidly reduces the labourer's weight and health till he literally dies from starvation and deprivation. There is no longer any question of the need for medium-term reproduction of individual labour power. It is true that the average productivity of such labour is abysmally low. But as long as the supply of slaves is abundant, an operation of this order has a rationality of sorts. Ancient Roman senators and contemporary SS gangsters – not to mention eighteenth-and early nineteenth-century Southern plantation owners in the USA – made 'exact' calculations to discover where the precise limit of that 'rationality' lay. And while the SS gangsters were certainly the most criminal of all, they were by no means the least calculating. Like the Roman slave-owners of certain periods, they literally forced their slaves to work themselves to death.[18] All those who could work they did not kill outright. That was the precise function of the notorious extermination camps, 'selections' in which Dr Mengele and co. played their sinister roles.

More generally, the rationale of the extermination programme was drastically to reduce the population of Poland and the Ukraine – the German colonisation space – and to allow only those to survive who would become obedient slaves. The Jews were considered unfit for that role – something of a racist compliment to them.[19]

The overall picture of the ideology prevalent during World War II is thus sombre indeed. Internationalist or even simply humanist consciousness were at a historical low-point – so much so that many thought that an irreversible slide towards barbarism had already set in, Orwell's *1984* being the prototype of such premonition.

Such profound pessimism was premature. In the last analysis, the radical decline in globally rational behaviour which indubitably marked WWII was a reflection of the great defeats suffered by the international working class prior to, and during, the first years of the war. But after Stalingrad and Mussolini's downfall, a new and tumultuous rise of international working-class militancy occurred. The disappearance of the fascist dictatorships in Europe, and the victory of the Yugoslav and Chinese revolutions, were the clearest expressions of this modification in the global balance of class forces. The upsurge of the French and Italian labour movement in 1944-48; the landslide victory of the British Labour Party in 1945; the insurgency of national liberation movements throughout Asia which seriously weakened imperialism in the 1945-50 period – these must be added to them. Such upheavals ultimately made possible a limited and contradictory revival of working-class consciousness and genuine internationalism too, even if they had to start from a very low level.

Certain social forces and individuals saved humanity's and the international proletariat's honour during the Second World War. The Amsterdam workers launched a magnificent strike in February 1941 against the first anti-semitic measures of the Nazi occupation. The Yugoslav Communists built a proletarian brigade – much to the fury of Stalin – which succeeded in recruiting several thousand Italian, Austrian, Hungarian and German soldiers and volunteers into its ranks. The Danish resistance saved nearly all the Danish Jews from the Holocaust by transporting them overnight to Sweden. Small groups of Japanese leftists aided the Chinese guerrillas in Manchuria. An ex-militant of the Left Opposition, Lev Kopelev, succeeded in organising anti-fascist propaganda in the German language so efficiently that the German citadel of Grandenz surrendered without a fight to the Red Army. Having thus saved the lives of thousands of Soviet and German soldiers, he was promptly arrested and imprisoned by Stalin's NKVD for the hideous crime of 'cosmopolitanism'.[20] A tiny group of European Communists under the leadership of Leopold Trepper set up an information network in occupied France and Belgium which was worth several divisions for the Red Army, according to expert opinion. After the liberation of France, Trepper travelled to Poland where he was promptly arrested by the NKVD and kept in jail for several years.[21] Small groups of internationalist Communists, generally of Trotskyist conviction, combined anti-fascist resistance activity with a steadfast defence of working-class interests and a staunch internationalist attitude towards the individual German soldier and worker. Many of them paid with their lives for their stance, one much feared by the fascists. The whole leadership of the Dutch semi-Trotskyist RSAP and their best known representative, the co-founder of the Chinese and Indonesian CPs and former Dutch MP, Hendrik Sneevliet (Maring), were killed by the Nazis. The Italian fascists condemned to death the ex-General Secretary of the Greek CP Pantelis Pouliopoulos who, having become a Trotskyist-Internationalist, addressed the Italian soldiers of the firing-squad so persuasively that they refused to shoot him (the fascist officers present had to do the dirty work themselves).

These were small exceptions. But they demonstrated that under the ashes heaped upon the workers' class consciousness by Noske, Hitler and Stalin, a spark remained. From that spark, new flames would arise. What these proletarian internationalists embodied was the conviction that the war could end otherwise than by the restoration of ruling-class power or the emergence of new bourgeois states; that it could end otherwise than by the total victory of either of the two coalitions; that it could lead to the spread of victorious popular socialist revolutions. Such conviction was neither utopian nor did it discount the strength of the armies of the potential victors. It expressed an understanding of the instinctive wishes and spontaneous trends of tens of millions of workers and poor peasants over three continents. For it to be realized, sufficient organizational strength – including armed strength – and political capacity were required. But purpose and initiative could make all the difference. It was not the relative strength of their opponents which made the Yugoslav Revolution victorious and led the Greek to defeat, which saw a victory of social revolution in China and its defeat in Indonesia. Differences in the resolve and determination of the Communist Parties in these four countries were the decisive factors. And what was possible in Yugoslavia and China would also have been possible in some other European and Asian countries.

Part Two
Events and Results

10.

The Opening Gambit In Europe

Hitler's *Blitzkrieg* strategy called for quick victories against Poland and France – with the proviso of a successful 'peace offensive' making war with France unnecessary. Planning for both operations started early. They were completed in the summer-autumn of 1939. Naturally, the general staffs of all great powers have contingency plans for many – often contradictory – eventualities. In this case, however, something more was involved than just contingency planning.[1]

The war against Poland opposed completely unequal forces. Poland's defeat was inevitable as a result of her military and industrial inferiority. The only thing that might have saved the Polish army and state was an alliance with the Soviet Union as well as British and French imperialism. Soviet troops would have had to enter Polish territory to fight alongside the Polish army against Germany, thus forcing Hitler to send a significant contingent of the *Wehrmacht* and especially the *Luftwaffe* to the Eastern front. Even then, only a rump Poland would probably have survived in the Warsaw-Bialystok-Lwow triangle, whither the Polish army would have had to retreat before the German onslaught.

But this possibility was never seriously considered, neither by the Beck-Ryz-Smigly regime, nor by the French and British general staffs, nor by Stalin. The class hostility of the Polish landlords and capitalists towards the Soviet Union; class fear of the Red Army; suspicions about Stalin's further intentions; national tensions between the oppressed Ukranian minority, Poles and

Jews in Eastern Poland – these were too great for Warsaw to envisage the prospect of a real military alliance with the Kremlin. The refusal of the Polish regime to accept direct Soviet military assistance transformed the military negotiations between the Western allied general staffs and the Soviet government in the summer of 1939 into a farce.

In these circumstances, Stalin preferred to ally himself with the likely victor rather than with the probable victim. Even in the unlikely case of the Polish government accepting the Red Army into Poland, it is doubtful whether Stalin would have gone for a military alliance with that country and its Western allies. He had little confidence in their fighting capacity and was fascinated and awestruck by the power of the German military machine,[2] whose expansion far outstripped the tardy modernization of the Red Army. He therefore far preferred a neutral position for Russia, letting the two imperialist camps fight it out among themselves in a long war, and gaining time to strengthen the USSR's war industry and army. By acting thus, he undoubtedly helped Hitler commence hostilities by invading Poland. He also seriously underestimated the rapidity of the German victory there,[3] and later in the West – hence also the threat to the USSR of Germany controlling the continent of Europe from the Pyrenees to Bialystok and Wyborg, and from the Nordcape to the Dniester.[4]

As for the French army, weakly assisted by Britain, it had no intention of attacking the Siegfried line, or taking any offensive in the West. It prudently retreated behind the Maginot line and imprudently failed to cover the Sedan gap with strong contingents and adequate mobile reserve. Weak divisions composed of older veterans were located there instead, for reasons which are difficult to understand.[5]

So Hitler had his hands free to tackle Poland. He could concentrate the totality of his armoured divisions and most of the *Luftwaffe* on the Eastern Front, thereby making rapid victory certain. In their own way the Polish General Staff aided him by massing a large part of the Polish army near the frontier, where it became an easy target for great encircling operations. Stalin too lent a helping hand by cutting off the retreat road for the Polish army when it finally decided to withdraw, and by occupying the Polish Ukraine, thereby adding fuel to Polish anti-Russian sentiment. Nevertheless, the Polish army fought with great courage – surprisingly so, given the rottenness of the state and the explosive character of the social contradictions within Polish society. The war was not over in two weeks as German propaganda claimed: Warsaw surrendered on 2 October after resisting for four weeks (i.e. nearly as long as the much more powerful French army). However, German casualties were limited and the experience gained by the armoured divisions, the bombers and the gunners would be of great importance in subsequent operations in the West and Russia.

During the interlude of the *drôle-de-guerre*, Hitler feverishly prepared the offensive against France, based upon the brilliant strategic plan by von Manstein and Guderian. Instead of trying to encircle the French armies in Eastern France (as was done successfully in 1870 and tried unsuccessfully with the Schlieffen plan in 1914), the *Wehrmacht* would attempt to encircle them in the centre of the front by a bold breakthrough at Sedan and a quick rush for the English Channel. General Gamelin walked right into the trap by sending his crack mobile divisions into Holland and Belgium on 10 May 1940. The result was not a foregone conclusion, since the actual German superiority of forces was slight.[6]

But the German gamble paid off because of superiority in strategic conception and rapidity of military execution. French strategic doctrine, heavily influenced by Pétain, continued to cling to defensive dogmas.[7] The counter-offensive against the Sedan breakthrough was slow and piecemeal, partly due to the backwardness of French communications.[8] A second counter-offensive at Arras, linked to a last-minute effort to effect breakthrough of the Allied armies encircled in the north, failed for similar reasons: lack of coordination, speed and unity of purpose.[9]

The Dutch army was beaten after four days, the Belgian after eighteen and the British units pushed back to Dunkirk and the Channel after a fortnight. The French army was crushed in six weeks. In the middle of June 1940 Pétain and Weygand begged for an armistice. The war seemed all over on the Western front.

The *drôle-de-guerre* had been preceded by a British-German race to the Norwegian coast, the sea-lane via which Swedish iron ore was transported to Germany's war industry. The race was finally won by the Germans, who succeeded in occupying the whole of Norway. Denmark had fallen without attempting to resist militarily. In exchange, it gained something unique: the conservation of the general trappings of bourgeois-parliamentary democracy for two years under Nazi occupation.

For the war genuinely to end on the Western front, however, German imperialism had to secure British recognition of its gains. With a half-hearted attempt at diplomatic overtures, Hitler pre-

pared the invasion of Britain. What stood between him and final
victory in the West was not so much the Expeditionary Corps
under Lord Gort, miraculously repatriated from Dunkirk, but the
Royal Air Force and the Royal Navy.[10] No successful landing was
possible without absolute mastery in the air, given the formidable
superiority of the Home Fleet. At the beginning of the Battle of
Britain the *Luftwaffe* had a slight edge over the RAF in terms of
number and quality of aircraft, as well as the advantage of offensive
initiative – in the first instance against airfields and aircraft factories. Nevertheless, these were largely neutralized by the fact that
RAF fought over its own territory, had a superior information and
communications system (radar played a key role here) and
employed better tactics.

On 7 September 1940 the *Luftwaffe* abruptly stopped its concentrated attacks on RAF airfields in order to switch to massive
bombing of London. This allowed the British airforce to recover
its exhausted reserves and incorporate newly-built fighter planes
into its squadrons.[11] Several hypotheses have been advanced to
explain this sudden switch. The most convincing is that it was a
tactical move, aimed at drawing Fighter Command's attention
away from the airfields of southern England to the defence of the
capital. If so, it was a grave mistake since the British Air Marshal
Dowding did not respond as expected and the switch only gave the
RAF badly-needed respite. The German decision was due partly
to inaccurate information, which in July-August had underestimated the RAF's strength and now erred in the opposite direction, as well as long-term strategic considerations: the need to
conserve the *Luftwaffe's* strength for the forthcoming operations in
the Mediterranean or against the USSR.

By 13 November 1940 the *Luftwaffe* had lost 1733 airplanes in
the Battle of Britain out of the 2,200 it had committed to the battle.
By the end of March 1941, the losses rose to 2,265 planes, with
8,000 pilots or other flying personnel either killed, wounded or
missing. In contrast, the RAF lost 915 planes up to November
1940. What really saved Britain was Hitler's determination not to
limit himself to a purely European war but to go for world hegemony[12] – i.e. to attack the Soviet Union. For that he needed
aircraft which accordingly could not be used against the British
Isles.

Once the Battle of Britain was lost and Operation Sea Lion
cancelled, the *Blitzkrieg* had to be extended to other areas, as time
was beginning to run out. The German High Command would

have preferred a mopping-up operation in the Western Mediterranean and North-West Africa. This indeed made sense from a strategic point of view, both in the short-and long-term. By taking Gibraltar and securing the Moroccan and North-West African coast up to Dakar, German imperialism would have created much more favourable conditions for a future onslaught against Egypt and the Middle East and against the Americas. But that operation (Undertaking Felix) hinged upon the consent of, if not active cooperation by, Franco and Pétain. Here formidable military-economic and political-psychological obstacles arose.

The Spanish army had been severely weakened as a result of the Civil War. The country's economy was in ruins. There was starvation in several regions. The same applied, *mutatis mutandis*, to Vichy France's army and economy, both in the rump metropolis and in the colonies. Under these circumstances, any military large-scale operation would have to be fully funded, armed and supplied by Germany itself, whose lines of communications were already considerably stretched (the distance Bordeaux-Dakar is longer than that of Berlin-Stalingrad). It also meant putting large quantities of arms at the disposal of forces about whose reliability as allies Hitler had the gravest doubts (they could be turned against Germany either by the generals themselves or by the soldiers – the vast majority of both the French and Spanish masses were hostile to an outright alliance with Germany). The reluctance of Franco and Pétain fully to commit themselves to active military co-operation with Hitler was intensified by the outcome of the Battle of Britain: doubts began to arise in the minds of these conservative diehards about whether the German upstart adventurer could really win the war. Hitler himself did not feel like committing great resources to Undertaking Felix, since he would need them once the operation against the Soviet Union commenced. So, after hesitating for some months, Operation Barbarossa, planned as early as July 1940, became the next *Blitzkrieg*.

Hitler's obsession with the conquest of the Ukraine (which made sense from the viewpoint of the more aggressive sectors of German imperialism), and a nagging doubt about the USSR's real industrial strength, explains the concentration of efforts on Eastern Europe and the Soviet Union. For him, as for Roosevelt, the Mediterranean and the Near East were not of such great strategic importance.[13]

Of course, Churchill was of a quite different opinion: after the Battle of Britain, he and Dill, Chief of the Imperial General Staff, made their strategic decision to commit a substanial part of the British army (including Britain's only surviving armoured division) to North Africa. For the British bourgeoisie, the loss of Egypt and Middle Eastern oil would have meant as much as losing the British homeland, for the homeland would come next. So the Mediterranean became British imperialism's main theatre of war and would remain so for three years.

Whilst preparing the largest aggression in its history – the invasion of the Soviet Union – the German bourgeoisie was faced with unanticipated challenges, occasioned by its allies rather than its foes. Misjudging the world situation in 1940, and believing that the war would soon end, Mussolini – against Hitler's advice – declared war on France and Britain in order to claim a slice of the victor's cake. He followed this up with badly-prepared operations in North and East Africa and Greece, as a result of which he quickly lost Ethiopia to an inferior British army and was beaten back by an even weaker Greek one. The Germans had to come to his rescue, which meant diverting resources from the Eastern front to the Balkans and the constitution of the *Afrika Korps*. The losses incurred by the Reich were relatively slight (except in the case of Crete), but the diversion was serious in terms of the time lost. At this stage General Halder, the central strategist of the *Wehrmacht*, did not think that this would create problems, expecting the Red Army to be smashed in a couple of months, well before the winter season. But in the event postponement of Operation Barbarossa for six weeks meant that the German army, like Napoleon's before it, had to deal with the Russian mud and winter before an assault on Moscow.

In the final balance-sheet of the opening gambit in Europe, clearly won by Hitler, the cost of victory also has to be included. Here a basic rule of war was demonstrated: the more battles are fought which do not end the war, the more the marginal cost of partial victories weighs upon the final outcome. German imperialism won an easy victory in Norway, but its navy's losses in that war made Operation Sea Lion both materially and psychologically impossible without a prior defeat of the RAF. Holland was overcome in four days and Crete taken in seven, but the loss of paratroops and glider planes made a similar approach to Malta impossible.[14] The victory against Poland was easy, but the two hundred or so Polish pilots who escaped to Britain may well have made the difference between victory and defeat for Fighter Command in September 1940; and the Polish secret service brought to Britain the key to the German military code which, together with a similar breakthrough by USA in deciphering the Japanese Navy's code, gave the Western Alliance a decisive intelligence edge over their foes throughout the war. So a nemesis of power does, after all, operate in military history and, through it, in the history of class struggle – in world history taken as a whole.

11.

The Unfolding World Battle

In the second half of 1941, Hitler's assault on the Soviet Union and the Japanese attack on Pearl Harbor transformed what was previously an essentially European conflict into a world war. Though Southern Africa and South America remained outside the actual zones of operation, they were nevertheless indirectly very much involved. An important naval battle took place at the estuary of the River Plate. The largest South American country, Brazil, entered the war as a satellite of the USA in the summer of 1943. South Africa became a key naval base for protecting Britain's remaining safe route to India. Kenya eventually became the Middle Eastern headquarters of the British army as soon as Cairo was threatened, with the port of Kilindini (Mombasa) designated to serve as a British naval base in the Indian Ocean after the Japanese bombing of Trincomalee in Ceylon. Throughout the war India remained the main logistical base for the British forces in the Middle East, while itself becoming a theatre of military operations, in the Assam and Naga Hills, following the Japanese conquest of most of Burma.

Germany's attack on the Soviet Union not only endowed the war with a new geographical dimension; it partially modified its social character as well. For whilst it is true that the German imperialists were out to plunder other countries, seizing mines, factories, banks almost ubiquitously, this transfer of ownership affected other capitalists. In the case of the USSR, by contrast, the property to be plundered was not capitalist but collectively owned.[1] Hence the intended appropriation involved a social counter-revolution on a gigantic scale. A parallel can be drawn here with armies of the European monarchies in 1793 which, had they defeated the French revolutionary army, would have restored the *ancien régime* – i.e. the social and economic privileges of the nobility and clergy – except that in 1941 it would have been a foreign nobility.

The aim of Operation Barbarossa was the destruction of the bulk of the Red Army west of the rivers Dwina and the Dnieper, i.e. cutting off its retreat towards the Don and the Volga through a series of huge pincer-like encirclement operations. It was based upon a series of presuppositions, some of which drew upon accurate military intelligence and judgement while others involved a total miscomprehension of the situation in the Soviet Union. The first assumption, which proved largely correct, was that Stalin would be taken by surprise: that for this reason the bulk of the Red Army would be concentrated relatively near the frontier; that it would be unprepared for the attack; and that most of the air force would be destroyed on the ground.[2] The second assumption – only partially correct – was that the Soviet army would be no match for the *Wehrmacht*; that its commanders would find themselves completely overwhelmed by the speed of the attack; that much of its equipment and manpower would be destroyed; and that its will to fight would thus be broken. In reality, however, while defence was disorganized, especially in the central sector of the front which bore the brunt of the *Blitzkrieg*, causing huge human losses, from the outset Soviet resistance was much stronger than the German command had foreseen. As a result, Germany's own losses were much higher than planned, and the momentum of the offensive checked. The *Wehrmacht* lost around a million men even before the battle of Moscow began.[3] In addition, the Soviet medium tank T34 came as an unpleasant surprise, since it was superior to German models (only later would the modified *Tiger* and *Panther*, incorporating the lessons of the battle-field, redress the balance). The third assumption, which proved quite wrong, involved much too low an estimate of Red Army reserves, both of man-power and military equipment. The German staff had planned for 200-220 divisions of the Red Army, of which at least 150 were to be destroyed in the first two months of the war. After that, the war would be reduced to simple mopping-up operations. But although the German army did initially annihilate some 150 divisions of the Red Army, its opponent was nevertheless able to raise its fighting strength to nearly 300 division (4.7 million men) by the end of the year.[4] So whilst the *Wehrmacht* won four impressive battles, (Bialystok-Minsk; Smolensk; Kiev; Vyazma-Bryansk) during the summer and autumn of 1941, it nevertheless failed to capture or destroy the bulk of the Soviet army. Taking into account mobilized as well as potential soldiers, only thirty-five per cent of the Red Army perished in the first wave of the German offensive.

At the start of Barbarossa, General Halder, chief of the German General Staff and, together with von Manstein, the top strategist of the German armed forces, expected the USSR to be defeated within four weeks. Von Ribbentrop told his Italian counterpart Ciano that the collapse would come within eight.[5] The American War Department thought that Germany would need between one and three months to beat Russia. The British military believed that the occupation of the Ukraine and the capture of Moscow would take three to six weeks.[6] Isaac Deutscher was one of the few observers to adopt a more realistic perspective from the very beginning.

After the success of the first large-scale pincer movements, Hitler, Keitel, Halder and von Brauschitsch proclaimed that the Soviet army had been smashed. On 2 October 1941, in a speech given at the Berlin *Sports Palace*, Hitler informed his audience that 'the enemy was already beaten and would never rise again'. The chief of the German press, Dietrich, stated a week later that with the destruction of the Army Group Timoshenko, 'the decision has fallen in the East'. On 10 October the Nazi official daily, *Völkischer Beobachter*, carried a headline across much of its front page proclaiming: 'The Battle in the East has Been Decided', adding that 'Stalin's armies have disappeared from the earth'. This was not so much mendacious propaganda or empty boasting as self-delusion. Dietrich confirmed afterwards that this early announcement of German victory in the East corresponded to Hitler's settled conviction. Subsequent proof to the contrary came as a great shock.[7]

This does not mean that the blows delivered to the Red Army were minor ones, nor that they were the result of some deliberate strategy of Stalin's. Indeed, the defeats suffered in the summer and autumn of 1941, and again in the spring of 1942, were horrendous. The USSR came close to collapse.[8] 30,000 of its industrial plants and 40,000 miles of railroad were destroyed and the losses in agriculture were such that in 1945 Soviet agricultural output was only half of its pre-war level. No political or military leadership would have planned such a sacrifice, which in any case made no sense in military terms.[9]

That the Battle of Moscow was finally won by the Soviet Army was due to a number of factors. The *Wehrmacht* lost valuable time thanks to the stiffening of the Red Army's resistance in September-October 1941 and Berlin's tactical hesitations before the final attack. The Muscovite working class mobilised unforeseen reserves, energy and militancy for the defence of the capital. The German army began to feel the effects of lengthening supply lines and the disorganization caused by the bad weather. Above all, Stalin found himself in a position to divert a significant proportion of battle-hardened Soviet forces from the Far East after receiving authoritative information that Japan would remain neutral in the German-Soviet war.[10] The successful defence of Moscow was thus intimately linked to the attack on Pearl Harbor.

Hitler had been stung by the news of the Soviet-Japanese Neutrality Pact, coming as it did so soon after the formulation of Barbarossa. The German-Japanese alliance was never a real military alliance. True, Germany declared war on the USA four days after the Japanese moved against Pearl Harbor;[11] but this was less an act of solidarity than a consequence of the desire to intensify the battle in the Atlantic against US cargo ships now becoming vital to Britain's survival. After the German failure to take Moscow, and the start of the first Soviet strategic counter-offensive in January 1942, Tokyo grew worried lest Germany became involved in a long and exhausting campaign in Russia, hence weakening the thrust against Britain and the USA. They therefore tried to persuade Berlin to negotiate with Moscow. Berlin, in turn, argued strongly in favour of a Japanese blow at Vladivostock, to be followed by an offensive in the direction of Lake Baikal, in order to finish off the Soviet Union together. Neither side prevailed.

Japan's decision to secure the oil and raw materials of South-East Asia led directly to the attack on Pearl Harbor, in order to prevent the American fleet from coming to the assistance of the European colonialists. Once the decision was taken, neutrality vis-à-vis the Soviet Union logically followed. Ironically, the victor of Pearl Harbor, Admiral Yamamoto, had been the most sceptical of all the Japanese warlords about a war with the USA. From the start he warned against underestimating American strength and set a short-term goal for all military operations on the grounds that the war would be won in one year or definitively lost.[12] At the outset Japanese army and navy commanders had differed on how to respond to the increasing pressure of the economic blockade conducted by American and British imperialism. The army had favoured a war against the USA because it feared the alternative collision with the Soviet Union and because it wanted to have its hands free to crush China. This meant neutralizing the USSR and cutting off Western supplies to Chiang Kai-Shek. The navy, on the other hand, preferred to keep out of the war with the USA and concentrate on European possessions in South-East Asia. Once the decision for a combined operation was taken (i.e. attacking Pearl Harbor *and* moving south against Britain, France and Holland), the army and navy swapped roles: the navy pushed for an ever-wider circle of operations, whereas the army wanted to concentrate on consolidating the gains in China and South-East Asia.

The victory at Pearl Harbor was vitiated by two important mistakes. Admiral Nagumo, who led the task force, first failed to ensure that the US carriers were destroyed by the attack.[13] He then failed to arrange for a second attack out of fear for the safety of his task force, though nobody could have threatened it at that moment. He thereby allowed the USA to salvage half of its ships (among them four battleships) which, though damaged, were not actually sunk. As a result, and despite the initial great success, Japan would be master of the Central and Southern Pacific for only six months – after which the US fleet, expanded through a feverish shipbuilding programme, could threaten the Imperial forces in the Central Pacific and at the South-Eastern tip of the defence perimeter.

If the Soviet-Japanese non-agression pact seems reasonable in the given circumstances, the positive military alliance between the Soviet Union and Britain of July 1941, subsequently joined by the United States, appears to be another matter altogether. Why should one imperialist power ally itself with a workers' state against another imperialist power? Today, with Soviet Union having become a world power, doubt as to the wisdom of that decision is proportionately greater in the bourgeois camp. It certainly came as a shock to Hitler, who was incredulous for several weeks. In the conjuncture, however, it made sense – a case of choosing the lesser evil. Unwilling to fight the war on the European continent, the British and Americans saw the Alliance as one that would simultaneously weaken both Germany and the Soviet Union, after which they would come in for mopping-up operations. To ensure that the USSR would bear the brunt of German aggression without collapsing under it, the two countries offered material aid. It was a small price to pay for preventing Germany controlling Europe and therewith her future ability to crush Britain and challenge the USA for world hegemony.[14]

It was the global character of the war and the goal of world hegemony which inspired the Anglo-American alliance in the first place and made its extension to the USSR a rational choice for the Western bourgeoisie. In a letter to Roosevelt written on 15 June 1940, Churchill summarized what was at stake with great clarity: 'Although the present government and I personally would never fail to send the fleet across the Atlantic if resistance was beaten down here, a point may be reached in the struggle where the present ministers no longer have control of affairs and when very easy terms could be obtained for the British islands by their becoming a vassal state of the Hitler empire. A pro-German government would certainly be called into being to make peace and might present to a shattered or a starving nation an almost irresistible case for entire submission to the Nazi will. The fate of the British fleet, as I have already mentioned to you, would be decisive to the future of the United States because if it were joined to the fleets of Japan, France and Italy and the great resources of German industry, overwhelming sea power would be in Hitler's hands . . . This revolution in sea power might happen very quickly and certainly long before the United States would be able to prepare against it. If we go down you might have a United States of Europe under Nazi command far more numerous, far stronger, far better armed than the new world.'[15]

While there was undoubtedly an element of panic-mongering in this warning – intended to procure more US aid than was currently forthcoming – Churchill's basic reasoning was sound. If one added to the picture the vast material resources of the Soviet Union, and the geopolitical gains accruing to both Berlin and Tokyo in the event of her defeat and/or break-up, the argument for an alliance with Moscow became irresistible. From the British and American point of view, all they had to do was keep the Soviet Union in the war; the delay in the opening of the Second Front, real difficulties notwithstanding, was motivated by this long-term objective: to let Germany and the Soviet Union exhaust one another.[16] The Western Allies could choose when and where to engage Germany, and their choice was governed more by political, than military, considerations. The Soviet Union, by contrast, enjoyed no such luxury: given her terrible suffering, immediate military aid was much more important than long-term political gains. From the outset the issue of the second front was therefore a real test of the nature of the Alliance, the Soviet people paying in blood for the relatively modest food and military hardware aid programme from the West.

Finally, one should add that Churchill was not completely unconstrained in his decision to extend support to the Soviet Union after 22 June 1941. Refusal to come to her aid or an attitude of studied neutrality would have provoked enormous opposition, especially in the working class. Furthermore, at that point in time it was not at all clear how Britain could win the war without the gigantic Soviet effort in the East;[17] the whole situation of 'national unity' could have been imperilled by an incorrect decision – and Churchill was lucid enough not to make such a mistake.

12.

Towards The Climax

1942 saw a general buildup of forces in all the major warring states, the fortunes of war swinging first one way and then the other. By the end of the year there were two strategic victories. The *Wehrmacht* was defeated at Stalingrad. In the Pacific the US Navy scored a resounding victory against Japanese carriers at the Battle of Midway. This historic victory at Midway gave the United States the initiative in the Pacific, just as victory at Stalingrad would later give the Soviet Union the initiative in Eastern Europe.

1942 was also the year in which a definite shift in the balance of power within the Western Alliance occurred in favour of the United States. In March 1942 the two powers had divided the world into three strategic areas: the Pacific, to be the concern of the USA; the area between the Mediterranean and Singapore, to be the responsibility of Britain; and the Atlantic and Western Europe, to be shared between the two. Not only did this arrangement allocate China and Australia – two traditional areas of British influence – to the American sphere; but once the Japanese Navy began to venture west of the Malaya Barrier, the British were forced to seek American aid in the Indian Ocean as well. The Mediterranean also became a *de facto* shared responsibility after the landing of the Western Allies in North Africa in November 1942. In contrast, the American chiefs firmly kept their British colleagues out of decision-making in the Pacific.[1]

Economically, too, Britain was becoming dependent on the United States. This was one of the main reasons why Churchill and

General Allanbrooke were preoccupied with the defence of Suez and the need to free the Mediterranean sea lane to Egypt and India. The long-term implications of economic dependence escaped neither London nor Washington. In February 1942 the British were forced to sign a Mutual Aid Agreement in which they pledged, in return for Lend Lease, to work for a multi-lateral system of world trade after the war.[2] That the voice of America was becoming increasingly dominant in Allied councils was something about which Britain could do very little, since the very American economic and military might that was now eclipsing Britain's imperialist interests was what kept her in the war. The British were forced to listen with good grace to the increasingly loud affirmation of American leadership of the Alliance by the US bourgeoisie.[3]

The British Treasury, advised by Keynes, was very much aware that the country would need some $4 billion of US aid on easy terms to plug the expected deficit in the first post-war years. In addition, some $7 billion worth of military supplies were required to keep Britain in the war after 1943. Such help 'in a manner and to a degree unparalleled in international terms', in the words of a senior Foreign Office official, meant 'parting with political authority and control' (in Churchill's words). This was likewise understood by US State, Treasury and War Department officials who tried to link the question of aid to Open Door Policy in military (bases, jurisdiction over certain islands) and economic considerations (exploitation of resources; opening of markets) in all areas of the world under British control. De facto Britain became a second-rate power, the Second World War laying the basis for 'the special relationship' between it and the United States.[4]

To their military and economic pressure the Americans now added a political dimension: condemnation of the policy of colonialism practised by Western imperialist states, which was perceived by the US public as one of the main causes of defeat in the Far East. This defeat had been astonishingly rapid. By the end of January 1942 the British and Australian defence units had retreated from the Malay peninsula into Singapore, only to surrender themselves in mid-February to General Yamashita.

Hongkong, the symbol of global British commercial interests, and Singapore, the very heart of the Empire's defence system in the Far East, were now both in Japanese hands. Then, at the start of April, the Philippines were taken – a heavy blow to the American pride.[5] By mid-May nearly all of Burma was under Japanese occupation. The Burma road to China was now cut and only the

expensive air route across the Himalayas remained for the supply
of China and the American forces there. British India was threatened in turn. This series of great Japanese successes represented a
major turning-point in the history of Asia, which no subsequent
defeat would completely erase; for once the West was humbled by
the East.[6] Only the American victory at Midway checked Japan's
military momentum.

The collapse of British power in the Far East was not just a
question of the Empire's weakness there. After all, Japan had
managed to conquer this huge area with less than 200,000 men. (In
comparison, the British Imperial Army lost 140,000 soldiers at
Singapore, most of whom became prisoners of war.)[7] Rather, the
defeat indicated the subject peoples' unwillingness to fight for the
British cause. The Japanese victories reflected the decomposition
of the political and social fabric of British Imperial rule. The army
in Malaya had been hit by large-scale mutinies.[8] In Kedah, the
masses had risen against the Sultan; his son, Tengku Abdul
Rahman (later Prime Minister of Malaysia), kidnapped him and
presented himself to the occupiers, offering to broadcast a radio
appeal to the population not to resist.[9] In Burma, the Burmese
deserted the army created by the British en masse: even before the
Japanese army got to Rangoon, British rule had taken a heavy
battering.[10] Thailand became distinctly pro-Japanese in the hope
of preserving the social status quo.[11]

All these events represented a grave danger to the British
presence in India. Already on 2 February 1942 Churchill was
writing to General Ismay: 'The reinforcement of India has become
most urgent. I am deeply concerned with the reactions to Japanese
victories throughout Asia. It will be necessary to have an additional
number of British troops in India. These need not be fully formed
divisions, as they are for internal security against revolt.'[12] Indeed,
revolution was knocking at the door of British India. After the
failure of Stafford Cripps' attempt to pacify the Indian National
Congress,[13] Gandhi and Nehru launched a campaign of mass civil
disobedience in July 1942 to force self-administration for India, as
a step towards complete independence. The Indian bourgeoisie
took this step with great reluctance, since it never intended to wage
a real war on Britain.[14] At the start of the Second World War, India
was without a nationally-based army, and the weak force around
Chandra Bose, who wanted an alliance with Japan, was a small,
ineffectual nucleus for a potential army.[15] The native leadership
was forced to act, not only because of the great opportunity which

British defeat offered to their nationalist cause, but also because of the pressure of a rising tide of mass indignation at the grave deterioration of the food and economic situation, of which the great Bengal famine was the most horrific example.

Nehru described these pressures graphically: 'With the fall of Penang and Singapore, and as the Japanese advanced in Malaya, there was an exodus of Indians and others and they poured into India . . . Then followed the flood of refugees from Burma, hundreds of thousands of them, mostly Indians. The story of how they had been deserted by civil and other authorities and left to shift for themselves spread through India. . . . It was not the war which caused discrimination in treatment between Indian and British refugees . . . . Horrible stories of racial discrimination and suffering reached us, and as the famished survivors spread all over India, they carried those stories with them, creating a powerful effect on the Indian mind.'[16] And even more precisely: 'In Eastern Bengal, in a panicky state of mind, in anticipation of an [Japanese] invasion, tens of thousands of river boats were destroyed . . . . That vast area was full of waterways and the only transport possible was by these boats. Their destruction isolated large communities, destroyed their means of livelihood and transport, and was one of the contributory causes of the Bengal famine.'[17] (The 1943 Bengal famine cost 3,400,000 deaths according to a University of Calcutta study.)[18]

Churchill, full of venom towards the movement for Indian independence, and also partly out of sheer racialist prejudice, decided against any help to alleviate the mass sufferings. Under these circumstances, Gandhi and Nehru thought it wiser to channel mass indignation through the movement of civil disobedience than risk losing control over popular forces to a more radical nationalist leadership or even a revolutionary one. The war in the Far East thus made its own specific contribution to the Indian struggle for independence.[19]

The Japanese conquests put the question of the future of erstwhile colonies after the war on the agenda. For the United States, whose long-term interest in China and now in South-East Asia as well was greatly enhanced by the war, the destruction of colonial rule provided the stimulus for reviewing its own prospects once the Japanese competitor had been eliminated from the imperialist contest. Early on in the war Roosevelt had declared himself an 'anti-imperialist', and at American insistence the Atlantic Charter proclaimed 'the right of people to choose the form of government under which they will live'. Churchill, following the legacy of Versailles and the policy of colonial imperialism which the war was rendering redundant, chose to interpret this point as applicable only to the European peoples. For the Americans, however, it was a declaration of their intent to prevent the restoration of the European colonial empires after the war was won.[20] Thus 1942 was the year in which the United States began to formulate its own grand design for Asia.

Japan had pushed its line of conquest not only to the South-West but also to the South and South-East, occupying Guam, the Marshall and Gilbert Islands, New Britain, Rabaul, the New Hebrides, most of the New Guinea and the Solomon Islands. The purpose was not so much to occupy Australia, which, Yamamoto correctly assumed, would be the spring-board for the American counter-offensive. Rather, it was to cut off its supply lines from the USA: Midway, New Guinea, Samoa, Fiji and New Caledonia were targeted in turn. At the beginning of May, however, the US Navy prevented Japanese occupation of Port Moresby in New Guinea and a month later came the victory at Midway. Following Midway, the US Army and Navy began a counter-offensive at Guadalcanal in the Eastern Solomon Islands which, while making slow progress, became a terrible drain on Japanese shipping and supply lines.

While the war in the Pacific captured the imagination of the American public much more than the European contest, exactly the opposite was true of Britain. For the British population, the bombing and the threat of invasion came from Germany and this concern with the German enemy would deepen with the war: eight times as many Britons died in the war with Germany as with Japan. For the British political and military leaders as well, control of the Mediterranean was linked to the defence of British interests in the Middle East which, apart from supplying oil – the bloodstream of the tank and airplane war – was also the sea bridge to India. The urgency of freeing the Gibraltar-Suez-Aden supply route increased with the drain on the country's naval and financial resources caused by having to use the much longer and less secure route via the Cape. In fact, so heavy was this drain that, combined with the losses suffered in the Atlantic, it brought Britain nearer to defeat in the summer and autumn of 1942 than in the summer of 1940.[21]

Thus, although the British commitment to the war in the Far East remained – because of raw materials and the defence of

Australia and New Zealand – it was the conflict with Germany which commanded the attention of the British Chiefs of Staff. Yet British defeats in the Far East, and the poor performance of the troops in North Africa for much of 1942, helped to encourage the ever-present tendency in American military councils to increase operations in the Pacific: by the end of 1942, 346,000 US troops would be serving there (150,000 more than originally planned) – a figure roughly the same as in North Africa. Official US policy never changed; it continued to treat Germany as the main enemy. But the US military always saw the Mediterranean as an area where, prior to the invasion of Europe from the North West, the diversionary momentum had to be balanced against the scope and tempo of diversionary operations in the Pacific prior to the invasion of the Japanese homeland.[22]

British imperialism was troubled by Hitler's attempt to cash in on the growing anti-British and anti-Russian sentiment in the Middle East and Iran attendant upon German military successes in 1941-2. In 1942 German diplomacy placed considerable pressure on Turkey (and its fanatically anti-Communist army) to allow the passage of German troops through Anatolia in order to attack Soviet forces in the Caucasus and the British troops defending Al Alamein from the rear. At the same time overtures were made to the Shah of Iran in the name of class and national interests against the traditional British imperialist and Russian Communist foes. Hence the fate of the two fronts – in the Soviet South West and in North Africa – became concretely linked: the Western Allies' ability to maintain themselves in the Mediterranean crucially depended on the Red Army's determination to block the German drive to the oil fields of Baku. For, if successful, it would not only have ensured plentiful fuel supplies for the German war machine (and throughout the war oil was the Achilles' heel of the *Wehrmacht*) but would also have lined up Turkey and Iran behind Germany, thus changing the whole geopolitical balance between the Mediterranean and India to Britain's disadvantage. Churchill and Roosevelt sought Stalin's guarantee that the Red Army would stand its ground in the Caucasus, and dangled before him the prospect of increased supplies via Iran rather than along the uncertain Northern route to Murmansk.

Hence in 1941 and in 1942, the outcome of the war against Germany, of the war as a whole, continued to depend on developments on the Eastern Front. For Hitler the war against the Soviet Union remained an absolute priority; European Russia was to be his India – the consolidation of German power in this part of Europe was the royal road to Germany becoming a world power. German forces in North Africa were consequently given only token and hesitant support, and this factor more than any other allowed the Western Allies to triumph in the Mediterranean in 1942.[23] By the end of the year British naval and air superiority had been restored there, severing the supply lines to Rommel's *Afrika Korps*. Egypt and Suez were secured. Mission accomplished, the Western Allies' counter-offensive, directed at Italy via Sicily (Europe's 'soft underbelly', as Churchill dubbed it), was launched.

1942 was the year in which the Soviet Union once again came to the verge of defeat. At the end of 1941 Stalin, intoxicated by the successful repulse of the German advance on Moscow, became convinced that the Red Army would break the enemy in the new year. At his insistence *Stavka* almost immediately adopted a plan for an all-out counter-offensive which was to strike simultaneously at the three German Army Groups (North, South and Centre) along a thousand-mile front. The scale of the proposed operation was incompatible with current Soviet resources of skilled manpower and *materiel*. In addition, it was strategically unsound: both Zhukov and Voznesensky, then in charge of the war economy, were against it. They proved correct. Once the intitial surprise wore off, the German commanders were able to stabilise the front line, leaving the Red Army with no strategic superiority anywhere at the end of March. Worse was to follow. In April Hitler took the decision to push towards the Caucasus so as to deprive the Red Army of grain and oil, and to cut off its easterly supply lines. Operation Blau, scheduled to begin on 28 June, was conceived as a double-pincer movement which, driving to the Donets and the Don, would meet at Stalingrad and, having snuffed out all Soviet resistance, would isolate Russia from Iran and the Allies.

Almost as soon as the decision was taken in Berlin, Stalin had the main outlines of the German plan in his hands. Once again he disregarded reliable intelligence and continued to conduct the summer operations on the hypothesis of a German offensive aimed at Moscow. When, at the start of that spring, the Soviet Chiefs of Staff turned to contemplate military arrangements for the summer, they had pressed hard for a policy of strategic defence which would allow powerful resources of trained and well-equipped men to be built up: through a superhuman effort, the factories in the Urals were by then producing new tanks, guns and mortar which made the reconsitution of the Red Army's armoured forces possible. Yet Stalin was once again able to override his generals' proposals in favour of his own policy of 'simultaneous attack and defence' – i.e. a policy of generalised confusion.[24] In the event, only one local offensive was unanimously supported: Timoshenko's drive to Kharkov. German intelligence, under Gehlen's able direction, was fully aware of the absence of any coherent strategy on the other side. The Red Army's disastrous defeat at Kharkov (largely due to Stalin's insistence that the offensive be continued well after it became clear that it had failed) was only one consequence of this. For while Moscow fixed its eyes on Kharkov, the German drive to the Caucasus was attaining maximum velocity: Crimea fell with terrifying rapidity. By mid-June the Soviet Army had concrete evidence to demonstrate how wrong it had been about German intentions: yet it took another month before Stalin would accept that Hitler's sights were fixed on Stalingrad.

When, in early July, the Panzer armies crossed the Don and Voronezh fell into German hands, the battle for Stalingrad began to take shape. Conscious of the dreadful predicament of the Red Army, Hitler now broke off the concentrated drive to Stalingrad in order to effect one final encirclement of the Soviet forces at Rostov. But although the town fell, the Red Army – in its first orderly and planned retreat of the war – escaped destruction, having suffered fearful punishment. In August the German Army Group under List overran Kuban and proceeded with a double-pronged drive along the Black Sea Coast and towards the great oil centres of Grozny and Baku. With the Transcaucasian mountains in the *Wehrmacht*'s sights and the Black Sea Fleet on the point of destruction, the fateful possibility that Turkey might enter the war on Germany's side confronted the Soviet leadership.[25] The threat of a total collapse and disintegration of the Red Army galvanized the Soviet command. 'Mass political work' in the army, whose morale had been badly shaken by defeat after defeat, was reorganized. Mass conscription of Communist Party members was greatly accelerated. An angry revolt of the younger officers resulted in the military command securing an all-important margin of autonomy from the political administration (run by the NKVD). Zhukov, Vasilevsky, Rokossovsky and a score of other able commanders now rose to the top, with Zhukov obtaining the post of first deputy defence commissar.

The high command reverted to the dual command Supreme Commander–Front Command, with Zhukov and Vasilevsky bridging the gap between the two. At the front, the unitary command, which had been abandoned during the great crisis of the autumn of 1941, was reintroduced.[26] A real and rapid modernization of the Red Army was now in the offing: tank-mechanised corps, air corps, air armies and a long-range bomber force emerged to provide the much needed strike power. Slowly and painfully, after defeats and despair, the Red Army was turning into a viable and modern fighting machine. Its decisive test would come at Stalingrad.

The second consequence of the German success in the summer of 1942 was the Soviet campaign for the opening of the second front in Europe by the Allies. At the end of 1941, flushed with victory at Moscow, and believing that the war was practically won, Stalin had presented the British emissary Eden with his plans for a reorganization of Europe. The British government, not wishing to offend its Soviet ally at this stage (for fear that Moscow might sign a separate peace with Berlin), chose to procrastinate. Now, six months later, with four-fifths of the total German army deep into Soviet territory and the Red Army in danger of collapse, Stalin abandoned all his post-war aims and solicited Western help in the shape of a second front which would draw off at least forty German divisions. Molotov travelled to London, Washington and back to London in the late spring and summer of 1942, without receiving a satisfactory reply. The best the Soviet Union could hope for was a second front in 1943, something on which the Americans appeared keen but to which Churchill paid no more than lip service. Though the Soviet Union could expect increased aid in food and military equipment, it was made clear to Molotov that the Red Army must fight alone – or go under – at Stalingrad.

When, that October, Hitler brought the German summer offensive to a close, he made an exception of Stalingrad and the Caucasus. By the end of the following month, however, Soviet victory at Stalingrad was in sight. In the second half of December the plan for a Soviet counter-offensive – Operation Uranus – was ready. On 1 February 1943 Field-Marshal von Paulus, the German commander at Stalingrad, surrendered. The tide of German victories was halted. The Red Army's triumph at Stalingrad and later at Kursk and on the Pruth made the Soviet Union a world power.

13.

The Decisive Turning-Points

In early November 1942 the Western Allies began their landing in French North Africa. In February 1943 Japanese expansion in the Pacific was halted by the US Navy. In the same month Germany's advance came to an end with the Red Army's victory at Stalingrad. Thus, within a few months the Second World War turned to the advantage of the Allies. They had now conquered the initiative and would not lose it again. Battles at Tunis, Kursk and Saipan rounded out the turn.

As a result of these battles Vichy France would cease to be even a pseudo-independent entity. The place of France (its alignment in Europe) and, flowing from it, the future relationship of Europe to the United States would be placed on the political agenda. Italy would be invaded by the Western Allies and, in its own way, set the pattern for the future arrangement of spheres of influence on the European continent. The downfall of Mussolini and the withdrawal of German troops from the Balkans would enable, for the first time since 1938, the reemergence of a sector of the European working class – in Italy, Yugoslavia and Greece – as an autonomous protagonist in the global drama.

The tremendous increase in the Western Allies's material resources through the reconversion of the US's industrial mass-production potential into weapons output, as well as the systematic and increasingly efficient husbanding of the USSR's huge industrial capability, and reserves of manpower, fighting spirit and military command, made it inevitable that the tide would sooner or later turn after Germany's and Japan's failure to convert their *Blitzkrieg* victories into a final kock-out. Now the time of *Blitzkrieg* was over. The moment had come for confrontations between ever greater concentrations of mechanised weapons – in the first place, tanks and airplanes – and their production and utilization on the battlefields with maximum efficiency and tactical skill. Goebbels formula of *total war* now became a reality: *total war* replaced *Blitzkrieg* to the inevitable and progressive disadvantage of Germany and Japan.[1] From their bases in Britain and the Mediterranean the Western Allies would submit Germany and Italy to round-the-clock bombings.

It was not purely coincidental that the decisive battles of the war occurred so close to each other. In part it was due to conscious planning. The battles of El Alamein and Operation Torch (the Allied landing in North Africa) had been coordinated from their inception. So had the approximate date of the US counter-thrust in the South Pacific. The central planners of Anglo-American strategy, Generals Marshall and Alanbrooke had, after a deal of bickering, decided to devote roughly thirty per cent of Allied resources to the war in the Pacific, and the rest to the war in Europe and the Middle East. A good deal flowed more or less automatically from these decisions. Whilst there was no joint military planning between the Western imperialist powers and the USSR, the Red Army's resistance at Stalingrad and the Terek, in the Caucasus, was obviously bolstered by the German defeats in the Mediterranean and the increase in Western supplies they facilitated. So the general links between the counter-offensive in the Mediterranean, on the Eastern Front and in the Pacific are not hard to establish.

Beyond these links, specific battles were of course conceived, fought and won. Montgomery won the battle of El Alamein by achieving tremendous superiority in guns, air power and tanks. He had over 1,200 guns at his disposal against Rommel's 200, 700 tanks to Rommel's less than 200, and absolute mastery in the air, following a deliberate build-up of forces during the summer and autum of 1942 and the progressive starving of Rommel's *Afrika Korps* of regular supplies (including oil and ammunition). The battle of El Alamein destroyed the Italian North African Army. But part of the *Afrika Korps* was able to escape. Montgomery did not succeed in surrounding it, either at El Alamein itself or at Mersa Matruh where this had been successively planned, preferring not to over-extend his supply lines.

The success of the North African landing, Operation Torch,

largely depended upon the collaboration of the local French military chiefs. The Western Allies initially transported only one hundred thousand troops, who had to cover a huge coast line and the immediate hinterland between Casablanca and Tunis. There were more than a quarter of a million French troops in this area, besides the remnants of the *Afrika Korps;* possible German-Italian reinforcements also had to be considered. Though the French units were badly armed they were nevertheless well-trained and could have complicated the projected operation. Without first consulting the British, Roosevelt moved to obtain, if not the support, then at least the acquiescence of French military and political leaders who, only days before, had been cooperating with the Germans; the 'Darlan Deal' was thus concluded.[2] When, after Darlan's assassination, the Americans were pressed for an alternative, they chose the arch-conservative General Giraud as the representative of French authority in North Africa.[3]

The question of who would be recognised as French spokesman in this 'liberated' territory of France had significant implications vis-à-vis the future legitimacy and role of a reconstituted French state. Giraud had many qualifications in American eyes: he was anti-communist, anti-German and anti-British. In contrast, de Gaulle's close involvement with London and his ambition – and potential – to represent the French nation made him highly suspect to Washington. The difference between Giraud and de Gaulle, between the United States and Great Britain, also centred on the question of whether France would be weak or strong after the war, i.e. whether a capitalist Europe would be pro-American or relatively independent of the USA. The British bourgeoisie clearly understood at this point that Britain would not be equal in power or influence to the USA and the USSR and therefore sought to constitute a kind of West European bloc. And since France was the key to British success in bringing together smaller West European states, Britain began to agitate for the restoration of France as a Great Power.

But the main reason for the difference in approach was Roosevelt's miscomprehension of the real social and political balance of forces in France consequent upon the growth of the Resistance movement. Giraud and de Gaulle became co-presidents of the French Committee of National Liberation (CNL), which assumed the power and structure of a government-in-exile. For the majority of the French population, and in the first place the French working class, Giraud was identified with the intention of perpetuating an

authoritarian, anti-working-class and anti-republican regime after
the defeat of Vichy and Germany. A 'national front' explicitly set
on the restoration of bourgeois-parliamentary democracy,
including all the basic freedoms the labour movement had enjoyed
in the Third Republic, was the only realistic alternative for the
French bourgeoisie to an uprising of the French working class
following the collapse of Nazi occupation – a possibility only the
PCF could neutralize.[4] De Gaulle and Churchill displayed greatly
superior political judgement to Roosevelt's, since they based themselves on the experience of a politically independent European
labour movement which Roosevelt had never known. A Giraud
solution would not have been 'pro-American'. It would have been
unrealisable, or, worse from a bourgeois point of view, could have
led to civil war.

The war in North Africa brought rapid success in Morocco and
Algeria thanks to the cooperation of the French military, and
Dakar came as an additional prize. It failed in Tunisia, however, as
a result of the French Admiral Esteva's manoeuvres.[5] His initial
intention to remain neutral collapsed with the arrival of the
Germans, who entered Tunis in order to erect a protective shield
for the retreating *Afrika Korps*. After a bloody battle Tunis was
taken only in May 1943.[6]

The key battle of 1942-43 was the battle of Stalingrad. The
attack of the German Sixth Army under Von Paulus commenced
on 28 June 1942 and reached the outskirts of Stalingrad exactly one
month later. The Red Army's defence of the Volga metropolis was
improvised under conditions of near panic. But with the participation of the workers of that great industrial city, it rapidly
assumed epic proportions. Wave after wave of German assaults
came within an inch of taking the whole city and were stopped each
time as the Red Army and the Stalingrad workers counter-attacked
and kept a sector of their city – a factory, a bridgehead – free. Their
long and heroic resistance enabled the Soviet General Staff
(*Stavka*) to prepare a counter-offensive. A considerable reserve
force had assembled behind the Volga-Don front, concealed from
the enemy. While General Halder was becoming increasingly
concerned about the vulnerability of the long flank north and south
of Stalingrad, *Stavka* had succeeded in assembling forces which
assured it of superiority in numbers and fire power. By November
1942 the following distribution of forces obtained on the 'Stalingrad axis':[7]

	Soviet	German and Axis
tanks	894	675
guns and mortars	13,540	10,300
aircraft	1,115	1,216
manpower	1,005,000	1,011,000

It should be stressed that whilst increasing Soviet reserves, shorter supply lines, US military assistance (especially in trucks and tanks), rapidly diminishing German reserves and the internal weakness of the Axis allied armies (Rumanians, Hungarians and Italians) all influenced the outcome of the battle, the decisive element was the long resistance of the Stalingrad defenders. It was this resistance which depleted German reserves and gave *Stavka* the necessary time to plan and organize in minute detail the encirclement of the Sixth Army. That resistance in turn clearly reflected a social phenomenon: the soldiers' and workers' superiority in urban, house-to-house or barricade fighting. Already, during the Spanish Civil War, a similar observation could be made of the battles of Barcelona and Madrid in 1936. Chuikov, the commander of the Soviet Sixty-Second Army, which formed the backbone of Stalingrad's defence, would later write: 'City fighting is a special kind of fighting . . . . The buildings in the city act like breakwaters. They broke up the advancing enemy formations and made their forces go along the streets . . . . The troops defending the city learned to allow German tanks to come right on top of them – under the guns of the anti-tank artillery and anti-tank riflemen; in this way they invariably cut off infantry from the tanks and destroyed the enemy's organized battle formation.'[8]

The brilliantly conceived Stalingrad operation, Operation Uranus, was based on the possibility of two breakthroughs, to the north and to the south of the city. Starting on 19 November in the north and one day later in the south, it succeeded within four days: the Sixth Army was surrounded and, despite a desperate counter-attack mounted by Von Manstein, it would never re-establish contact with the bulk of the German forces nor be adequately supplied by the *Luftwaffe*.

By the end of the Soviet counter-offensive the *Wehrmacht* had lost a quarter of a million soldiers, the *Luftwaffe* most of its reserves on the Eastern front, and a huge quantity of tanks, guns and ammunitions.[9] The political and psychological gains of the liberation of Stalingrad extended far beyond the immediate military results. Thereafter, an important part of the German officer corps and the German bourgeoisie, not to speak of a broad section of the German people, lost the belief that the Third Reich could still win the war. As for Stalingrad itself, Chuikov, who was made a Soviet Marshal after the victory, committed the following picture to memory: 'The city burned, covered in black smoke and in pulverised stone. From the summit of the Kurgan Hill, which was called Height 102,0 on our maps, we could see but the skeletons of buildings, ruins and mountains of bricks. Stone had not resisted the assaults, but men did. Each ruin, each skeleton of buildings, each pit, each stack of bricks, became a defensive stronghold. The most stubborn fight was conducted for every couple of metres, for every floor of building, and not only for streets or parts of streets. Mamayev Kurgan (a hill) was the site of the most obstinate battle. After the war it was calculated that more than a thousand shells or shrapnel splinters hit every square metre of Kurgan. The earth was overturned by iron and lead.'[10] The scale of the battle of Stalingrade can perhaps be grasped better if one recalls that Soviet losses in this single encounter were larger than those of the United States in the whole of World War II.

However, from the standpoint of military strategy, there was a flaw in Operation Uranus. The Soviet army had in fact, begun a double pincer operation, the first – successful – designed to cut off the forces of the German Sixth Army at Stalingrad, the second – aiming at the Don estuary at Rostov – intended to cut off the whole German Army Group A in the Caucasus. The latter encirclement failed. One and a half million German and allied soldiers were saved from annihilation. This was not only due to Von Manstein's undoubtedly skilful manoeuvres[11] but to the stubborn defence of Sixth Army at Stalingrad for two months in the face of extreme adversity as well. Contrary to a legend spread by the German generals, Marshall Chuikov correctly stresses that Hitler's resolve to stick to Stalingrad at all cost was not as irrational as it seemed. A quarter of a million troops were sacrificed in order to save more than a million. Three hundred and fifty thousand Soviet soldiers were tied down around Stalingrad by the Sixth Army's resistance; they could have made all the difference to the Red Army's capacity to take Rostov rapidly and cut off Army Group A.[12]

The Battle of Stalingrad, like all the important turning-points of the war – the Battle of the Meuse, the Battle of Britain, the beginning of Operation Barbarossa, the attack on Pearl Harbor, the battles of Midway and El Alamein, the landing in Casablanca/

Algiers, the landing on Guadalcanal, Operation Overlord, the attack on Arnhem and the breakthrough on the Vistula, to name only some of the most important – is further confirmation of the crucial role of surprise, hence of inadequate enemy military intelligence, in the success or failure of such sweeping operations. Whilst the *Abwehr* espionage service in the USSR and the normal reconnaissance services at the front – the *Fremde Heere Ost* – had frequently warned since summer 1942 that the Soviet counter-attack would occur sooner or later between Voronesh and the Kalmuck *steppe*, they failed to discover the full extent of Red Army preparation – the build-up of a reserve striking force of nearly fifty divisions.[13] Why this failure occurred remains a mystery, just as similar mysteries surround the surprise effect of all the other successful operations mentioned. Again, a likely, though no means certain, hypothesis is that army leaders – and in this Hitler was neither better nor worse than Gamelin/Daladier, Stimson/Knox, Stalin/Voroshilov, Tojo or Eisenhower – are predisposed against information which completely contradicts their established strategic concepts and thought habits, especially when political prejudice and dogma combine with outdated military doctrine.

The Battle of Midway, which restored US naval superiority in the Central Pacific, is another example of the vital role of intelligence during the Second World War. In this case, however, the reasons for Admiral Yamamoto's failure are clear. The US Navy had broken the Japanese code and possessed full advance knowledge of his plan to draw the American naval force into a fatal show-down battle around Midway, the feinted invasion plan being the bait to catch the US aircraft carriers unawares and destroy them with planes launched from the Japanese carriers lying in wait, away from the supposed landing Armada. But the trapper was himself ensnared once the plans became known to Nimitz. The US carriers operated to the rear and not in front of the main Japanese task force. They concentrated not on the defence of Midway Island, but on catching the Japanese men-of-war. They had an additional piece of luck when the Japanese planes interrupted their initial attacks to reconvert from bombs to torpedoes. It was during that fateful interval that the US planes struck in one devastating blow and sank four Japanese aircraft carriers, which had made the mistake of operating in close formation.[14]

Henceforth, any Japanese hopes of effacing the US navy from the Central Pacific and thus preventing a serious attack on the outward perimeter of the conquests of 1941 and early 1942 – and, later, on these conquests themselves – were finished once and for all. The way was clear for a generalised American counter-offensive: the battles of Guadalcanal, southern New Guinea, the Solomon Islands, New Britain and the Gilbert islands would give US forces the necessary experience as well as bring them to the outward perimeter of the Japanese Empire itself.

The Japanese high command sacrificed tremendous resources at unimportant points of the peripheral war, obstinately refusing to cut their losses and withdraw to the inner line of defence. A fundamental split between the army and the navy supervened. The army's priority was to cover its positions in Indonesia and the Philippines through offensive operations in New Guinea. The Imperial Navy, on the other hand, was preoccupied with defence of its great naval base at Truk Island, covered by its strongholds in the Solomons. These differences over strategy paralysed the Japanese high command for a fatal six months.[15]

A similar difference in strategic conception arose between General MacArthur and Admiral Nimitz. MacArthur favoured concentrating all efforts upon the reconquest of the Philippines – in the final analysis, for political reasons. He understood the discredit suffered by the Army – and Western imperialism in general – as a result of the crushing defeats of early 1942. He was afraid that without a spectacular victory there the Philippines would be permanently lost to the USA. Nimitz, on the other hand, understood that the Japanese were capable of tremendous defensive efforts in strongholds like Rabual, Singapore, Indonesia and the Philippines, and wanted to bypass them through island hopping, aiming straight at the Japanese homeland. In the end both commanders were allowed to follow their favoured course, with a two-pronged attack towards Japan, but with the US Navy carrying the main burden of the military roll-back.

The US landing at Guadalcanal thus became the first important test of strength between the combined forces of the USA and Japan, less because of any particular strategic importance possessed by the island, than because of Japanese obstinacy in trying to hold these distant positions[16] – something which led to a terrible drain on Japanese resources and a profound demoralization of the army's command.[17]

14.

The War of Attrition

1943 and early 1944 saw a war of attrition develop on the Eastern front in Europe, in the Mediterranean, in the Far East and over Germany, like a slow build-up to the final onslaught on Germany and Japan, which would occur in the second half of 1944 and in 1945. The tide had turned to the advantage of the Western Allies and the USSR. But the reserves which the Axis powers could mobilise were much larger than initially assumed. Their previous conquests had provided them with a lot of space from which to withdraw before the war could hit directly at their homelands. Withdraw they did, but rather slowly, in good order and – at least in the case of the *Wehrmacht* – with a deal of military skill. So the war dragged on, with an increasing waste of men and material, and awful costs for the whole of humankind.

But the outcome was never in doubt. In the war of attrition, the Axis' enemies held a trump card: the virtually unlimited resources of US industry. While Germany and Japan ran into greater and greater difficulties as a result of their increased losses, ongoing mobilisation of soldiers and expanding output in the USA permitted the Western Allies not only to replace such losses but to build up their strength for a successful invasion of Europe.

The situation of the USSR was intermediary between that of the Western Allies and that of the Axis powers. The tremendous losses of territory, soldiers and weapons incurred between summer 1941 and autumn 1942 made it difficult to replace additional human and material losses in 1943 and early 1944. On the other hand, the transplanted armaments factories and factories newly built after

June 1941 started to produce at full capacity in 1943. Together with the Anglo-American weapons delivered to the Soviet Union during the eighteen months of the war of attrition, this enabled the Red Army to build up the necessary reserves to launch successive and progressively more effective offensive operations against the *Wehrmacht*. So a certain stalemate set in on the Eastern front between the systematic German retreat and the real but still limited offensive capacity of the Soviet forces.

This relative stalemate explains why it took the Red Army eighteen months to free Soviet territory of the Axis occupying forces and cross the Polish, Rumanian and Hungarian-Slovak borders. But in this time the USSR's military power steadily increased and Germany's steadily declined, so that a qualitative turning-point was reached in the second half of 1944 with the Jassy-Kishinev offensive which marked the beginning of the end of the *Wehrmacht* on the Eastern front.[1]

A useful index of the gradual attrition of German forces on the Eastern front is the comparison of the *Wehrmacht's* losses and replacements;[2] the Battle of Stalingrad represents a point of no return:

From December 1941 till September 1942

Losses	Replacements
1,688,100	1,169,300
	(replacements 69% of losses)

From July to October 1943

Losses	Replacements
654,000	279,000
	(replacements 43% of losses)

Nowhere were these characteristics of the war of attrition more clearly visible than in Italy. Immediately after the collapse of the Italian army and the *Afrika Korps* in May 1943, the invasion of Italy was on the agenda. In the face of some opposition from American and British generals, Alanbrooke and Montgomery planned a direct thrust from Tunis to Sicily and Calabria, which was executed in summer 1943 without much resistance or cost. it enabled the Anglo-American armies to accumulate valuable new experience for the final invasion of Western Europe.

In Sicily, General Patton's tactical talents as a leader of armoured break-through columns – he was the US equivalent of the German General Guderian and applied de Gaulle's theories –

came into their own. But the tactical military successes needed to be put at the service of a broader strategic and political purpose. And here failure was virtually total. What initially looked like a rapier thrust into the heartland of Europe became a long-drawn-out, painful and costly war of position and attrition towards the Centre and the North of the Italian peninsula, lasting nearly twenty months.

The nearer the war came to the Italian homeland, the closer Mussolini came to being overthrown. For the Italian ruling class, the problem was no longer how to share in the spoils of war; it was clearly on the losing side of any move to redivide the world into spheres of imperialist influence. The key question now was how to save its basic property and class power in the homeland itself, where mass discontent was becoming ubiquitous and where revolutionary explosions were on the agenda, the opposition forces in the underground – in the first place, the CP and the *Partito d'Azione* – gaining in confidence from the *Duce's* military defeats. The king and the court clique, who shared responsibility with big business for allowing the fascists to take power in the first place and for their major crimes thereafter, were faced with the problem of saving the dynasty at any cost. One can say that from the fall of Tunis onwards, the Italian ruling class anxiously prepared a reversal of alliances – something of which Hitler was well-informed and conscious.[3] *Mutatis mutandis*, the same pattern would soon repeat itself with all the other minor European allies of German imperialism, – Rumania, Finland, Bulgaria and Hungary successively. The German counter-moves likewise more or less consisted of attempts to preempt the military disasters which such reversals of alliance might entail by occupying the territory of the former 'ally' and installing pure *Quisling* governments in the place of relatively authentic governments of the native ruling classes. The counter-move would fail in Rumania and Bulgaria (it was never really tried in Finland). It would be largely successful in Italy and Hungary, in the first place as a result of inept manoeuvering by the native ruling class, in part as a result of lack of prompt initiatives and reaction by Germany's foes.

In Rome the court and army command around Badoglio experienced no real difficulty in overthrowing Mussolini thanks to their accomplices inside the fascist Great Council. As soon as the *Duce* was removed from the scene, secret negotiations were started with the Anglo-Americans.[4] An armistice agreement was quickly achieved. The real problem was to coordinate the diplomatic-military volte-face with the allied landings in Italy. Following the landing in Calabria, a second one at Salerno was planned to coincide with the Italian army cutting off the German forces south of Rome if not south of Florence. But the *Wehrmacht* took pre-emptive action. The court and army command panicked. The king ignominiously negotiated his personal safety and his family's for important military concessions to the *Wehrmacht*, enabling it to occupy not only Rome but the whole stretch of territory from Salerno to the capital.[5] The tactical surprise of the Salerno landing was squandered through inept hesitation by American commanders.[6] The end result of the tragi-comedy was a real tragedy: more than two-thirds of Italy fell under Nazi control exercised by a reign of terror. It cost the Italian people (and the Allied armies) tens of thousands of dead and terrible material destruction before the *Wehrmacht* capitulated on 25 April 1945.

In Italy, the ruling class and British and American imperialism had certainly underestimated German reserves and capacity for reaction, as well as the skill of German military commanders like Kesselring. But underlying the miscalculation was a deeper social cause for the new war of attrition into which they inadvertently blundered in Southern Europe. Their class interest was confronted with a real dilemma: how to liquidate fascism whilst preserving the foundations of the bourgeois state, i.e. their political class rule, indispensable for neutralising or, if necessary, confronting mass mobilisations and the threat of revolution. This generated intensifying political contradictions, in which the Soviet bureaucracy, mindful of its own interests, gradually began to intervene through the intermediary of the PCI.[7] Hence the inextricable complications of the game. Hence the failure of so many maneouvres.[8]

A similar relative stalemate occured on the Eastern Front. After the disastrous defeat suffered by the *Wehrmacht* at Stalingrad, the German army concentrated on securing the withdrawal of its forces from the Don, the Kuban and the Caucasus without a new disaster. But Hitler and von Manstein – who was now de facto in charge of the whole Southern front – wanted at all costs to prevent the Red Army from retaining the initiative. After an offensive along the whole front in 1941 and an offensive limited to the Southern front in 1942, in 1943 the Wehrmacht was only capable of attempting to take the offensive on a small sub-sector of the Central front: a good indication of the evolution of the balance of forces. The chosen sector was the Kursk salient, where the Soviet High Command had kept important forces ready for a breakout, and which the *Wehrmacht* now thought of cutting off. A formidable quantity of weaponry – probably the largest of the Second World War – was concentrated in this limited territory: 4,000 tanks on the Soviet side against 3,000 tanks and self-propelled guns on the German.[9]

The German attack had major flaws. There was insufficient concentration of forces to establish the local superiority necessary for a real breakthrough.[10] Moreover, it lacked the element of surprise: the Soviet High Command was apprised of the plan and timing of the attack.[11] The German Army had again under-estimated the power, flexibility and leadership gradually acquired by the Red Army since the winter of 1941-42. The use of mine-fields in depth as anti-tank obstacles and of anti-tank guns under a single command against a single target were very efficient new tactics applied by the Red Army command against Operation Citadel in the Kursk salient. So the breakthrough failed.

The Battle of Kursk is seen by many historians as the decisive turning-point on the Eastern Front, more so than the Battle of Stalingrad. After Stalingrad, the *Wehrmacht* could still conceivably regain the initiative. After Kursk, it had lost it forever. At Stalingrad, the *Wehrmacht* lost a quarter of a million men but relatively little armour. At Kursk, it lost its key armoured form-ations. These would never be reconstituted on the Eastern Front (although they would be partially in the West). After Stalingrad, the German High Command still had several options open. After Kursk, only one option remained: orderly retreat, sacrificing space for time so as to delay for as long as possible the moment when the Red Army would cross the border of the homeland itself, hoping in defiance of their better knowledge that some political miracle would forestall that catastrophe.

The Soviet High Command had two priorities in the offensive which followed its victory at Kursk: to break through around Leningrad and to liberate the Donets and the Ukraine. Both objectives were dictated by obvious socio-economic consider-ations. They took precedence over the central stategic task of destroying the German Army in the East. So the *Wehrmacht* could manage an orderly retreat without major Soviet breakthroughs and battles of encirclement. They came closer to disaster at Krivoi Rag and Tcherkassy. But skilful manoeuvering prevented a collapse at the front. Disaster would strike later, at Minsk, at the Pruth, and in Kuckland (. . .).[12] Operations during the spring, summer and autumn of 1943 and the winter of 1943-44 gradually led to these disasters, involving as they did a gradual depletion of German forces, the disappearances of reserves and the Soviet achievement of ever greater superiority in manpower, aircraft, tanks and fire-power.

In the meantime, a new war of attrition had struck Germany in the shape of the systematic destruction of its major cities through carpet bombing. Air-Marshalls Tedder and Harris had been consistent advocates of this form of warfare for several years, inspired as they were by the Douhet doctrine. Churchill plumped for it as a substitute for the rapid opening of a second front in France. Roosevelt followed suit for similar reasons. From the outset, the objectives of the offensive were unclear and contradictory.[13] The idea that bomber attacks would cause the German people's nerves to snap, and lead to a general breakdown of morale and hence a readiness to end the war immediately, at any cost, proved utterly mistaken. Subborn persistence – if not indignation – rather than demoralisation, was the net effect of the resulting wholesale destruction and massive losses imposed on defenceless civilians. The only demoralisation occurred inside the *Luftwaffe* (particularly affecting Goering and his immediate cronies) and, to a lesser extent, inside the High Command, where the failure to adequately protect vital war industries was recognized as a harbinger of defeat.

The second objective, that of forcing Germany to its knees by destroying specific sectors of the war industry (in the first place, synthetic oil, synthetic rubber and ball bearings), could probably have met with great success had the British and American air forces concentrated on these targets,[14] instead of conducting inhuman raids on the civilian populations of large cities, like the incendiary bomb attacks on Cologne, Hamburg and, later, Dresden.

The following table indicates the extent to which Allied bombs were concentrated upon civilian targets:[15]

A Period	B Total weight of bombs dropped on Germany	C Of which on Industrial sites and submarine bases	C as % of B
1942 (quarterly average)	11,443 t.	446	3.9%
first quarter 1943	27,920	1,818	6.5%
second quarter 1943	46,377	4,796	10.3%
third quarter 1943	60,018	5,133	8.6%
fourth quarter 1943	52,734	10,130	19.2%

On the other hand, the Allied air offensive against Germany did have the effect of forcing the *Luftwaffe* substantially to withdraw planes (especially fighters) from the Russian front for the defence of the homeland:[16]

	Disposition of Luftwaffe			
	May 1943		October 1943	
Eastern front	3,415	50.7%	2,312	37.6%
Western front	1,115	16.5%	1,153	18.8%
Italy	909	13.5%	571	9.3%
Balkans	299	4.4%	583	9.5%
Germany	998	14.9%	1,526	24.8%

This third objective was to weaken the German war machine by a general disorganisation of communications and industrial capacity. To come anywhere near attaining this objective, British and American air power would have needed considerably greater forces than it had at its disposal throughout 1943 and the first half of 1944 (which is why Tedder and Harris constantly harped on the necessity of qualitatively increasing the output of bombers). Its forces were sufficient to achieve that objective only in a limited geographical sector. The obvious choice of sector was the area behind the intended landing sites of 1944 and that goal was by and large achieved in North-West France and Belgium in spring 1944.

The impossibility of achieving the third objective throughout the whole, or even the major part, of Germany was increased by a steady improvement in German air defences during the attacks. Anti-aircraft guns became more and more efficient. German fighters now enjoyed the same advantages of the 'inner line' as the RAF had possessed against the *Luftwaffe* during the Battle of Britain. They inflicted heavier and heavier losses on the attackers – especially on the US airforce, which had opted for daytime bombing as against the nocturnal raids of the RAF. The question of sufficient fighter cover for the bombers' raids came to the forefront. The Mosquito and Mustang planes proved the most efficient in this field.

Finally, there was the objective of causing a general disorganisation of German society, a breakdown of urban life, a malfunctioning of all the elementary mechanisms of industrial civilisation. In this respect, carpet bombing was largely successful.[17] So much so that working-class strength was sapped and the possibility of a massive upsurge in German workers' militancy (not to mention a German revolution) – a persistent fear not only of the Nazis and German imperialists,[18] but of the Allies as well – gradually vanished.

The paradoxical outcome of the war of attrition in the air over Germany and Western Europe throughout 1943 and the first half of 1944, was that the decisive losses for the German war machine were not those inflicted by enemy bombers on their civilian or military targets, but those occurring in the aerial battles themselves. By trying to protect the German factories and cities against Bomber Harris, the *Luftwaffe* lost such a large proportion of its own fighter planes that the Western Allies could conquer total hegemony in the air over Normandy and Northern France in the summer and autumn of 1944 – one of the main reasons they won the Battle of Normandy.

In the Far East, the war of attrition developed simultaneously in the Western, Eastern and Northern sectors. In the West, the Imperial Japanese Army had, to all intents and purposes, lost the initiative at the Burmese-Assam border. The Anglo-American imperialist forces tried to initiate the reconquest of Burma with the assistance of American-trained Chiang Kai-Shek forces, led by the US general Stillwell. In 1943 these plans came to nothing. In 1944, they began to enjoy some success with victory at the Battle of Myithyiha.[19] In the Northern sector, the Japanese Army stubbornly continued its attempts to break up rump China and advance towards Chungking, Chiang Kai-Shek's wartime capital since 1938. Chinese resistance gradually increased, with mounting support from the US airforce and growing attrition of the Japanese army as a result of steadily lengthening lines of supply and progressively decreasing air cover. Nevertheless, the Chinese still suffered grave defeats in 1943-44. But it was in the Eastern sector that the war of attrition assumed its fiercest form. Having taken the initiative at Guadalcanal and cleared the main Japanese base in the South Pacific at Rabaul, Nimitz's and MacArthur's island-hopping slowly progressed towards the Japanese homeland. Bloody landings at Saipan and Tinian were followed by the nightmare struggle for Iwo Jima in the Bonins. In each battle Japanese resistance was fierce, but US naval superiority more overwhelming.

After the aerial assasination of Admiral Yamamoto, Japanese naval strategy had become more hesitant. Following much soul-searching, Admiral Koga imposed the 'New Operations Policy' in the fall of 1943. A new inner line of defence—to be held at all costs—was established from Timor through the Marianas to Manchuria.[20] Replenished naval airpower was massed to inflict a decisive blow against the US fleet sometime in spring or summer 1944. In the event, the vital defence perimeter was soon breached at the Mariana Islands. After the notorious 'turkey shoot' off Truk Island, which cost the Japanese three hundred planes, Koga's successor, Admiral Toyota, decided to concentrate his entire fleet of nine aircraft carriers between Saipan and the Phillipines. He hoped to take the Americans by surprise in the course of their landing operations in the Gulf of Leyte. But the US commanders were appraised of the Japanese strategy, and once again the trapper was trapped. Despite the initial advantage of their nearby air bases in the Philippines, the Japanese were overwhelmed in the great battle of attrition that began on 19 June 1944.[21] The significant US losses were quickly replaced by the burgeoning shipbuilding capacity of the West Coast (where industrialists like Henry Kaiser had adapted Fordist mass production methods to ship construction). By contrast the limited capacity and restricted supplies of Japanese industry made a recuperation impossible. The battles of Leyte Gulf and Lingayen Bay resulted in the virtual destruction of Japan's operational naval forces. What had been the world's largest navy in December 1941 had been destroyed by superior industrial power and economic mobilization.

15.

The Final Onslaught

The Anglo-American landing in Normandy on 6 June 1944; the August 1944 and January 1945 offensives of the Red Army which brought it from the Dniester to the Danube and from the Vistula to the Oder, respectively, capturing Hitler's industrial base in Silesia; and the conquest of the Philippines between the Battle of the Leyte Gulf and the landing in the Lingayen Bay (November 1944-February 1945) – these opened the final onslaught on the home-lands of German and Japanese imperialism which would culminate in their collapse in May and August 1945. All these offensives ended in crushing defeats for the foes of the Allied powers. Only in Italy did the *Wehrmacht*, under the guidance of Kesselring – its most skilful field commander besides von Manstein – succeed throughout 1944 and the first three months of 1945 in preventing any break-up of its front.[1] Professionally, the Western Allied commanders proved themselves inadequate to their task, in spite of numerical and material superiority. It was only in April 1945 that Italy was finally cleared of German forces.[2]

The landing on the Normandy beaches, by far the biggest amphibious operation in the history of warfare, was a daring and outstanding organizational feat. In six weeks' time one and a half million men and tremendous quantities of weapons, ammunition, supplies, means of transportation, building material, bridges, petrol, etc. were brought onto the continent. Conditions were so risky that the chief British planner, General Alanbrooke, doubted its outcome until after it had achieved initial success. There were indeed tremendous obstacles – in the first place, minefields and heavy artillery positions, as well as cleverly combined machinegun nests – to be surmounted by the Allied troops on the very beaches where the invading forces landed.

Moreover, the Germans had at least one *Panzer* division on the spot, which forestalled Montgomery's attempt to seize the town of Caen at the outset. (It took the British army more than four weeks to achieve that initial objective.) In general, the German Army was superior in the professional skill of its commanders. It also had qualitatively superior weapons at its disposal. These were factors which undoubtedly could have defeated the Allies, or at least led to a protracted war of position.[3] But these disadvantages for the invading army, and the very real risks involved in the gigantic undertaking, were outweighed by a number of decisive advantages.

Foremost among them was absolute Allied air superiority. The *Luftwaffe* was no more able to impede the landing operations than the German Navy. Allied landing craft and shipping were able to cross the Channel at will. Had they not, Operation Overlord would have failed. Allied air superiority also involved a constant hammering at the German lines of communication behind the front – in the first place, the bridges across the Seine, the Somme and the Loire, the railway system throughout Northern France and Belgium up to the Meuse and the Rhine, and the highways throughout France. This made the movement and concentration of German reserves extremely costly and hazardous. A second bonus for the Allies was the failure of the German High Command to settle immediately on the type of defence with which to oppose the landings. Rommel was in favour of an immediate concentrated counter-blow at the disembarkation points, while von Rundstedt – fearing the effect of Allied bombings on any troop and armour concentration – favoured a more flexible response: he did not believe that the Allies would be able to effect a quick breakout.[4]

In the event, things went rather differently from how either the German commanders or the Allied planners had expected. The Allied infantry was pinned down by stubborn German resistance in a narrow beachhead for much longer than foreseen, making large manoeuvres difficult. Montgomery's first attempt at breakthrough in the east failed. The second attempt by Patton at Avranches succeeded. But complete encirclement of all the German forces in Brittany, southwest France and Normandy did not occur. It would take the Allies sixty days to reach the Seine. In the end, in the absence of any long-term strategic conception other than a slow whittling down of enemy reserves, German resistance began to collapse. With the collapse of the German front at the Seine, the Western Allies moved with lightning speed to capture Liege and Antwerp. General Blumentritt, Chief of Staff of the German Army in the West, wrote: 'There were no German forces behind the Rhine, and at the end of August our front was wide open.'[5] The war came within an inch of ending in autumn 1944.

Two monumental strategic blunders by the Allied High Command saved the situation for the *Wehrmacht*. After much dispute and through Eisenhower's arbitration, the American-dominated southern wing of the Allied offensive against Germany opted in favour of a gradual thrust through the heavily-defended Moselle area, instead of moving further North – territory which was largely unfortified and where the German Army had twice achieved a massive breakthrough with much less armour than was now possessed by the US Army. Simultaneously, the Mont-gomery-led northern wing tried a breakthrough over the Rhine at Arnhem, but with the forces which were only a fraction of those necessary to effect the operation and despite the existence of large reserves. The insufficient impetus of Operation Market Garden was compounded by utterly inadequate intelligence: its com-manders ignored the fact that a crack *Panzer* division was actually on the spot at Arnhem, that the paratroopers would drop right on top of it, and that they would be cut to pieces by superior armour and firepower.[6]

The immediate purpose of the German Ardennes offensive was logistical: to capture Liege and Antwerp and, with them, huge Allied supply dumps, in the first instance oil, of which the *Wehrmacht* and the *Luftwaffe* were already desperately short. As for the broader strategic objective, this was based on the hope that the internal contradictions of the Allied camp, and especially the prospect of Soviet occupation of Eastern and Central Europe, would convince the Anglo-Americans to go for a separate peace. As Hitler told his generals in December 1944: 'In all history there has never been a coalition composed of such heterogeneous partners as that of our enemies. The states which are now our enemies are the greatest opposites which exist on earth: ultra-capitalist states on one side and ultra-Marxist on the other; on the one side a dying empire – Britain; on the other side a colony, the United States waiting to claim its inheritance. These are states which diverge daily. . . . If we can deal it a couple of heavy blows, this artifically constructed common front may collapse with a mighty thunder-clap at any moment.'[7]

Hitler's calculation was rooted in a stubborn conviction – maintained against his generals' advice (founded on accurate intelligence) – that the Soviet Army would not be able to recover as fast as it did and strike a blow on the Eastern Front which would take it to the German frontier and within thirty-five miles of Berlin by early February 1945. The Ardennes offensive did ultimately inflict heavy casualties on the British and American troops – but with disastrous strategic results for the German bourgeoisie. What happened was exactly what the military conspirators of 20 July 1944 on the one hand, and Churchill and his colleagues on the other, wanted to avoid: the arrival of Soviet troops on German soil and the Soviet occupation of Hungary, Austria and most of Czechoslovakia.

So these German tactical victories were, in reality, huge political defeats. The battles of Arnhem and of the Ardennes confirmed that military victories are not ends in themselves, but means of obtaining political goals which must be clearly understood and prioritised. The same applies, *mutatis mutandis*, to Kesselring's successful resistance against the Allies' attempts to effect a breakthrough in Italy. Contrary to an opinion expressed by many experts, including General MacArthur, the Italian front was far from being a military 'diversion', i.e. a squandering of forces on a secondary theatre of war which might have been better employed in France or the Pacific.[8] Given the existing superiority of the Allied armies on these two fronts, the diversion to them of the thirty Allied divisions stationed in Italy would not have made any difference to the outcome of the war. But the successful breakthrough of these divisions in the spring, summer and autumn of 1944 towards the Po valley and, from there, through the Ljubljana gap would have changed the map of Europe. Anglo-American forces would have arrived in Budapest, Vienna and Prague much earlier than the Red Army.

Kesselring's 'victories' were in reality victories for Stalin. Of course, the inept military command of the Allied forces in Italy deserves equivalent blame to that laid at Kesselring's door by those capitalists who bitterly regret that it was Russian soldiers who liberated Central Europe – at a heavy price in blood – from the Nazi butchers. It was only in April 1945 that the German forces in Italy were crushed – and by then the fate of Central Europe had already been settled. The successive interruptions to the Red Army offensive from the battles of Kursk and the Donetz to the recapture of Kiev, Smolensk, Minsk, the Baltic countries and Odessa, can be readily understood. The Red Army remained short of motorised transport. Huge problems with the supply and repair of the tank divisions employed accordingly arose after each important advance. Hitler's 'scorched earth' policy made supply on the spot nearly impossible. After the liberation of the Donetz and the Ukraine, not a single big factory there could produce military goods before the war's close. With each successive retreat of the *Wehrmacht*, its own supply lines became shorter. As German war production was still intact – or rather, increasing – in spite of carpet bombing (the high-point of tank, airplane and artillery'output was reached in summer 1944), the *Wehrmacht* in fact received greater reinforcements than the Red Army. Its weakest link was man-power, not material. But after the terrible toll of the previous three years, manpower started to become scarce in the USSR too. More and more women had to be drafted into the Army to make up for the loss of male soldiers.

German field commanders proved to be skilful in retreat and in organising local counter-offensives which repeatedly eroded the Red Army's build-up of reserves in advance of planned offensives. The most successful of these surprise counter-thrusts were made in April 1944 in Southern Poland and in August 1944 on the Vistula.

Once again, however, the German Army only gained time in these holding operations, with no obvious strategic purpose. The Red Army had such a porpose: to drive the *Wehrmacht* all the way back to Berlin. This took longer than initially foreseen, but it was by and large successful. And it entailed some brilliant operations, especially the Battle of Minsk, in which nearly two hundred thousand German soldiers were trapped and which broke the Army Group Centre of the *Wehrmacht*; the recapture of the Baltic states, which led to the encirclement of a large German army in Kurland (the northern tip of Latvia); and the breakthrough over the Vistula and on to the Oder in December 1944-January 1945.

From a strategic point of view, Malinovski's and Tolbukhin's offensive on the Pruth, begun on 20 August 1944, was even more decisive. By breaking up the *Wehrmacht's* Moldavian positions in a few days the whole situation in Southeast Europe was transformed. The defection of Rumania and Bulgaria from the Third Reich became inevitable. Admiral Horthy tried to engineer a similar defection in Hungary, but just failed. Above all, the whole Southern Army Group of the *Wehrmacht* – nearly a million

144

soldiers! – collapsed in a military disaster worse for the Nazis than Stalingrad. All Churchill's schemes for arriving in the Balkans before the Red Army were rendered impracticable. It was not at Yalta that the ruling classes of Southeast Europe were 'sacrificed'; they were crushed on the battlefield, together with their erstwhile German allies, on the Pruth.

In the meantime, a terrible tragedy evolved further to the North on the main Minsk-Berlin axis. Spurred on by the ambiguous appeals of Red Army commanders, motivated by the desire to liberate their capital by their own efforts and to establish a more favourable balance of forces for the London-based Polish government-in-exile vis-à-vis the Lublin regime set up by Stalin, and also anxious to obtain the maximum amount of weapons for self-defence against ongoing repression by the NKVD, the Polish underground *Armija Krajowa* (dominated by the social-democratic PPS rather than by bourgeois reactionaries) rose in Warsaw against the German occupation forces when the Soviet army reached the Vistula. The uprising was based upon a doubly-incorrect assumption: that the Red Army would join, or at least help, them (Stalin had promised this when meeting Mikolayczik the first day of the uprising – a promise he repeated in a telegram sent to Churchill on 15 August 1944); and that the *Wehrmacht* had been decisively weakened along the Vistula. In fact, the *Wehrmacht* assembled a still impressive force to counter both the Red Army's drive and the Warsaw insurrection. And Stalin blocked all help to Warsaw, letting the Germans do the dirty work of liquidating the *Armija Krajowa* he would otherwise have had to do himself. As a result of that double miscalculation, the uprising was crushed by the Nazis, in spite of the heroism of the combatants. Their butchers took a terrible revenge: 'After two months of merciless fighting, sixty-two days of unending horror and atrocity, with 15,000 men of the 30 to 40,000 of the *Armija Krajowa* dead, the population forcibly evacuated or murdered on the spot, 150,000 to 200,000 civilians immolated out of one million, the dead entombed in the ruins and the wounded lying untended on the roads or suffering their last agonies in cellars, surrender could no longer be delayed. On October 2 (1944) the fighting ceased: the Poles were collected for deportation or extinction in the gas chambers, after which the Germans bent to the maniacal labour of levelling Warsaw to the ground.'[9]

The Red Army's halt at the Vistula lasted five months. The move from the Vistula to the Oder would occur in January 1945. In the beginning of March 1945, the *Wehrmacht* would launch its last major offensive on the Eastern front – similar to the Ardennes offensive in the West – around Lake Balaton in Hungary, in order to cover the approaches to Vienna. After some initial success, the offensive broke down, as in the Ardennes, because of a lack of fuel and reserves.[10]

After the defeats in the Ardennes, at the Oder and in Hungary, German resistance was ready to collapse. The two main industrial supply centres for the army – the Ruhr and Silesia – were progressively cut off from the bulk of the German armed forces and occupied shortly afterwards. All German reserves had been used up. Hitler again hesitated over committing his main forces to a desperate last-ditch defence around Berlin or in a mythical 'Alpine fortress' linked to Bohemian industry, but was unable to concentrate his forces on either of these two objectives. After the crossings of the Rhine by the US Army at Remagen and the British at Wesel in the North, the Western allies met the Red Army at the Elbe. Zhukov and Koniev moved their forces pincerwise towards Berlin, where the *Wehrmacht* made its last stand, inflicting heavy casualties upon the Soviet army but never putting the end result in doubt. Hitler killed himself on 30 April 1945. On May Day 1945 the Red Flag was flying over the *Reichstag*. A few days later, the German High Command surrendered.

Could the Anglo-American armies have arrived in Berlin before the Red Army, given the delay on the Soviet assault from August till December 1944? At the beginning of November 1944, the Red Army and the Western armies were roughly the same distance from Berlin, the Russians facing three million German soldiers with 4,000 tanks, the Anglo-Americans one million with 1,600 tanks.[11] On 11-15 April 1945, a similar situation was in the offing.[12]

Conflicting pressures were put on Eisenhower, some (above all, Churchill – but also Bradley) pushing him to take Berlin (even the use of General Gavin's paratroopers was envisaged); others (e.g. Patton) counselling a change of thrust towards the Dresden-Leipzig area and Prague. Besides political considerations – amongst which was not only the Yalta agreement, but also an attempt to bypass the British and not let Montgomery move quickly towards Berlin – there were two major military motives for Eisenhower's hesitations, which ended with the loss of the Berlin prize: fear of the frightful costs of street fighting in the German capital (he thought that the capture of Berlin would cost the Western Allies 100,000 men; in fact the Russians lost 300,000 in the battle for Berlin) and the need to transfer forces as rapidly as possible to the Pacific front.

Interviewed by Willy Brandt in 1958, Eisenhower said that if he could do things all over again, he certainly would have taken Berlin.[13] As things now stand, and given the available evidence, there is no way of comprehensively judging the issue.

In the Pacific, the final offensive against the Japanese Imperial Navy and Army occurred on two largely disconnected fronts, and with increasingly political, rather than purely military, purpose. At the Western perimeter of the Japanese zone of conquest, Mountbatten led Allied forces towards a slow reconquest of Burma; his main intention – by and large achieved – being to reestablish the British hold over Malaya and Singapore and to facilitate the reconquest of Indochina by the French and of Indonesia by the Dutch imperialists. Hurley in China was writing to Roosevelt: 'The British, the French and the Dutch in the Far East are bound together by a vital interest, namely repossession of their colonial empires . . . . , because without their empires they would be impoverished and weak. This interest is also binding because it is based on the desire of the British to expand to the Far East the same character of imperial hegemony of the three great imperialistic nations as they have arranged for the control of Western Europe . . . . You may therefore expect Britain, France and the Netherlands to disregard the Atlantic Charter and all promises made to other nations by which they obtained support in the earlier stages of the war.'[14]

In Indochina such moves were preempted by the Viet-Minh's general insurrection and seizure of Saigon and Hanoi, from which they had to withdraw, however, under heavy combined pressure by British, French and Chiang Kai-Shek's military forces. But they withdrew, not to surrender, but to engage in a stubborn popular war in the countryside which, via Dien Bien Phu and at least in part thanks to the sanctuary they gained after the victory of the Chinese revolution, would lead them back to Hanoi in 1953.

In Indonesia, the Japanese military command helped Sukarno and Hatta to make a plea for independence on the eve of the Japanese surrender. The Dutch organised a war of colonial reconquest against the national liberation struggle, which also became intertwined with social revolution, although to a lesser extent than in Indochina. After some oscillation and several incipient betrayals by a largely corrupt national bourgeoisie, but given the tremendous disproportion of forces involved as soon as armed mass mobilization began to spread in a population of over one hundred million, Dutch imperialism had to withdraw.

At the Eastern perimeter of the Japanese Empire, MacArthur and Nimitz pressed on towards the Japanese homeland. After Saipan, the Japanese ruling class understood that it had lost the war and began to look for a political solution. A first prudent move in that direction was the elimination of General Tojo as Prime Minister. Feelers were put out in Moscow, Ankara and Stockholm for a way to achieve armistice. Meanwhile resistance continued and even stiffened, with *kamikaze* heroism and the mass suicide of soldiers (as in Iwo Jima), of soldiers and civilians (as in Okinawa).[15] The Japanese Navy lost its last operational reserves at the Battle of Leyte Gulf in the Philippines. The Japanese air force was practically wiped out of the skies.

Nevertheless, the US High Command was worried lest an invasion of the Japanese homeland result in heavy losses. The fear was founded on the experience of Saipan, Iwo Jima and Okinawa: stubborn resistance and suicide missions for which, MacArthur and Marshall feared, there were millions of willing candidates in Japan itself. At Iwo Jima and Okinawa, the US forces lost 70,000 men, more than in Normandy. Their fear was reinforced by the existence of a still powerful and largely intact Japanese Army in Manchuria, some 750,000 men strong, which could be brought home at the last minute to oppose the US invasion force. For this reason, the US High Command and political leaders were in favour of the Soviet Union joining the war against Japan three months after the end of the war in Europe. This was the basic motivation for Roosevelt's conciliatory tone towards Stalin at Yalta.[16] They calculated that in all probability the Kwantung Army would stand and fight the Red Army, in order to prevent a crossing of the Yalu into Korea or even a landing in Japan, in the rear of the defence force fighting against the US invasion.

However, US air raids – especially the incendiary bomb attack which largely destroyed Tokyo – had so broken Japan's will to resist that the end of war seemed imminent. The USA and USSR now switched their positions, with Stalin keen to join the war against Japan (the Soviet Union declared war on Japan on 8 August) in order to get his hands on whatever booty he could find in Manchuria and Korea, and the USA trying by every means to delay the Soviet Union from joining in the final kill.[17] In the event the division of Korea into two zones of occupation along the 38th parallel, which led to the creation of two separate states, was unilaterally decided upon by Washington and inscribed in the

General Order No.1 concerning the conditions of surrender of the Japanese armed forces imposed on the Emperor.[18]

There is little doubt today that the dropping of the atomic bomb on Hiroshima and Nagasaki was motivated more by political than military considerations.[19] It played no role, as was trumpeted at the time, in reducing US casualties: Japan was on the point of surrender anyway.[20] If its purpose was to assist the Tokyo court clique's desperate attempt to overcome last-minute resistance to capitulation among the military diehards, then the power of the bomb could have been demonstrated by its use on an uninhabited island. General MacArthur emphatically states: '(At the end of April 1945) . . . my staff was unanimous in believing Japan was on the point of collapse and surrender. I even directed that plans be drawn up "for a possible peaceful occupation" without further military operations. . . . Japan had already been gutted, the best of its army and navy had been defeated, and the Japanese homelands was now at the mercy of air-raids and invasion'.[22] The gruesome killing of a quarter of a million human beings was carried out for no other purpose than a political show of strength directed much more at US allies, particularly the Soviet Union, than at Japan. It was a major crime against humanity in a war which was not short of them.

A detailed, sometimes moving narrative of what happened in Japan prior to the dropping of the atomic bombs, of the peace overtures already under way, of the utter falsity of the thesis of the 'risk of one million American dead' (recently rehashed by Nixon) is provided in *The Day Man Lost:* 'At night, while the rest of the people huddled hungry in bombed out dwellings, those in power entertained one another at luxurious dinner parties, parties that often turned into nightlong orgies. It is hardly surprising that *yamatodamashi* was on the wane. This increasing demoralisation of the people was what chiefly preoccupied Prince Konoye who feared that if, or when, Japan lost the war, the masses would turn to communism as a panacea. . . . The only way to retain the (old imperialist) system . . . was to terminate the war as swiftly and painlessly as possible.'[23]

By the time the atomic bomb was dropped on Japanese cities, the Americans had already clarified for their own benefit and also, where appropriate, for that of their wartime 'friends', the three basic postulates of their policy towards defeated Japan: that the occupation of the Japanese mainland would be a purely American affair; that the occupying power would retain the Emperor as a 'symbol of authority'; and that a Japan sympathetic to the United States was desirable to check the Soviet presence in Asia. As in Western Europe so also in the Far East, the USA sought to prevent any transfer of power to the local Resistance: the General Order No. 1 ensured that the collapse of Japanese power in Korea, the Philippines, the Dutch East Indies and Indochina would not benefit the resurgent nationalist and Communist Left. However, since only actual occupation would guarantee the fulfillment of American aims, the USA made peace with the archaic forces of colonialism or corrupt conservatism in order to restore the desirable *status quo ante bellum* now everywhere in its death throes. Washington's global policy in the Far East met with little opposition in Moscow and it was the Chinese Revolution that decisively altered the geopolitical balance in Asia against US design.

16.

The Outcome

The crushing of German, Japanese and Italian imperialism; a decisive weakening of their French and British counterparts; the decline and fall of 'direct' colonialism in general; the emergence of US imperialism as a hegemonic power in the world; the emergence of the USSR as a world power and its military control over Eastern and Central Europe; the impetuous rise of national liberation movements in the colonies and semi-colonies, increasingly inter-twined with social revolution as in China; the resurgence of the organized labour movement on the continent of Europe, with a high level of militancy – especially in 1944-48 period; similar developments in Japan and the USA, though at a lower level of class consciousness; the outbreak of the Cold War essentially as a test of strength between the United States and the Soviet Union, and the resulting 'campist' ideology among broad layers of the international labour movement – this was the world that emerged from World War Two.

Was this outcome decided at Teheran, Yalta and Potsdam? Was it, in other words, the product of diplomatic horsetrading, 'mistakes' or even 'betrayals'? To a large extent it was determined on the battlefield. The division of Europe along the Stettin-Trieste line was clearly contrary to long-term interests of British and American imperialism. Yet it was an inevitable result of the Soviet Union bearing the brunt of the war against Hitler. In 1945 the Western powers were in no position to change the de facto situation in Eastern and Central Europe – except in a marginal way. They could of course have refused to abandon parts of Saxony and Thuringia (as Churchill urged Eisenhower), areas to which their troops had gone and which lay beyond the frontiers decided upon at Yalta as demarcation lines between Soviet and Western zones of occupation. This Washington refused to do, for at the time it still thought it needed Soviet troops in China. But if it had listened to London, the outcome would probably have been less favourable than what did emerge, since the USSR would probably have refused to let the Western allies enter Berlin and Vienna – cities crucial to their position in Central and Southern Europe, but where they had no troops on 8 May 1945. If Eisenhower had sent US troops beyond the Elbe into regions where the Red Army was not yet present in the first days of May – essentially Mecklenburg and Bohemia – in spite of previous agreements, nobody can predict what would have happened. The Cold War would certainly have broken out earlier. The repercussions in the West and East alike would have been formidable.

Again, on balance, the gains for capitalism would have been marginal, the risks momentous. The Yugoslav partisans would have kept Trieste. The Italian partisans could have taken over Milan and Turin. The revolution in Greece might have been victorious. A huge explosion could have occurred in France. Big disturbances may have broken out in the US Army and in Britain, not so much because of sympathy with the Soviet Union – although that was very much present – but out of general war weariness. It is more than likely that US leaders chose what was – for them – the lesser evil.

By and large, both armies remained where they were at the end of the war. Given the class character of the Soviet state, there was no way of altering the state of affairs through political or diplomatic means. It was only possible to change it by continuing the war, i.e. by transforming it into a war between the USSR and the USA. For obvious reasons – war weariness in the USA and Britain; the risk of civil war in Europe; economic exhaustion of the USSR – this was not a realistic prospect for any of the major powers. So, politically and diplomatically the situation largely became frozen where it stood militarily in May 1945 – as far as Europe was concerned.

Naturally where it stood militarily was not determined solely by force of arms: several miscalculations by the imperialist and bourgeois powers led to the final outcome. The basic miscalculation was the German bourgeoisie's. Had it capitulated in the summer of 1944 – or had the 20 July 1944 conspiracy against Hitler been successful[1] – the map of Europe would have been quite different today. When German historians and politicians, and some of their covert Anglo-Saxon brethren, blame Roosevelt's insistence on 'unconditional surrender' for the Red Army's occupation of Eastern Germany, Czechoslovakia and Hungary, it is a typical case of cutting one's nose to spite one's face. After all, what was involved was their own property and state power. Bourgeois political and military leaders who end up losing half of their state through pride, or because they hope – against all the evidence – to regain through last-minute political upheavals what they have lost on the battle-field are simply a bunch of incompetents who do not defend their class interests properly.

This is not to say that the 'unconditional surrender' formula was a wise one from the stand-point of the Allies (neither Churchill nor Stalin were in favour of it). It certainly prolonged the war by generating in the German High Command (though less so amongst big capital) a certain psychological resistance to suing for peace. But in the first place it prolonged the war at the expense of the German bourgeoisie, which should have known better. After all, the remnants of the Third Reich under Admiral Doenitz ultimately *did* surrender unconditionally in May 1945. Would it not have been wiser, from their own point of view, to have done so in the summer of 1944, when there was still not a single soldier – and especially no Russians – on German soil?[2]

Something similar might be said of the Polish ruling class, especially its main political personnel. For two years Mikolajcyzk's government-in-exile stubbornly refused to accept the Curzon line on the eastern frontier for post-war Poland, as had been demanded by Stalin since the very first negotiations with Britain, and quickly accepted by Churchill. It likewise refused to face the new realities by declining to include a sufficient number of pro-Moscow representatives in its cabinet. At the outset Moscow was ready to accept four out of sixteen; then it demanded half; and finally Mikolajcyzk was offered four places in the Lublin government – which he accepted, just as he ended up accepting the Curzon line. From the point of view of the Polish bourgeoisie it would obviously have been preferable to have made a deal with the Soviet Union as early as 1942 (not to mention prior to the war), when the *Armija Krajowa* was still intact, and the Red Army was very much outside Polish territory. Though one cannot predict what kind of deal would have been struck then, it certainly would have been no worse for the Polish ruling class than what emerged in 1945. That class's complete lack of realism, its chief characteristic ever since the formation of an independent Poland after WWI, was based on an incorrect assessment of Soviet strength. As Hopkins reported to Roosevelt in March 1943 after Eden's return from Moscow: 'Poland has very large ambitions after the war and Eden says that privately they say that Russia will be so weakened and Germany crushed that Poland will emerge as the most powerful state in that part of the world.'[3]

The example of Czechoslovakia confirms that even unqualified 'friendliness' towards the Soviet government *ab initio* did not save the local bourgeoisie around Beneš from ultimate expropriation. Yet this was not a foregone conclusion in 1945; it was the product of the development of the Cold War in 1946-47.[4]

An argument is often advanced to the effect that Eisenhower and Montgomery deliberately delivered 'millions of Germans' to 'Soviet totalitarianism' through their refusal to accept armistice on the Western front alone. This is pure demagogy. The records show that a de facto one-sided surrender in the West did transpire which enabled the Western Allied armies to advance further east than they would otherwise have done.[5]

The fact of the matter is that far from concentrating all their forces against the USSR, Hitler and the *Wehrmacht* High Command had built up a huge army in the West, clung to their western conquests (including Norway, Denmark and Holland) to the very end, used their final reserves (the most efficient new tanks and airplanes) to conduct a mighty counter-offensive in the Ardennes in the winter of 1944-45, and had even withdrawn significant forces from the Eastern front for that purpose. (According to Diana Shaver Clemens, at the beginning of 1945 185 German divisions were positioned on the Eastern front, and 147 on the Western front and in Italy – i.e. more than forty per cent of total German forces.)[6]

If, as a result of that momentous miscalculation, the Russians, and not the Western imperialists, arrived first in Berlin, the German bourgeoisie should lay the blame where it belongs: on its own political blindness – for sure, Hitler's in the first place, but also that of all its main military commanders and of most of its political representatives as well.

Behind that blindness lay typical imperialist arrogance – refusal to acknowledge defeat and the stubborn clinging to the hope of a last-minute 'political miracle', i.e. the hope that the inevitable 'cold war' would transform itself into a new 'hot war' between Western imperialism and the USSR before the 'hot war' with Germany was over. Such obstinacy was that of reckless gamblers, characteristic of broad layers of German imperialism's leading personnel since its inception (for historical reasons which have been explained many times). If the gamble was lost – as it was bound to be – the loser could not lay the blame on those players who had come out better than he did from the whole horrific game.

It was, however, true that from the autumn of 1943 onwards, authoritative representatives of German big business and banking consciously prepared for a radical change of economic orientation and foreign economic policy in the direction of integration into a world market dominated by US imperialism. This involved a good deal of medium- and long-term planning, a reconversion of arma-ments industry into civilian production, the preparation of an export drive, and a radical currency reform in order to make the German *Mark* convertible once again.

Many, if not all, of these plans were implemented in the 1945-48 period. The people involved in the planning – Erhard, Emminger (later chief of the *Deutsche Bundesbank*) and Abs, chief of the *Deutsche Bank* (the main West German private bank) and grey eminence of Konrad Adenauer – where those who later actually implemented them. It took place, essentially, in the Ministry of Economic Affairs (*Reichswirtschaftsministerium*) and in the Working Group for Questions of Foreign Economic Relations (*Arbeitskreis fur Aussenwritschaftsfragen*). The participants were shielded from repression by the fact that the person in charge of the ministry was Ohlendorf, assistant SS chief of the body responsible for internal security (*Reichssicherheitshauptant*).[7] Despite his anti-Marxist orientation, the author Ludolf Herbst accurately sums up what was at stake: 'The main concern was . . . the conservation of the capitalist economic and social order. Inside big industry there existed a clear consciousness of the fact that the future of capitalism in Germany decisively depended on the way in which the recon-version of a war economy into a peace economy was conducted.'[8] Yet the German bourgeoisie proved itself incapable of taking the political-military measures necessary to implement these projects in time: this was the price paid historically for its decision to deliver political power to the Nazis and the military clique in 1932-33.

Simultaneously, General Alanbrooke, Chief of the British Imperial Staff, was writing in his diary: 'Should Germany be dismembered or gradually converted to an Ally to meet the Russian threat of twenty years hence? I support the latter and feel certain that we must from now on regard Germany in a very different light. Germany is no longer the dominating power in Europe – Russia is. She has . . . vast resources and cannot fail to become the main threat in fifteen years from now. Therefore, foster Germany, gradually build her up and include her in a Federation of Western Europe.'[9] This was indeed the plan that the West was contemplating for Germany.

The Rumanian ruling class was another case in point. It delayed its switch of alliance until the very last minute, when the Red Army had already broken the German Army Group South. Thus it could not prevent the switch being accompanied by the Red Army's occupation of its country. With no possibility of the West coming to its aid, Stalin's henchman Vyshinskii became the real master of the country and the eventual expropriator of the Rumanian ruling class.[10] One can remark the sorry fate of ruling classes which become embroiled in regional and global balances of forces which they can neither control nor alter, except marginally. Yet this helplessness is, to a significant degree, self-inflicted, for it reflects the lack of support for the particular ruling class within the country. This was manifestly the case in Rumania, whose ruling class had historically displayed considerable opportunism, being successively dependent on Prussian power, French diplomacy, German economic and military interests in the area, and finally on the Red Army. Hated by the masses, the Rumanian ruling class was scarcely in a position to mobilize large-scale peasant resistance to Vyshinkskii's 'revolution from above'. In the last instance, it fell because of its own inner rotteness.

The ease with which first Germany, and then Russia, regained control over Eastern Europe after its reconstitution in 1918 was ultimately based on the profound political, social and economic weakness of the bourgeois order there. In this preponderantly agricultural part of Europe,[11] undercapitalization, low labour productivity, unemployment and hunger accompanied ruthless and venal ruling classes. For the most part these ruling classes had collaborated with Nazism, either via formal military alliance or by participation in many of its crimes during the dark years of 1941-42. Long before the Soviet Union embarked upon the policy of 'structural assimilation', the old political and economic structures of Eastern Europe had been destroyed by the war. The Soviet leadership mainly saw the problems of Eastern Europe through the prism of its own determination to prevent the resurrection of a traditionally hostile ruling class; and in this, of course, the total collapse of much of East European society was working to its advantage. To the United States, on the other hand, the question of Eastern Europe was one of principle only; the rise of the 'national security state' meant that all political and economic blocs, all spheres of influence not directly under US control, were seen as inimical to it and its conception of an integrated world captialism. Ready to use its enormous capital resources to pull Eastern Europe back into the Western fold, the United States had little to offer its people on the political plane.

From the standpoint of the long-term interests of the working class, not to mention the interests of world socialism it would of course have been preferable if the masses of Rumania and the other East European countries had been able to liberate themselves, through their own forms of struggle. The Soviet bureaucracy's 'revolutions from above' bequeathed an ugly political legacy, which has profoundly marked the post-war situation, not only in this part of Europe, but throughout the world. But this issue in turn had been largely pre-determined by what happened in the twenties and thirties, i.e. by the internal crisis of the Comintern and the growing passivity of the labouring masses. Moreover, the ruthless anti-working class and anti-Communist repression of the East European and Balkan ruling classes had contributed to the negative choice made in the international Communist movement, which resulted in the victory of the social revolution conducted through a military-bureaucratic apparatus instead of authentic popular revolutions. This has been the main cause of political instability in this part of Europe since the war.

The observation that nowhere were any substantial territorial gains surrendered in exchange for political concessions is confirmed by comparing the outcome of the war in the Pacific to that in Europe. If the Red Army entered the war against Japan at the last minute, it was not in response to an actual invitation by the United States – though the pressure from Washington was real enough until it became clear that Japan's surrender was a matter of weeks. It was in order to obtain assets which could influence the post-war arrangements in the Far East that the Soviet bureaucracy seized and conserved its hold over South Sakhalin and the Kurils. It wanted to hold on to Port Arthur too, but here the Chinese Revolution intervened. Soviet presence in North Korea led to the partition of that country, just as the absence of Soviet troops (and British, for that matter) in Japan led to an exclusively American occupation there.[12]

Soviet troops were in Manchuria when the war ended and they left (having seized quite a lot of booty) because they could not have stayed anyway – not in the midst of a civil war between Communists and Chiang Kai-Shek whom the Kremlin formally supported.[13] It was faced with an insoluble dilemma: it could not fight alongside Chiang's army against the People's Liberation Army; it did not want to fight alongside PLA against Chiang's forces; it could not stay neutral in a massive civil war unfolding before its eyes. The only way out of that dilemma was to withdraw – which it did.

As for Iran, the Red Army withdrew from occupied Azerbaijan in exchange for a withdrawal of the imperialist armies from the rest of the country. This was a political *do ut des*, fundamental to the whole war and post-war strategy of the Soviet bureaucracy.[14] In the Middle East, Italy, Greece, Turkey and Iran Stalin ended up by bowing to Churchill, and later to Truman, and he expected Washington and London to do the same in the case of Eastern Europe. The US, on the other hand, pursued its policy of excluding not only its class enemy, but also its closest ally, Britain. Admiral King, one of main American strategists, was not the only one to oppose all aid from the Royal Navy in the 'mopping up' operations against Japan. Britain was excluded from sharing in the occupation of Japan, and in the Middle East Truman did not intervene solely to stop Stalin: what followed was a rapid substitution of the USA for Britain as the regional hegemonic power.

If the way in which World War Two reshaped the map of Europe and the Far East was largely decided on the battlefield, and not on the conference tables at Yalta and Potsdam, military-diplomatic realpolitik was disrupted and partially neturalized by the irruption of independent class forces onto the political area – class forces, that is, not controlled by Big Power military commands or governments. The most telling case is that of Yugoslavia. At the Moscow Conference of October 1944 Churchill proposed to Stalin that the Soviet bureaucracy and British imperialism enjoy equal influence there: 50%-50%. The Yugoslav workers and peasants, and the Yugoslav Communist Party under Tito's leadership, dissented. They swept aside all attempts to impose a coalition government which would retain the capitalist mode of production and completed their socialist revolution as early as the end of 1945. The refusal of the Yugoslav working masses and the CP to submit to Soviet *diktat* was a key element in the future rift between Tito and Stalin.

Likewise in Greece, despite Stalin's compliance with Churchill's demand that it be completely assigned to the British sphere of influence, the masses had other ideas. A long civil war followed, which they eventually lost mainly because the Greek CP – unlike its Yugoslav counterpart – fatally submitted to Stalin's orders and its own political illusions, surrendering its arms in the sinister Varkiza agreement of February 1945, with all the horrific consequences that followed.

In France, and especially in Italy, a huge upsurge of working-class militancy put some considerable strain on the collaboration of the French and Italian CPs with the bourgeoisie in the framework of a restored capitalist order. Contrary to Stalin's expectations and American hopes, in Britain the population turned Churchill out of office in the first post-war elections, giving a landslide victory to a Labour Party with a clear mandate for radical reforms and granting independence to India.

Even in Eastern Europe, independent class activity put some constraints on Kremlin's plans – at least temporarily – in East Germany, Czechoslakia and Hungary.[15]

In Indonesia and Indochina, all manoeuvres by imperialism and the Kremlin to restrict the huge national liberation movements to the horizon of 'reformed' colonial empires failed. Long wars ensued which, in the case of Indochina, would eventually develop into socialist revolution, and, in the case of Indonesia, end in bloody defeat.[16] In China especially, imperialism and the Soviet bureaucracy showed themselves unable to contain or suppress peasant uprisings in the Northern plains and to halt a civil war which would result in the victory of the Chinese Revolution.

17.

The Aftermath

The Second World War had hardly ended when the Cold War began. The evolution of the first into the second transpired quickly and without interruption – so much so that some historians and radical ideologues of both the right and the left have argued that the Second World War never really ended or – what amounts to the same thing – that the Third World War started in 1945.

These views are, of course, exaggerated. Hitler's and Tojo's hope that the military alliance between the Western imperialist powers and the USSR would break up at the last moment, and that a reversal of alliance would then become possible, did not materialize. Military collaboration within the Alliance continued right up until the immediate aftermath of the surrender of Germany and Japan. Whatever tensions developed between Washington, London and Moscow arose within the framework of the Alliance; they did not lead to its break-up. Only once the common foe was utterly crushed did the question of who should shape the world thereafter come to overweigh all other considerations.

When did the Cold War actually start? This question has been debated among historians, openly in the West, more indirectly in the East (given the importance of historical revision to the bureaucracy) and the 'world communist movement'. Some Communist and Soviet authors date the beginning of the Cold War from the death of President Roosevelt, thereby perpetuating the myth of a 'peace-loving' Roosevelt as distinct from an 'aggressive' Truman – a myth with no factual foundation whatsoever. Others date it from the proclamation of the Truman Doctrine or from the launching of the Marshall Plan.[1] A distinction must be made, however, between what were actually two successive stages of the Cold War.

During the first stage, the conflict was over political and military control of Eastern Europe. Control ('governments friendly to the Soviet Union') had by and large been granted Stalin at the Moscow and Quebec conferences and at Yalta. The US Under-Secretary of State Summer Welles wrote a few months after Yalta: 'The Soviet government is as legitimately entitled to promote a regional system in Eastern Europe, composed of cooperative and well-disposed independent governments among the countries adjacent to Russia, as the United States has been justified in promoting an inter-American system of twenty-one sovereign American republics of the Western hemisphere.'[2] Whilst the proposed settlement gave the Western imperialists, and in the first place the British, some minor say in shaping the political, and especially the economic, destiny of these countries, it did not involve either a quick withdrawal of Soviet occupying forces or the occupying power's total 'neutrality' vis-à-vis their eventual political evolution.[3] That the occupying powers would influence the post-war politics of occupied countries was clear from the way the Western Allies ran Italy, from whose government the Soviet Union was pointedly excluded. The arrangement in Eastern Europe, as in Italy, by and large reflected the military balance of forces on the European continent as it prevailed in October 1944-February 1945. The failure of the Western Allies to break into Germany from Italy, their inability to cross the Rhine quickly after the Normandy invasion, and, above all, the effects of the German Ardennes counter-offensive on their military goals – at the time when the Red Army was sweeping into the countries of Eastern Europe – led to the political 'spirit of Yalta'.

In the spring and early summer of 1945, however, the balance of forces changed. The American Army was now firmly entrenched on the European mainland – in firepower, mechanized weapons and industrial infrastructure, it was the most powerful in the world. There was now a growing consensus among US leaders that 'the time had arrived to take a strong American attitude towards the Soviets, and that no particular harm can now be done to our war prospects even if Russia should slow down or even stop its war effort in Europe and Asia'.[4] By the late summer the USA had developed the atomic bomb and was able – given its new string of military bases – to deliver it anywhere in the world. The temp-

The Meaning of the Second World War   161

tation to use this superiority to retrieve what had been 'granted' to
Stalin was very great indeed. That Roosevelt died and Truman
took his place made little difference: this development was inevitable. Encouraged by Churchill and by his own military and
political staff, Truman began his term of office by frontally chal-
lenging the Yalta consensus. Harriman, his ambassador to
Moscow, openly questioned Soviet control over Rumania and
Bulgaria, even though it was exercised in Rumania through a king
who was by no means a purely nominal head of state and there was
little question of Bulgarian popular loyalty to the Soviet Union.[5] In
Hungary free elections did take place in 1945, which were lost by
the Communist Party. The same happened in Austria. In Czechoslovakia the elections were also free, and while the CP became the
strongest party, it could not govern alone. In all these countries,
with the exception of Bulgaria, the coalition governments were not
communist controlled in 1945-46.

Yet there was mounting pressure on the Soviet Union at
Potsdam to move towards 'real' coalition governments in Eastern
Europe. Churchill, who had become obssessed by the danger of
communism in Europe, and used every opportunity to stiffen the
will of the US officials in their dealings with the Soviet Union, was
'completely carried away' on hearing of the successful test explosion of the atomic bomb.[6] The news reached Truman at Potsdam;
according to Churchill, he became 'a changed man. He told the
Russians just where they got on and off and generally bossed the
meeting.'[7] And since Poland, for obvious geostrategic reasons, was
pivotal to the new East European order, it was chosen as the test of
whether the Soviets would subscribe to the American-dominated
world or whether they would pursue a distinct strategy of their
own. For the Soviet Union, however, Poland was an unnegotiable
issue. Given that it had no troops there, the United States could do
little in the case of Poland. Greece was to prove a different matter.

Greece came to the US's attention after the decision of Congress
to stop the Lend-Lease arrangement with its European allies.
Britain responded by scaling down its economic and military
presence in Greece – then in the throes of a civil war. The Treasury
argued for a withdrawal from Greece. 'Nor even, if we *had* the
money, am I satisfied that we *ought* to spend it this way . . .
propping up, even with American aid, weak states in the Eastern
Mediterranean against Russia', the Chancellor of the Exchequer
wrote to Attlee in November 1945.[8] The collapsing *Pax Britannica*
provided the opportunity for the American Empire to assert itself:

by now it was primed for problems of this kind. Within the new anti-communist consensus, Greece was presented as a question of the American nation's survival. Navy Secretary Forrestal told Truman: 'If we were going to have a chance of winning, we should have to recognise it as a fundamental struggle between our kind of society and the Russian.'⁹ The Russians, he argued, would respond to nothing but power. Marshall, the new Secretary of State, argued likewise: 'It is not alarmist to say that we are faced with the first crisis of a series which might extend Soviet domination to (Western) Europe, the Middle East and Asia'.¹⁰

On 12 March 1946 Truman delivered a speech before a joint session of Congress which, in addition to requesting $300 million for Greece and $100 million for Turkey, presented events in the former as a global struggle 'between alternative ways of life': 'It must be the policy of the United States to support free people who are resisting attempted subjugation by armed minorities or by outside pressure.'¹¹ The proclamation of the Truman Doctrine can be seen as the commencement of the first phase of the Cold War.

To diplomatic-military pressure after the war the United States added economic blackmail. US imperialism emerged from the war with huge industrial, agrarian and financial capacities at the time when all its potential competitors were economically prostrate. This was especially true of the Soviet Union. Horowitz quotes a very telling description by *The Observer*'s Moscow correspondent and Russian expert Edward Crankshaw: 'To travel, painfully slowly, by train on the newly opened railway from Moscow to the new frontier in Brest Litovsk in the days after the war was a nightmare experience. For hundreds of miles, for thousands, there was not a standing or living object to be seen. Every town was flat, every city. There were no barns. There was no machinery. There were no stations, no water-towers. There was not a solitary telegraph-pole left standing in all that vast landscape, and broad swathes of forest had been cut down all along the line as a protection against ambush by partisans. All along the line lay the twisted rails pulled up by the Germans, who had worked with special trains fitted with draghooks as they moved West. In the fields, unkept, nobody but women, children and very old men could be seen – and these worked only with handtools.'¹²

All major powers emerging from the war hoped for US economic and financial assistance. So did the Soviet Union.¹³ What each power particularly wanted, however, was assistance that would not entail reduction of independence and the capacity to determine its own policies as perceived by its ruling classes and castes. But that is precisely what Washington was not prepared to concede in 1945; its suspension of direct grant aid via Lend-Lease was a heavy blow to Churchill, de Gaulle and Stalin alike. The refusal of American loans made the question of German reparations even more important for the Soviet bureaucracy.[14]

The Soviet armed forces started to strip their zones of occupations of an important part of their industrial equipment. They did so in East Germany. Likewise in Manchuria. When they started to act similarly in Rumania, Bulgaria and Hungary, conflicts with the local bourgeoisie and non-Stalinist wings of the labour movement were bound to increase. The seeds of the second stage of the Cold War were being sown.

But things were not so clear at the outset. The question of whether or not the heavy industry of the Ruhr should be dismantled was not predetermined. A minority wing of the US bourgeoisie, represented by Secretary of the Treasury Henry Morgenthau, had favoured such a move. Not unimportant sectors of the British and French bourgeoisie thought likewise. Even inside the British Labour Party, there was some hesitation.[15] In the event moves towards a dismantlement of the Ruhr commenced. They became the focal point for the first revival of the German working class, which struck in a mass protest throughout the Ruhr against these barbaric acts. Since Stalin hoped for some of the proceeds, heavy pressure was put on the CP, both in the Western and Eastern zones of occupation, to oppose the strikes.

In West Germany the uninterrupted decline of German Stalinism commenced (the CP there had still enjoyed surprising influence in the immediate post-war period).[16] In Eastern Germany, Stalinism was the main source of working-class discontent, and neutralised the popular appeal of Communist-Socialist unity, especially as it entailed an increased production effort by the working class for the purposes of creating a new fund of 'primitive socialist accumulation' to rebuild industry and the country. This would eventually lead to the 16-17 June 1953 workers' uprising in East Germany – which forced the Kremlin to put an end to the plunder of Eastern Europe.[17]

In this context, mention should be made of the wholesale and indiscriminate expulsion of eleven million Germans from East Prussia, Pomerania, Silesia, Poland and Czechoslovakia – an indefensible act. Yet this was not just Stalin's, but an all-Allied, answer to the post-Versailles irredentism of the German minorities in Eastern Europe, as well as a precondition for the adoption of the Oder-Neisse frontier for Poland.

When American imperialism decided against maintaing Germany, Japan and Italy in a state of economic prostration and moved towards the Marshall Plan and the monetary reforms of 1948, the second stage of the Cold War became unavoidable. Through the operation of the Marshall Plan and the European Payments Union linked to it, participating countries were integrated into a world market ruled by the law of value, with the US dollar as universal means of exchange and payment, and US political and military power the secular arm of that saintly rule. For Stalin, the choice was clear. Either the countries under the Kremlin's military and political control would be economically reabsorbed by international capitalism, or they had to be structurally assimilated to the USSR – i.e. capitalist property had to be abolished there.[18]

The decision was not an easy one for the Soviet bureaucracy. Nor was it taken universally and dogmatically. The cases of Austria and Finland indicate that a compromise solution – governments neutral and friendly towards Moscow, but retaining capitalist property relations – was possible.[19] Although no definite proof exists, there is a mass of circumstantial evidence to suggest that in exchange for neutrality and demilitarisation, the German bourgeoisie could probably have obtained reunification of its country, under predominantly capitalist property relations, albeit with a large public sector like Austria, in 1955.

Stalin's successors, especially Malenkov, seem to have made moves in that direction. Overtures were made to Kurt Schumacher, the leader of German social-democracy, who would probably have emerged as the Chancellor and dominant figure of a united Germany, replacing both Adenauer and Ulbricht. But the hypothesis was never tested in practice. Dulles, Eden, Bidault and Adenauer blocked it successfully, each of them for his own particular reasons. So the division of Germany and of Europe into two different socio-economic systems – and thereafter into two different military alliances – became fixed and institutionalised.

In Japan, Truman and MacArthur moved in a similar direction in 1948. But there the outbreak of the Korean War was the decisive turning-point. Japanese industry became the main material basis for the imperialist war against the Chinese Revolution. From that point on, it embarked upon the path of accelerated economic growth which it has pursued ever since.

Exactly when the Soviet bureaucracy opted for creating a *glacis* of client states at its Western borders structurally assimilated to the Soviet Union – i.e. characterised by the overthrow of capitalist state power and property relations through military-bureaucratic compulsion ('revolution from above', with little or no significant popular revolution – is an interesting question.[20]

For the first eighteen months of the German-Soviet war, while the Red Army was essentially on the defensive, Stalin does not seem to have had any post-war plans beyond attempting to secure from Churchill approval for the Soviet frontiers of 1941, i.e. recognition of what had been obtained through the Hitler-Stalin pact: the Baltic States, the Western Ukraine and Western Byelorussia as well as Bessarabia and the Northern Bukovina. Churchill and Eden hummed and hawed – as did Roosevelt, under pressure from a vocal Polish-American lobby in the Democratic Party. But generally, they were inclined to accept these proposals – with the proviso that the Polish government should ratify them.[21]

After the victory of Stalingrad, Stalin began to change course. Maisky was recalled as Ambassador from London and nominated vice-commissar (later vice-minister) of Foreign Affairs in charge of post-war status-of-Europe negotiations. His brief centered on the question of reparations. Later Litvinov joined him.

Indeed, throughout 1943 – including the Teheran conference – and the first half of 1944, reparations and the German question were at the forefront of diplomatic negotiations and conflicts between the Western imperialist allies and the Kremlin, much more so than the Polish or Eastern European questions. The emerging military configuration in Eastern Europe was still far from clear. The second front was now a certainty. The Allied armies were already advancing through Italy to Central Europe. The value of the German and North Italian 'prize' involved in these moves – in the first place the industrial bulwarks of the Ruhr, Southern Germany, Saxony, Berlin and Silesia, and those of Milan and Turin – was much greater than Poland, Rumania, Bulgaria, Hungary, Yugoslavia, Greece or even Czechoslovakia.

The failure of Allied armies to break through towards Milan and Vienna in the second half of 1944; the failure of Montgomery's thrust across the Rhine in autumn 1944; Malinovsky's and Tulbukhin's Yassy breakthrough; Tito's victory in Yugoslavia – these radically altered the situation. Now, for the first time, it became likely that the Red Army would be in Budapest, Vienna, Berlin and Prague before its Anglo-American counterparts. Yet who would be first to Hamburg, Munich and Milan was still in doubt. Thus the question of the division of Europe into military zones of occupation and influence moved to the centre of the diplomatic stage and was at the heart of the Moscow and Yalta horsetrading.

Negotiations were based on an essentially realistic estimate of the military balance of power in Europe in January 1945. That balance had shifted somewhat at the expense of the Western imperialists as a result of Tulbukhin's breakthrough on the Pruth front and Hitler's Ardennes offensive.[22] We are probably not mistaken in thinking that it was in the late summer of 1944 that Stalin, Molotov and others began to envisage a takeover of several Eastern European countries by the Soviet bureaucracy – though which ones precisely was by no means predetermined. Stalin acted in an essentially pragmatic manner in all cases. His ambition extended to seizing territorial opportunities with a minimum of risk (including that of confronting popular revolutions). This was not new. Already in 1939-41, the opportunity to seize the Baltic states, the Western Ukraine and Belorussia, and Bessarabia as a result of the Hitler-Stalin Pact had presented itself. In 1944-48 the opportunity to impose pro-Moscow political regimes in most of the Eastern and Central European was seized. But it was a strictly military-bureaucratic operation, based upon de facto agreements with imperialism – i.e. the division of Europe and Asia into spheres of influence – and with no intention whatsoever of 'stimulating' international socialist revolution.

The clearest proof that the latter option was off the agenda is offered by what happened in the rest of Europe. Stalin abandoned the Greek ELAS forces and the Greek CP to a slow erosion, and then final defeat, at the hands of the Greek bourgeoisie and British and US imperialism. He imposed upon Thorez in France and Togliatti in Italy a line of total capitulation to the rebuilding of a bourgeois state and a capitalist economy. So there was a genuine *do ut des* involved in the post-war arrangements between, first, Stalin and Churchill, and then Stalin, Roosevelt and Churchill. The gains of capitalism were certainly greater than those of the Soviet bureaucracy.

Why did the Cold War not turn into a hot war, except in Korea and even there, very significantly, without the direct participation of the USSR? Powerful sectors of the US bourgeoisie were in favour, if not of an all-out military trial of strength with the Soviet Union, then at least of constant 'brinkmanship'. If such brinkmanship was by and large avoided – although it did occur, later, in

Korea and reemerged over Dien Bien Phu – it was basically for political reasons. In spite of Truman's and Forrestal's heavy pressure, the US Congress did not accept conscription in peace-time in 1945. The American army in Europe was largely demobilised in the autumn of 1945. The eventuality which obsessed Churchill, of the US army leaving Europe, almost transpired.[23] For sure, it was strengthened again after the proclamation of the Truman Doctrine, when the United States set up bases in Greece and Turkey, and with the conclusion of the North Atlantic Treaty after the erruption of the Korean War. But in the interlude, the remaining US forces in Germany and Austria were insufficient to start a war against the USSR.

More fundamental than such technical reasons, however, was a socio-political one. In the period between the dropping of the atomic bomb on Japan and the full-scale unfolding of the Cold War, American imperialism was faced with an increasingly complex series of crises. The GIs began to demonstrate and went to the verge of mutiny in order to be repatriated. American labour struck in the largest and second most militant strike wave in American history. Civil war unfolded in Greece. French and Italian labour rose, largely independently of, and even against, their social-democratic and Stalinist leaders – an upsurge which climaxed in an insurrectional general strike in Italy on 14 July 1948 following an attempt on Togliatti's life. Civil war raged in the most populous country in the world, China. The second most populous country in the world, India, was in the throes of bloody post-independence convulsions and it was by no means certain that there, as in Indonesia, the local bourgeoisie would be able to retain control. On top of all that, it was scarcely certain that the huge American industrial machine, bloated by wartime investment, would be able to reconvert to civilian production without running into a deep crisis of overproduction.

The conclusion to be drawn from this list of headaches for American imperialism and international capitalism is obvious. In spite of its absolute military superiority and its industrial-financial hegemony, US imperialism was unable to face all these crisis and conflicts and risk a 'hot' war with the USSR at the same time. The Soviet Union was already the second largest military power in the world, its army battle-hardened and flushed by a sense of self-confidence and success.

Owing to its defeat of European fascism, it enjoyed enormous prestige in the eyes of the working class. Above all, however, it was the rise of working-class militancy in the heartlands of world capitalism and the successes of world revolution in China, Yugoslavia, Greece, Indochina, and Indonesia which, however uneven, nevertheless proved sufficiently strong to save world peace and the USSR. The Pentagon was forced to restrain itself, lest these explosions multiply. And at a more modest level, the election of the Labour government in Britain in 1945 acted as a restraining factor.[24]

In the last instance, it was a question of priorities. US bourgeois leadership had to draft a post-war strategy, the first task being restabilization of capitalism in Western Europe, Japan and at home. It allocated itself the role of world gendarme of capitalism, but would limit its intervention to local wars, i.e. limited wars of counter-revolution. Having extinguished the Greek push for independence and revolution, it turned its attention to Korea. And this would remain the pattern: whilst remaining in the military planners' dossiers of war games and war preparations, all-out onslaught on the USSR has been off the agenda for a whole historical period. It is not on it even now.

US imperialism could restrain itself because it had a way out economically. The option it chose in 1946-48 was to concentrate its efforts on the political and economic conslidation of capitalism in the main imperialist countries, and to grant them sufficient credit and space for development to initiate a world-wide expansion of the capitalist economy, on the basis of which capitalism would be politically and socially stabilized in its main fortresses. To that priority, other goals were subordinated – including the 'saving' of China from communism and 'rolling back' the USSR to its pre-war frontiers and impotence. Aided by local social-democratic and Communist parties in a manner markedly reminiscent of the labour bureaucracy's strategy after World War One, the US project proved pretty successful for exactly twenty years: from 1947-48 to 1967-68.

18.

The Legacy

The legacy of destruction left by World War II is staggering. Eighty million people were killed, if one includes those who died of starvation and illness as a direct result of the war – eight times as many as during World War I. Dozens of cities were virtually totally destroyed, especially in Japan and Germany. Material resources capable of feeding, clothing, housing, equipping all the poor of this world were wasted for purely destructive purposes. Forests were torn down and agricultural land converted into wasteland on a scale not witnessed since the Thirty Years War or the Mongol invasion of the Islamic Empire.

Even worse was the destructive havoc wreaked on human minds and behaviour. Violence and barbaric disregard of elementary human rights – starting with the right to life – spread on a larger scale than anything seen during and after World War I – itself already quite disastrous in this regard.

The climax to the rise of barbarism was the advent of the Bomb – a veritable epitome of late capitalism's basic destructive thrust. Since 1945 the shadow of final annihilation has hovered over humankind's fate in the form of the ominous mushroom cloud. That shadow itself is already poisoning hundreds of thousands of human beings, – their bodies and their descendants[1] – and poisoning their minds. Even the direct long-term radiation and fall-out results of nuclear bombs or experimental explosions are incalculable – and largely unknown.

Was all the destruction pointless? Has international capitalism

emerged from World War II with all the fundamental contradictions which led to the conflict unresolved – not only structurally, but even conjuncturally? Many observers would have categorically denied such a statement ten years ago, when it seemed
that in contrast to the inter-war period, the international capitalist
economy had experienced two decades (in the Anglo-Saxon countries, nearly three) of unprecedented growth, interrupted only by
minor recessions, and a long historical period of high levels of
employment and impressive rises in the material standard of living
of the toiling masses in the imperialist countries.

Today, it is obvious that the twenty to twenty-five years of the
postwar boom were only an interlude, a 'long expansive wave' of
the capitalist economy following the 'long depression' of the inter-
war period, which will itself be followed by a 'long depression' of
even longer duration than the 1913-39 period.[1]

To be sure, that interlude witnessed a new leap forward of the
productive forces – the third technological revolution – and a great
increase in the material wealth and average skill and knowledge of
the international working class, not to mention a big expansion in
the number of wage-earners. Even if the material and intellectual
progress was very unevenly divided as between the more and less
developed capitalist countries, it enlarged the base from which
world socialism can be built. The material preconditions for a
socialist world of plenty and a global withering away of the social
division of labour between 'bosses' and 'bossed' were much more
considerable in 1970 than in 1939, let alone 1914. They are even
more so in 1985.

At the same time, however, the price humankind must pay for
the delay of world socialism, for the survival of decaying capitalism, becomes more and more frightening. The tendency for the
productive forces to be transformed into forces of destruction not
only asserts itself periodically in crises of over-production and
world wars.[2] More and more it asserts itself unrelentingly in the
fields of production, consumption, social relations, health (including mental health), and above all in the uninterrupted succession of
'local' wars. This global price in human suffering, death, and
threats to the very physical survival of humankind, is again staggering. It outstrips anything seen during the First or Second
World Wars.[3]

Two outstanding examples are sufficient to underscore this
point (many others could be quoted). Since 1945, not a single year
has passed without 'local' wars occuring in some part of the globe,

often in many parts simultaneously. Most of these are imperialist counter-revolutionary wars of intervention against unfolding national liberation movements and unfolding or victorious social revolutions. The total number of victims of these already equals or surpasses that of World War I.

The perversion of human consumption and human wants through profit-oriented standardised mass production is imposing a growing burden of illness and death upon humankind. Not only does it involve a simultaneous growth of overproduction and artificial curtailment of food production in the West, and of hunger and starvation in the South. It also involves a rising flood of useless, harmful, poisoned consumer goods, including poisoned food, in the West itself. The result is a dramatic increase in so-called 'civilization diseases', like cancer and coronary occlusion, caused by poisoned air, water and bodies. Again, the death toll is staggering. And the threat which poisoned air, seas, water and forests pose to the very physical survival of humanity is similar to the threat of nuclear world war.

In that sense, the Second World War indeed solved nothing, i.e. removed none of the basic causes of the intensifying crisis of survival of human civilization and humankind itself. Hitler has disappeared, but the tide of destructiveness and barbarism keeps rising, albeit in more variegated forms and a less concentrated way (if World War III can be avoided).[4] For the underlying cause of that destructiveness remains. It is the expansionist dynamic of competition, capital accumulation and imperialism increasingly turned against itself, i.e. boomeranging from the 'periphery' into the 'centre', with all the destructive potential this expansion and self-assertion harbours in the face of growing resistance and defiance from millions, if not hundreds of millions, of human beings.

The militarization of the United States reflects the permanence of that expansionism and destructiveness, specific historical circumstances notwithstanding. Joseph Schumpeter asserted against Marxists that the roots of imperialism were essentially pre-capitalist, semi-feudal—absolutist-militarist – and not capitalist business interests.[5] He tried to prove his point by noting that the world's strongest capitalist country, the United States of America, had no army or military establishment to speak of. He went so far as to reiterate that argument, first advanced immediately after World War I, during World War II, in his classic *Capitalism, Socialism and Democracy* (1943 – one of the few bourgeois historical studies of the last fifty years worth mentioning, and vastly superior to Popper's critique of Marx, let alone von Hayek's anti-socialist rantings.)[6]

It is true that the historical specificity of US capitalism – its frontier in North America and the weakness of the client states in its Latin American sphere of influence – made it possible for it to expand geographically with comparatively little use of force (significantly less, in any case, than was employed by various European capitalist powers or Japan). Later, after World War I, the tremendous industrial and financial superiority of US imperialism again made 'peaceful' expansion (not without the use of the 'big stick' here and there, of course) a more efficient way of ruling than outright territorial occupation and large-scale military adventures.

The outcome of World War II changed all that. To begin with, the very global hegemony US imperialism had conquered implied that it increasingly had to play the role of world *gendarme* of capitalism. In this way, the contradiction between the internationalisation of the productive forces and the survival of the nation-state was partially and temporarily surmounted. But it was impossible to perform that role without a powerful and expanding military establishment. US imperialism literally had to confront all the contradictions of international capitalism – and, increasingly, to confront them with repressive threats and means.

Under capitalism – especially imperialism and its 'late-capitalist' phase, characterised by huge quantities of capital permanently in search of additional fields for investment – an expanding military establishment means a burgeoning sector of industry and capitalist firms geared to weapons production. These have a vested interest in such production, for they receive a large slice of the profits, guaranteed by the state, thanks to constantly escalating armaments output. Hence the birth of the 'military-industrial complex', to quote the phrase aptly coined by Eisenhower, himself a general turned President of the United States.

So Schumpeter was quite wrong, and Marxists correct after all, in the (exemplary) case of the United States. For all its historical peculiarities and 'uniqueness', the militarisation of the United States directly derived from the needs of US Big Business and imperialism, albeit with half a century's delay behind Britain, France, Germany, Japan and Italy.

But that is by no means the end of the story. Powerful as it was, US imperialism could not single-handed simultaneously confront the Soviet Union, the process of permanent revolution in the colonial and semi-colonial countries, and a periodically restive and explosive working class in several imperialist countries, with its own manpower and military resources. It needed allies and it had to cultivate them, in the first place financially. As a result, US imperialism saw the law of uneven and combined development assert itself for the first time against the United States.

When the US launched the reconstruction and consolidation of West German and Japanese imperialism (just as it had previously assisted in the reconstruction and consolidation of their French and Italian counterparts), it initiated a process which, as a consequence of the defeat and destruction these powers had suffered, offered them the possibility of achieving faster growth in average industrial labour productivity and a more modern industrial profile than the USA itself. Thus the build-up of the American military machine also performed the function of pressurizing the US's reluctant allies not to overstep certain bounds of financial, commercial and industrial autonomy within the alliance – a function which was itself gradually undermined by a change in the financial and industrial balance of forces to the detriment of US imperialism. So in spite of American military hegemony, the 'reign of the dollar' and predominant American ownership/control of multinational corporations did not last longer than twenty years after World War II. And if one bears in mind the growth in Soviet industrial and military power, which broke the American monopoly on nuclear weapons and the means to deliver them in the 1950s, the 'American Century' scarcely lasted for more than a decade. Bretton Woods, the reign of the dollar,[7] the reign of US-controlled multinational corporations, did enable American and world capitalism to avoid economic collapse on the scale of the Great Depression after 1945-48. But they were gradually eroded, eventually leading to the long depression which commenced at the end of the 1960s and the beginning of the 1970s.[8]

The postwar boom itself was not the automatic result of US imperialism's opting for 'peaceful' commercial and financial expansion, i.e. the Marshall Plan, massive capital exports, and everything that flowed from them. Its precondition was the termination of the post-war workers' upsurge in several key imperialist countries, especially Italy, France and Japan, where the militancy was largely channelled by the CPs and therefore perceived as a direct threat by American imperialism. But it occurred in the USA too,[9] if at a lower level of politicisation and radicalisation.

Under these circumstances, the class struggle in the key capitalist countries and on an international scale became intertwined with the evolution of relations between the great powers and the Cold War in a specific – and discontinuous – manner. Some of the main industrial struggles were largely divorced from the latter – for example, the post-war strike wave in the USA and the first massive wildcat strikes in Belgium and France, which resulted in the CPs having to leave the coalition governments under working-class pressure (and not under that of American imperialism or the European bourgeoisie). But the partial defeats of these struggles, combined with growing repression by capital (of which the Taft-Hartley Act and the gradual erosion of union strength in the USA was the most significant example), and the turn made by the CPs from government coalition politics to ultra-leftist gestures, led to a general decline in working-class militancy – even in Britain, where the Labour government, with a large parliamentary majority and important reform legislation behind it, had the best chance of avoiding fundamental disorientation. Whilst the stabilization of capitalism in the main imperialist countries enabled the boom to commence on a favourable basis – the retreat of the first post-war wave of workers' radicalisation and militancy – it imparted a peculiar twist to the developing balance of class forces, quite unlike that after 1923.

No working class in an imperialist country suffered a crushing defeat. While the Cold War caused great ideological and organizational divisions inside the labour movement, it also forced imperialism to pay a high price for keeping its 'home front' relatively quiescent. As a result of the post-war boom in Western society – accompanied by a new growth in wage labour, i.e. industrialisation – and of workers' rising expectations and consistent efforts to realise them via trade-union struggles and political initiatives (except in the USA), the strength of the organized labour movement constantly grew in the imperialist countries. It reached unprecedented levels, both in and outside the factory. For a period, this very growth seemed to fuel the boom by spreading mass consumption of consumer durables and the purchase of housing. But from a certain peak, symbolized by May 1968, the contradictions between that growth and the normal functioning of the capitalist economy became obvious.

On the other hand, the very conditions in which the 'American century' was ushered in – the reign of the multinational corporations and the implications of the third technological revolution in the field of raw materials (a gradual substitution of man-made for 'natural' ones) – facilitated imperialism's shift from direct to indirect rule over the 'third world' (from colonialism to neo-colonialism) without any marked redistribution of world profits (world surplus-value) in favour of the third-world ruling classes. A constant drain of value from the South to the North continued to be the rule in the whole post-war period, fuelling both the 'boom' itself and a revolt against such super-exploitation in the shape of national liberation movements. The old colonial empires collapsed. But the attempt to stabilize a new, 'indirect' US Empire was gradually worn down.[10]

From this point of view too, then, the Second World War has solved nothing, at a structural level for capitalism. Capitalism stabilized and prospered in the West between 1948 and 1968. But the price paid was continuous crisis in the Third World and the build-up of increasingly explosive material in Western Europe, which erupted in 1968. The crisis of imperialism had not been solved. Neither had the crisis of capitalist relations of production. The respite could not be used to repair the dikes. The breaches were widening. And through them the flood of revolution would start to flow again. It remains the best chance – in fact the only chance – of avoiding World War III. Humankind can only be saved from destruction by establishing rational control over international and domestic affairs, i.e. by abolishing class and national conflicts and competition. And only a democratic socialist world federation can achieve that goal.

Notes

Chapter 1

1. Recently, a Soviet author has argued that this is a specifically 'Trotskyist' thesis, analogous to that held by bourgeois technocrats who try to 'justify the cosmopolitan endeavours of monopoly capital'. N. Vassetsky, 'Trotskyism in Alliance with Reaction', *Mirovaia Ekonomiy y Mezhdunarodnikh otnochenya (World Economy and International Relations)*, No.7 1985. Unfortunately for Vassetsky, this thesis is to be found in official Comintern documents voted by Lenin and all Soviet and international leaders. See *Theses, Resolutions and Manifestoes of the First Four Congresses of the Communist International*, London 1978.

2. The world economic crisis after 1929 had hit the Japanese countryside in particular. The domestic silk industry, which was one of the main sources of additional income for the peasantry, suffered badly when the price of silk thread and products collapsed in the USA. The introduction of the Smoot-Hawley Tariff in June 1930, which raised the import duty on Japanese goods entering the United States by an average of twenty-three per cent in 1930, was followed in 1931 by the United States overtaking Japan as the leading exporter to China. The British attitude to the Chinese war debt also caused problems for Japanese exports. Japan's reply was to launch 'an assault first on many of the West's private markets and subsequently on sources and raw materials'. (Jon Halliday, *A Political History of Japanese Capitalism*, London 1975, p.122.) See also H.F. McNair and D.F. Lach, *Modern Far Eastern International Relations*, 2nd edition, New York 1976, pp. 402-03.

3. Benoist-Méchin, the most radical and intelligent ideologue of collaboration with the Nazis in Vichy France, describes in some detail the oscillations and indecisions of Hitler's policy towards the French bourgeoisie engaged in large-scale economic cooperation with Germany, in *De la Défaite au Désastre*, Paris 1984

4. General Giichi became Prime Minister in 1927, the year in which the full blast of the financial crisis hit Japanese society. In his 1927 Memorandum (or Memorial), he called for a 'positive' policy of expansion, i.e. the domination of Asia and ultimately Europe by Japan. See Leon Trotsky, 'The Tanaka Memorial', *Writings of Leon Trotsky 1939-40*, New York 1973, pp. 169-80.

5. Hitler was quite conscious of the long-term conflict of interest between German

and Japanese imperialism. Following the rapid Japanese conquests in Asia, he stated: 'East Asia could have been kept if all the white states had formed a coalition. Japan wouldn't have moved against it'. *Monologe im Führerhauptquartier 1941-1944* p.163. Goebbels was even more explicit: 'Europe, and in the first place Germany, have a high standard of living, which has to be further increased. It will be faced sooner or later in East Asia with a bloc of 500 million people of yellow race with a substantially lower standard of living, a fact which will not be without effect on Europe.' (Ibid, p.264).

6. Hitler, op.cit., p.110. A vast literature exists on German imperialism's plans for world hegemony. The best summaries are Jochen Thiess, *Architekt der Weltherrschaft: Die 'Endziele' Hitlers*, Dusseldorf 1976 and Wolfgang Schumman & Ludwig Nestle (eds.), *Weltherrschaft im Visier: Dokumente zu den Europa-und Weltherrschafts planen des deutschen Imperialismus von der Jahrhundertwende bis Mai 1945*, Berlin 1975.

7. Robert E Sherwood, *Roosevelt and Hopkins*, New York 1950, p.151.

8. At the beginning of the Second World War, in his book *The American Century*, Henry Luce wrote: 'Roosevelt will succeed where Wilson had failed . . . . For the first time in history, our world of two billion inhabitants will form an indissoluble unity. For this world to be healthy and strong, the 20th century must become to the largest possible extent an American century.'

9. Gabriel Kolko, *The Politics of War: The World and United States Foreign Policy 1943-1945*, New York 1970, p.251.

10. See H.R. Trevor Roper (ed.), *Hitler's War Directives 1939-1945*, London 1966.

11. R.E. Sherwood, p.290.

12. Ibid., pp. 125-6.

13. A good summary of these necessities and constraints can be found in Robert Coakley and Richard Leighton's official USA history of the war, *Global Logistics and Strategy 1943-1945*, Washington 1968.

14. Goebbels summarized the aim of imperialism in his usual clear and cynical fashion: 'Objectivity, a sense of justice and sentimentality would only hinder the Germans in their world mission. This mission does not consist in extending culture and education throughout the world, but in taking wheat and oil away.' *Monologe im Führerhauptquartier 1941-1944*, p.362.

15. Some of this debate has recently been reprinted in Henri Weber (ed.), *Kautsky, Luxemburg, Pannekoek: Socialisme: la voie occidentale*, Paris 1983 and John Riddell (ed.), *Lenin's Struggle for a Revolutionary International: Documents 1907-1916*, New York 1984. Carl E. Schorske's *German Social Democracy 1905-1917: The Development of the Great Schism*, re-issued by Harvard University Press in 1983, can be consulted with profit.

16. There is someting totally irrational – and morally obscene – in people calmly accepting ten million soldiers – the flower of European youth – being killed in World War One, and approving war credits which financed that butchery, but stridently opposing revolutions in Germany, Austria, Italy or France which would have made World War Two impossible on the grounds that they might have cost thousands of deaths, which was not even certain.

Chapter 2

1. Leon Trotsky, *The Struggle Against Fascism in Germany*, New York 1971, p.126.

2. H.R. Trevor-Roper (ed.), Introduction, p.16.

3. E.M. Robertson, *Hitler's Pre-War Policy and Military Plans*, London 1964, p.84

4. Friedrich Forstmeier and Erich Volkmann (eds.), *Wirtschaft und Rustung am Vorabend des Zweiten Weltkrieges*, Dusseldorf 1981, p.47, and Dietrich Eicholtz, *Geschichte der deutsche Kriegswirtschaft*, Berlin 1984, vol.1, p.21

5. See T.W. Mason, 'Some Origins of the Second World War' in Esmonde Robertson (ed.), *The Origins of the Second World War*, London 1971 and 'Zunere Krise und Angriffskrieg,' in Forstmeier und Volkmann (eds.), pp. 158-59. In 1938 Goering, who was responsible for the German economy, said: 'There is a tremendous shortage of skilled workers. . . . This cannot be relieved through closing down of the factories which produce seemingly unimportant consumer goods. For when the workers can no longer buy consumer goods for their wages . . . this is the beginning of inflation, and that is the beginning of the end.' Quoted in Berenice A. Carroll, *Design for Total War: Arms and Economics in the Third Reich*, The Hague and Paris 1968, p.159.

6. A.J.P. Taylor, *The Origins of the Second World War*, London 1964, p.18.

7. 'At the beginning of February 1983 Hitler demanded of the Reichswehr leadership 'the strengthening of our fighting will by every means', and a few days later the Cabinet ratified his apodictic demand that the creation of employment basically serve military readiness. In the light of these and other facts, initial attempts to write the economic history of the early years of the Third Reich as a distinct phase of job-creation, prior to rearmament, have been abandoned.' Forstmeier and Volkmann, pp. 118-19. So much for Taylor's thesis of a phase of New Deal-type pump priming prior to 1936. The Reichswehr had asked for a military expenditure of 1.4 billion RM in 1932-33. Military expenditure in fact increased from around 1 billion RM in 1932 to 2.8 billion in 1934 and 5.5 billion in 1935, of which more than 1 billion was on the Luftwaffe. (Ibid., p.56). See also Dietrich Eichholtz, *Geschichte der deutschen Kriegswirtschaft*, vol. 1, 1939-1941, Berlin 1984, p.31.

8. Taylor, p.17.

9. Taylor's figure confused *investment* in war industry with total military expenditure. (Volkmann pp.29-30) quotes the figure of 70 billion RM without private investment in the armament industry, 75.5 billion RM with that private investment, and 81 billion RM if one adds private investment in heavy industry providing plant and equipment for the armament industry.

10. Taylor, p.250.

11. Hitler gave instructions to the *Wehrmacht* as early as 21 October 1938 to liquidate the rest of Czechoslovakia. This was repeated in an order to General Keitel on 17 December 1938. The Nazis spurred the Slovaks on to agitate for complete independence as early as 16-17 October 1938 in an interview between the Slovak leader Durcansky and Goering, noted in the Foreign Ministry documents. See chapter 13 of William L. Shirer, *The Rise and Fall of the Third Reich*, New York 1962.

12. Taylor, p.250.

13. Taylor, p.19.

14. The instruction to 'definitely liquidate the West' was given to the High Command of the *Wehrmacht* as early as 19 October 1939. Hitler instructed his generals to attack Britain and then France 'as soon as possible'. The instructions of October 1939 state that 'first, as large a part of the French army as possible had to be smashed'. The attack against Holland and Belgium was seen as a means to attain that goal, not vice-versa. Hans-Adolf Jacobsen (ed.), *Kriegstagebuch des Ober-Kommandos der Wehrmacht*, vol.1, Munich 1982, pp.45-59 R, pp.55-56 B.

15. 'With his generals watching sceptically, he could not again call off the attack on Poland, unless he had something solid to show; and this was still denied him by the Poles.' Taylor, p.333.

16. Taylor, p.336.

17. In order to cast doubt on Hitler's – and German imperialism's – long-term expansionist and war plans, Taylor has to discredit the co-called Hossbach Memorandum which reports a meeting held by Hitler with his high dignatries on 12 November 1937, at which these plans were presented in an open and full manner. (Taylor, pp.2-21). In reality three different questions are conflated by Taylor: 1) did Hitler's exposé actually contain the directives: war no later than 1942-43 in order to conquer the Ukraine?; 2) did those present attach importance to the meeting?; 3) does the so-called Hossbach memorandum give an adequate account of the meeting? By concentrating on point 3, and by conflating points 1 and 2 with 3, Taylor implies that there was no long-term plan of conquest and war. But that conclusion is totally unsubstantiated. On the contrary, at least six different German generals, independently of each other, drew attention to the importance of the meeting, confirming the contents of Hitler's speech and the grave conclusions they drew from it.

18. Max Gallo, *La cinquieéme colonne,* Paris 1970, p.234. Even earlier, in April 1937, according to a confidential report of the Wilhelmstrasse, Laval told a secret envoy of Germany that France needed a Pétain government. Raymond Tournoux, *Pétain et la France,* Paris 1980, p.39. There is important evidence that Pétain was a party to these conspiratorial endeavours. Cassius, *La Vérité sur l'Affaire Pétain,* Paris 1945, e.g. pp.88-89.

19. Charles De Gaulle, *Mémoires de Guerre, 1: L'Appel,* Paris 1956, p.37. De Gaulle also mentions that the talk all over Paris in April-May 1940 was that if Reynaud fell, Laval would take power with Pétain at his side. (p.36). In his memoirs, Paul Reynaud himself silently glosses over the opening he gave to the right; see *Au Coeur de la Mêlée,* Paris 1951.

20. Tournoux, p.57.

21. This basic option of the American ruling class was strikingly confirmed when the Republican Party – traditionally isolationist – chose as its presidential candidate in 1940 Wendell Willkie, whose world view hardly differed from that of Roosevelt. 'The Willkie-Welles-Luce group see the world as a vast market for the American producer, industrialist and trader. They are believers in the American century, energetic technicians and businessmen filled with a romantic, equally self-confident, economic imperialism, eager to convert the world to the American pattern', wrote Halifax to London in May 1942. Christopher Thorne, *Allies of a Kind,* London 1978, p.139.

22. 'From the 1932 low of $1.6 billion, US exports rose to $12.8 billion in 1943 and $14 billion in 1944. The figure of $14 billion in postwar exports – well over four times the 1939 level – therefore became the target of most wartime planners, and their calculated precondition of continued American prosperity.' Gabriel and Joyce Kolko in Thomas G. Paterson (ed.), *The Origins of the Cold War,* Lexington, Mass. 1974, p.244. In fact US exports reached $10 billion in 1954 and $20 billion in 1960.

23. Ibid., p.243.

24. A survey conducted by the Inspector-General of the Red Army infantry in the summer of 1940 established that 'of 225 new regimental commanders, not one had attended a full course at a military academy, only twenty five had finished a military school and the remainder, 200 in all, had merely passed a junior lieutenant's course.' John Erickson, *The Road to Stalingrad,* London 1975, pp.19-20. The lessons of the

war with Finland brought some respite to the military, encouraging, *inter alia*, the release of 4,000 officers from the Arctic labour camps. Much of what follows is based on the author's so far unsurpassed history of the Nazi-Soviet war.

25. Molotov's speech before the Supreme Soviet on 3 October 1939 contained the following scandalous formulation: 'If we are to speak of the major European powers today, Germany finds itself in the – position of a State that seeks the swiftest end to hostilities and the advent of peace, while England and France – which yesterday spoke against aggression – are today in favour of the continuation of the war and against the conclusion of a peace . . . . The English Government has declared its war aims as nothing more nor less than the annihilation of Hitlerism. It follows that in England . . . war-mongers have declared something like an ideological war on Germany reminiscent of the old wars of religion . . . . Those wars could not but bring economic decline and cultural ruin to the people that endured them – but they go back to the Middle Ages. Are not the ruling classes of England and France dragging us back again to the time of wars of religion, of superstition [opposition to Fascism equated with superstition! – EM], of cultural regression? . . . A war of this kind cannot be justified in any way. The ideology of Hitlerism, like any other ideological system, can be accepted or rejected – that is a question of political opinion (!). But anyone can understand that an ideology cannot be destroyed by force . . . This is why it is senseless, indeed criminal, to wage any such war for the elimination of Hitlerism.' *(Cahiers du Bolchevisme*, January 1940.)

26. See e.g. Pavel Jiline, *Ambitions et Méprises du Troisième Reich*, Editions de Moscou, 1972. – Stalins explicit request to Hitler not to have any Polish rump state reconstituted was made in the presence of Molotov at a meeting with the German Ambassador von der Schulenburg, on September 25, 1939 *(Nazi-Soviet Relations*, op. cit. p. 102.)

Chapter 3

1. Fritz Wiedeman, *Der Mann der Feldherr werden wollte*, Munich 1964, p.101. According to Joachim Fest, Walter Hewall reported Hitler as saying: 'With that people I cannot yet conduct war.' *(Das Gesicht des. 3 Reiches*, Munich 1980, p.77.) John Toland describes how, after Hitler's *Reichstag* speech of 1 September 1939 announcing the war against Poland, 'the streets outside were almost deadly quiet. The few people abroad were serious, as if oppressed by concern for the future. There were no signs of jubilation as on that August day, twenty-five years before, when the Kaiser announced his war'. *(Adolf Hitler*, New York 1976, p.78.)

2. Churchill was known to the British working class as a dedicated opponent of the Russian Revolution and an advocate, back in 1920, of military intervention to suppress it. He was also known for his active opposition to the General Strike of 1926, and as a man who had admired Mussolini, condemned the Republican cause in Spain and ridiculed Gandhi. A vigorous proponent of the British Empire, he was likewise a racist. His contempt for 'coloured' people was not just a matter of feelings: when the Bengali famine broke out in the autumn of 1943, in which millions of people died, Churchill was instrumental in preventing any effective relief aid. It should be noted that he was not challenged on this by his Labour Cabinet colleagues. On Churchill's relations with Mussolini, see Arrigo Petalco, *Dear Benito, Caro Winston*, Mondadori 1985. Even in the midst of the second world war, at the moment of the *Duce's* downfall, he didn't hesitate to write: ' . . . he had raised the

Italian people (!) from bolshevism in which it might have sunk in 1919, to a position in Europe such as Italy had never held before. A new impulse had been given to the national life. The Italian Empire in North Africa was built' (*The Second World War*, vol. 9, p. 45).

3. This was not a basic misjudgment of the situation. When food rations were reduced or food prices increased, the secret reports of the SS *Sicherheitdienst* noted 'serious complaints' in 'broad circles of the population', especially the poorer part and 'above all, the industrial workers'. See *Meldungen aus dem Reich*, Berlin 1984, for example vol.12, p.4451 (report of 9 November 1942); pp.4796-8 (report of 8 February 1943); and vol.9, pp.3496-7 (19 March 1942) when rations were actually cut. There was a big decline in the labour productivity of German workers in war industry, which fell below that of foreign labourers. William S. Allen in J. Schna-decke and P. Steinback (eds.), *Der Widerstand gegen den Nazionalsozialismus*, Munich 1985, p.860.

4. Isaia Berlain's despatches from the Washington Embassy to the Foreign Office regularly stress the importance of labor struggles in the USA during the war (*Washington Despatches 1941–1945*, edited by H. G. Nicholas. London, Weidenfeld & Nicholson, 1981).

5. On the siege of Leningrad, during which 630,000 people died, see Alexander Werth, *Russia at War*, London 1964, part 3. The inhuman treatment of Soviet prisoners of war in 1941-2 was an important factor in stiffening the Red Army's fighting morale. Some 2.8 million Soviet prisoners of war died between 22 June 1941 and 1 February 1942 as a result of starvation, lack of medical care and outright slaughter. See on that subject Christian Streit, *Keine Kameraden – Die Wehrmacht und die sowjetischen Kriegsgefangenen* – DVA, Stuttgart, 1979.

6. For example, Hitler initially thought that he could control Yugoslavia with two divisions, whereas, according to the German Army Headquarters records, fifteen were finally employed against the partisans. The number of those engaged against the Russian, the Polish and the Italian partisan movement was at least identical.

7. On the scale of the Italian resistance movement in 1943-45, see, *inter alia*, Paolo Spriano, *Storia del partito communista italiano,* Turin 1967; Roberto Battaglia, *Storia della resistenza italiana*, Turin 1964; Battaglia and Garritano *Breve storia della resistenza italiana*, Florence 1974.

8. The carpet bombing of cities like Dresden, Hamburg, Cologne and Tokyo, which caused more deaths than the atomic bombs dropped on Hiroshima and Nagasaki, was quite simply a crime against humanity. But this judgement can of course be made only by those who do not share moral responsibility for the German and Japanese death machines. For German and Japanese generals and leaders of the time to protest against such bombings, while forgetting their own criminal acts, is blatant hypocrisy. Did not the Führer's war directives call for the destruction of Kiev (a city bigger than Dresden) with all its inhabitants, and for the razing to the ground of Leningrad (a city bigger than Hamburg)?

9. Ludolf Herbst, *Der Totale Krieg und die Ordnung der Wirtschaft,* Stuttgart 1982, p.237.

10. Gunther Weisenborn, *Der lautlose Aufstand*, Hamburg 1962, p.30

11. Ibid., pp.133-34. These figures come from an official report to the Nazi Minister of Justice, Thierack, published in *Die Lage* – a confidential publication distributed exclusively to the leading cadres of the Nazi party.

12. Eugene Kogon, *The Theory and Practice of Hell*, New York 1960, p.251.

13. US Department of State, Foreign Relations of the United States, Documents, 1943, vol.3, p.26.

14. Robert E. Sherwood, op. cit. pp.711-12.

15. On the Chinese resistance movement, see Israel Epstein, *Unfinished Revolution,* Boston 1947; Jean Chesneaux, *Peasant Revolts in China 1840-1949,* London 1973.

16. In 1942 the Japanese General Okamura officially proclaimed the doctrine of *Senko Seisaku* or 'three everything': burn everything, kill everything, destroy everything.

17. A very similar development occurred in Yugoslavia where already in 1941, the *Chetniks* under Mihajlovic's command (recognized at the time as an Allied army) decided that it was the Communists rather than the Germans who were the main threat. Given the shocking attempt by many Western and even some Yugoslav historians, for example Veselin Djuretic, to rehabilitate Mihajlovic, it is necessary to reaffirm that there is no doubt that the *Chetniks* actively collaborated with the Nazis and Italian fascists, to prove this, one need only consult such official German documents as *Kriegstagebuch des Oberkommandos der Wehrmacht,* e.g., vol.5, pp.98-9, 168-71 and vol. 7, pp.637- 640, 706-07.

18. The *Hukbalahap* movement took up the cause of land reform during the Quirino Administration (1948-53); they were militarily attacked at the end of 1945. See R.A.E. Smith, *Philippine Freedom 1946-1958,* New York 1959. Benedikt J. Kerkutiet, *The Huk Rebellion,* Quezon City 1979; William J. Pomeroy, *The Forest,* Berlin 1965; Renato Constantino, *A History of the Philippines, New York 1975.*

Chapter 4

1. H.C. Hillman, 'Comparative Strength of the Great Powers' in Toynbee and Ashton-Gwatkin (eds.), *Survey of International Affairs 1939-1946: the World in March 1939,* London 1952.

2. In spite of their demagogic rantings against 'plutocracy', the Nazi leaders had an almost mystical veneration of gold, for the very practical reason that they needed it to pay for scarce raw materials imported through neutral countries. Hence, for example, they went to extraordinary lengths to retrieve the gold deposits of the Belgian and Dutch central banks (worth some 1.6 billion Swiss francs at the time) that had been switched over to the *Banque de France* in May 1940 and transported to Dakar after the fall of France. The history of this attempt reads like a thriller, complete with trans-Saharan caravans and espionage plots. This gold (whose current value would be some $5 billion) the Nazis could commercialize only with the complicity of the Swiss banking world, above all the Swiss central bank. Werner Rings, *Raubgeld aus Deutschland,* Frankfurt 1985.

3. In August 1936 Hitler drew up a memorandum in which he developed a plan for Germany's complete autarky within four years so as to render her fully 'capable of conducting war' (*kriegsfähig*) in 1939-40. Reproduced in *Vierteljahrsheft für Zeitgeschichte,* no 3, 1955, p.204.

4. Soviet exports to Germany in 1940-41 included 1,000,000 tons of wheat and oil; 100,000 tons of cotton; 500,000 tons of iron ore; 300,000 tons of scrap iron; and a large quantity of platinum and manganese. The Nazis were also offered the use of the Soviet transport system to import goods from Asia and Latin America. *Nazi-Soviet Relations: Documents from the Archives of the German Foreign Office,* Department of State, Washington 1948, pp 83, 109, 200.

5. The goal of the ill-fated Caucasus offensive of 1942 was the capture of the oil fields of Baku. Even the 1941 campaign against the Soviet Union was decisively influenced by the desire to capture the wealth of the Ukraine and Donets even

before the Red Army was decisively beaten.

6. In 1940, 90% of German imports of iron ore and 45% of total German iron consumption came from Sweden. Manganese and nickel had been stockpiled so that at the beginning of the war manganese reserves were sufficient for fifteen to twenty months and nickel reserves for six. Soviet deliveries for the duration of the Hitler-Stalin pact and the subsequent plunder of Soviet resources, together with small deliveries from Slovakia, kept the manganese reserves stable till the end of the war. Nickel came from the Petsamo mine in Finland until 1944. Chrome flowed from Turkey till 1943, then from the Balkans. 63% of German wolfram requirements were covered by imports from Spain and Portugal. Alan S. Milward, *Der Zweite Weltkrieg: Krieg, Wirtschaft und Gesellschaft 1939-1945,* Munich 1977 pp. 335-37.

7. Henri Michel, *La Seconde guerre mondiale,* Paris 1968, pp.332-33.

8. The clearing system meant that Germany did not have to pay its balance of payments deficit in foreign currency; the export firms of the trading partners were paid in national currency. The balances, at an exchange rate favourable to the *Reich,* were earmarked on paper for imports from Germany. But the more the German economy was transformed into a war economy, the less goods were available for exports, and the more the clearing system meant outright plunder, paper foreign debts 'compensating' for German imports.

9. Nicholas Kaldor, *The German War Economy,* paper read to the Manchester Statistical Society on 22 May 1946.

10. Milward, pp. 41-2.

11. Dieter Petzina, *Die Deutsche Wirtschaft in der Zwischenkriegszeit,* Wiesbaden 1977, p.151.

12. According to John Erickson, 'by November [1941] the loss of 300 factories to the enemy deprived the Red Army of what had been a monthly production of 8.5 million shell-cases, nearly 3 million mines and 2 million aerial bombs. The loss of chemical plants slowed up the output of explosives . . . the imbalance between gun production and ammunition output grew wider week by week. . . . Ammunition output began to fall in August and dropped steeply by the end of the year . . . Aircraft production toppled wildly from 1,807 in July, 2,329 in September to the catastrophic 627 in November. . . . For the second half of 1941, only a little more than half of the planned output of tanks was managed.' (*The Road to Stalingrad,* p.233.) All these figures come from official Soviet sources, above all the six-volume *History of the Great Patriotic War of the Soviet Union (Istoriya Velikoi Otechestvennoi Voiny Sovietskogo Soyusa 1941-1945),* Moscow 1960.

13. In a report to the *Stavka* on the eve of the Soviet counter-offensive at Stalingrad, Red Army Marshals Vasilevskii and Zhukov commended the vital contribution of the Soviet workers to the offensive: 'The concentration of forces and vital supplies has been due to the titanic work of rail and river transportation workers and to those whose assignments additionally ordered by the GKO, especially the expansion of the front area railway network, finished with what is merely an insignificant infringement of the stipulated timetable.' Erickson, p.459.

14. Total available resources of oil products declined from an average of 10 million tons in 1941, 1942 and 1943 to around 6 million tons in 1944. Eichholtz, *Geschichte der deutschen Kriegswirtschaft,* vol.2, pp.354-5. Disastrous shortages of aircraft and armour fuel ensued. See Albert Speer, *Inside the Third Reich: Memoirs,* London, 1970.

Chapter 5

1. David Fraser, *Alanbrooke,* London 1982, p.215.

2. Franz Mehring, 'Vom Wesen des Krieges,' *Die Neue Zeit* 33 (I), 20 November 1914, reprinted in *Gesammelte Werke*, Band 8, Berlin 1976, pp.291-92.

3. See 'The Collapse of the Second International' and 'Socialism and War' in *Collected Works*, Vol.21, Moscow 1964. Clemente Ancona has written an excellent essay, 'L' Influenza del *Vom Kriege* di Clausewitz sul pensiero marxista da Marx a Lenin' in *Revista Storica del Socialismo* 8, 1965. It stresses Lenin's heavy debt to Mehring.

4. From this point of view the ancient Chinese treatise by Sun Tzu, *The Art of War*, is superior to Clausewitz because more dialectical. It is based on the dictum: 'In order to win a war, know thine enemy and know thy self'. See the new translation by Samuel B. Griffith, Oxford 1963, with a Preface by Liddell Hart.

5. On the origins of the tank-based *Blitzkrieg,* see Jean Lacouture, *De Gaulle*, Paris 1964, vol.1, pp.225-28.

6. The Stalin Line was a loose combination of fortifications in Belorussia and along the Baltic republics' frontier, approximating some 400-450 km. According to Erickson, it consisted essentially of 'a belt of firepoints, some two kilometres in depth, with artillery emplacements especially reinforced to resist heavy shell fire'. After the Soviet occupation of Western Ukraine, Eastern Belorussia and the Baltic states, it was largely dismantled, without a new solid defence line being built-up – yet another disastrous consequence of the Hitler-Stalin Pact. Erickson, pp. 70-1.

7. The Eben-Emael fort was built so as to be able to cover with its artillery the whole railway and road network between Cologne-Aachen on the one hand and Liege-Maestricht on the other, i.e. to prevent a crossing of the river Meuse around and north from Liege up to the Dutch border. It was taken on the very first day of the *Wehrmacht's* offensive in the West (10 May 1940) because of a grave weakness in its defence perimeter. The fort's capture was planned with meticulous care and rehearsed many times on a terrain identical in every detail to the fort's actual surroundings. This combination of grand strategy planning and attention to minute detail is very characteristic of the mobile war operations of WWII.

8. Having demonstrated in 1939-41 the inability of its enemies to hold a defensive line of fortifications against superior firepower, the German general staff subsequently had no option but to withdraw behind precisely such a line of fortifications (the 'Atlantic Wall') in expectation of the Western Allies' landing on the continent of Europe.

9. See, for example, Charles Cruickshank, *Deception in World War II,* Oxford 1979. The extraordinary lengths to which Montgomery for one had gone to hide the general direction of his offensive in November 1942 are recounted with much bemused accuracy by General Bayerlein, one of Rommel's deputies during the battle of Alamein. S. Friedin and W. Richardson (eds.), *The Fatal Decisions*, New York 1956, pp. 104-05.

10. For the German advantage in rearmament prior to the war see Hillman *op.cit.*

11. Gordon Craig, *Germany 1811-1945*, Oxford 1981, p.722.

12. Britain forced its colonies to pay for the cost of war by making them keep the credit balances of their balance of payments blocked in British banks. In the case of India, this amounted to more than £1.1 billion. The parallel with the German system of 'clearings deficits' is obvious.

13. Tukhachevsky and his colleagues had advanced the theory of 'in-depth combat', which combined the use of a mass army with modern offensive warfare

based on a massive use of tanks. This doctrine was built into the 1936 Field Regulations, but completely dismissed as a result of the purge. Tukhachevsky and his colleagues have been completely rehabilitated in the Soviet Union; no one but the gullible or dishonest any longer pays the slightest attention to GPU-Gestapo fabrications 'proving' Tukhachevsky's guilt. Here again, Taylor is wrong when he says 'we do not know anything about it' (i.e. the innocence or guilt of Tukhachevsky) in op. cit., p.147.

14. John Erickson's *The Road to Stalingrad* gives a fair account of the price the Soviet people paid for Stalin's unwillingness to heed information flooding in from all sides on the imminence of the German attack. See, in addition, Vasilevsky's *Memoirs*, all the more significant given that he tries on the whole to defend Stalin's record, as well as Maisky's and Yeremenko's own accounts.

15. Stalin's decision to leave the conduct of war to his generals in 1942-44 was taken after his disastrous handling of the Kharkov offensive in the spring of 1942. This represented a major turning-point of the war, little noted by most historians.

16. Erickson, p.371.

17. Sun Tzu's above-mentioned treatise on war (see footnote 2) is often quoted to explain Chiang's passivity. Did not the ancient sage write that in the best war the enemy is defeated without a battle? In fact, this is a wholly inaccurate interpretation of what Sun Tzu said. In his treatise he points out the crucial importance of flexibility, i.e. shifting back and forth between defensive and offensive operations. In reality Tzu's work sounds highly modern and very much to the point regarding the war in China and the Second World War in general. Griffith argues that it directly inspired Japanes operations in Malaya in 1942 as well as Mao's war against Chiang. Griffith, pp.41, 51-5, 177-8.

18. Paul Reynaud, p.422.

19. R.E. Sherwood, p.426.

20. Franz Mehring, *Kriegsgeschiftliche Streifzüge*, December 1914, in op. cit. p.304.

21. Quoted in John Erickson, *The Road to Stalingrad*.

Chapter 6

1. James and Suzanne Pool, *Who Financed Hitler?*, New York 1978, chapter 3.

2. Eichholtz, vol.2, pp. 331, 336, 340.

3. John Toland, *The Rising Sun: the Decline and Fall of the Japanese Empire*, New York 1970; Robert Guillain, *Le Japon en guerre*, Paris 1979, p.226.

4. According to Max Hastings, the German 88 mm anti-aircraft gun used against tanks and artillery was most feared by American and British soldiers in Normandy. The same author gives a detailed account of superior German weapons used on the Western front in 1944. See his *Overlord*, New York 1984, pp. 192-93.

5. The Japanese air force nevertheless received several planes of advanced quality in 1944-45. But either they could not be mass-produced or they could not be used efficiently, due to the general decline in industry and the lack of carriers and skilled pilots. A.J. Barker *et al.*, *The Japanese War Machine*, Brussels 1978, pp. 142-44, (French edition). In his memoirs General MacArthur wrote: 'The Japanese never were able to solve the problem [of aircraft maintenance] . . . After the surrender and my arrival in Japan, I inspected some 8,000 Japanese aircraft which were found in airfields in the home islands. All of these were 95 to 98% complete, but not operational, because some small parts were unavailable. What an inestimable difference these 8,000 planes would have made to the enemy's war effort!' (*Remi-*

niscences, New York 1964, pp. 168-69.)
6. Guillain, p. 191.
7. Len Deighton, *Blitzkrieg,* London 1980, pp. 193-99.
8. Winston Churchill, *The Second World War,* vol.9, London 1964, pp. 63-5.
9. G.K. Zhukov, *Erinnerung und Gedanken,* Berlin 1976, vol.1, p.310.
10. Kolko, p.19.
11. Werth, *Russia at War,* pp. 181-82.
12. US expenditure on shipbuilding grew from $400 million in 1942 to $12.5 billion in 1943 and $13.4 billion in 1944. During the five years of the war, the USA built 4,900 merchant ships with a capacity of 51.4 million BRT compared with a total output of less than 1 million BRT by Japan. Milward, pp. 90, 101.
13. Paul Lund and Harry Ludlam, *The War of the Landing Craft,* London 1976.
14. Guillain, p.275. One should not however underestimate the damage caused by the *Kamikaze.* According to official American statistics published after the war, they destroyed 31 naval units, including 3 aircraft carriers, and hit 258, including 36 carriers, 15 battleships and 15 cruisers.
15. Ernest Mandel, *Late Capitalism,* London 1975, chapter 8.

Chapter 7

1. Railways were also central to such operations as the mass murder of the European Jews. Karl Wolff, Himmler's personal adjutant, wrote to the *Reichsbahn's* director Ganzenmuller on 13 August 1942: 'Dear *Parteigenosse* Ganzenmüller! In the name of the Reichsführer SS [Himmler], I thank you very much for your letter of 28 July. I have noted with special joy that for the last fortnight, a train with 5,000 members of the chosen people daily travels to Treblinka and so forth . . . '. Kempner, *Eichmann und Komplizen,* Vienna 1961, p.76. After 1955 Ganzenmüller became chief of the transport board of the Hoesch trust.
2. The Japanese army actually tried to establish a continuous Shangai-Manchuria-Singapore railway connection, using the Shanghai-Hang-chou, Zhengiang-Jianxi, Hunan-Guanxi, Vietnam and Thailand railways. The military offensive it launched against Changsa, Zhejiang and Jiangxi in the spring of 1942 had the aim of securing complete control of the rail link. Dick Wilson, *When Tigers Fight,* London 1982, p.207.
3. Clausewitz had long before made the point that 'the whole conduct of war is similar to the functioning of a complex machine with tremendous friction, so that combinations which are easily conceived on paper can be realized only through the greatest of efforts.'
4. Former Japanese Foreign Minister Shigemitsu describes in his war memoirs the deleterious effects of food shortages on Japanese morale. Mamoru Shigemitsu, *Die Schicksaljahre Japans 1920-1945,* Frankfurt 1959, p.325.
5. Besides the already quoted work by Shigemitsu, see also Guillain, pp. 162-63, 144-45, 150, and J. Livingston, J. Moore and F. Oldfather (eds.), *The Japan Reader: Imperial Japan 1800-1945,* especially the excerpt from 'Bridge to the Sun' by Gwen Terasaki, pp. 465-74.
6. Franco Giannontoni, *Fascismo, Guerra e Società nella Republica Sociale Italiana,* Milan 1981, p.26.
7. In *Krieg ohne Hass,* Heidenheim/Brenz 1950, pp. 104, 107-09, General Franz A. Bayerlein indicates that Rommel's strategy at El Alamein in November 1942 was entirely dictated by insufficient supplies. He was unable to conduct mobile warfare

for lack of gasoline and could not even destroy Montgomery's jumping off positions through shortage of ammunition. Michel (pp. 430-35) indicates how the ups and downs of warfare in the Western Desert were closely connected with the ability of the Malta-based RAF to interrupt Italian convoys to Libya.

8. 'A proposed scale of one ounce of sweets, two ounces of biscuits and one packet of chewing gum for every man of the assault forces necessitated the distribution of 6,250 pounds of sweets, 12,500 pounds of biscuits and 100,000 packets of gum'. (Hastings, pp. 33-34.)

9. John Toland, *L'Empire du Soleil Levant*, Paris 1970, p. 188; A.J. Barker *et al.*, *The Japanese War Machine*, p. 180. On the battle of the Atlantic see the book of that title by Donald Macintyre (London 1961). In 1942 the Western Allies lost 8,245 merchant ships as a result of naval warfare, 1 million BRT more than they built in new ships. In 1943 the loss of 3,611 ships (incurred predominantly in the first five months of the year) was compensated by the construction of so many new ships the allied merchant marine witnessed a net growth of 10 million BRT. The German Navy's losses increased from 85 submarines in 1942 to 237 submarines in 1943, again essentially during the first six months.

10. Germany built 222 new submarines in 1942 and 292 in 1943, so that its total underwater forces were actually stronger at the end of 1943 and the beginning of 1944 than they had been at the beginning of 1942. But they operated on a much smaller scale, and with much less destructive results. See *Hitler's War Directives*, pp. 56-9.

11. It seems that the long-term German strategy against Britain was based upon that assumption after the failure of Operation Sea-Lion in autumn 1940. According to Robert E. Sherwood, Rudolf Hess is supposed to have said after his flight to Scotland: 'I am convinced that in any event – whether an Eastern front persists or not – Germany and her allies are in a position to carry on the war until England collapses from lack of tonnage . . . . The convoy system, which, in the world war – but at the last minute – settled the U-boat war in favour of England, has in this war misfired. It could not prevent the big-scale sinking figures which must finally be fatal . . . an occupation of the whole island does not come into question – for Germany would be burdened with the feeding of the population. In the long run, only the most important airfields would be kept in occupation. All these would be hermetically sealed over a wide area from the population, so that the troops of occupation would not be affected by the misery of their starvation.' (Sherwood, p. 374.) In a message sent to Roosevelt on 7 December, 1940, Churchill himself estimated that 'the annual tonnage which ought to be imported in order to maintain our war effort at full strength is 43,000,000 tons; the tonnage entering in September [1940] was only at the rate of 37,000,000 tons and in October at 38,000,000.' *(Churchill and Roosevelt: The Complete Correspondence*, vol. 1, p. 104.)

Chapter 8

1. In addition to these radical innovations, the importance of the giant strides made by the medical sciences, in surgery and drugs, prior to and during the war should be stressed. Sulfonamides, penicillin and advanced surgery saved the lives of millions of wounded soldiers and civilians, who would have died in WWI conditions. Anti-typhus drugs made the Germany army less vulnerable to epidemics on the Eastern front. Cortisone was developed as a result of wartime research. DDT

made the American operations in malaria-infested regions of the Pacific physically possible. The Japanese armed forces, lacking some of the medical supplies made available by the progress of medical sciences, paid a heavy price for conducting the war in the jungle without them, their greater powers of physical resistance notwithstanding.

2. German science declined dramatically under the Nazis. The number of university students fell from 118,000 in 1932 to 51,000 in 1938 and the number of *Habilitationen* (postgraduate degrees giving right to full professorship) fell from 2,333 between 1920 and 1933 to 1,534 between 1933 and 1944. Grumberger, *A Social History of the Third Reich*, London 1974, pp. 401-08. Twenty per cent of all scientists and twenty-five per cent of all physicists were dismissed (they were generally at the top of their class). Alan D. Beyerchen, *Scientists under Hitler*, New Haven 1977.

3. Radar research had started in the USSR as early as 1934 but without conclusive results or proper backing. The 1936-38 purges only made things worse. Erickson, pp. 35-6.

4. Paul Carell, *Verbrannte Erde*, Frankfurt 1985, pp.53-5.

5. Lothar Gruchmann, *Der Zweite Weltkrieg*, Munchen 1982 painstakingly examines the effects of the Allies' ability to decipher German army and navy codes, and argues persuasively that these were not as great as often assumed. Operation ULTRA is analysed in F.W. Winterbotham, *The Ultra Secret*, London 1974 and Peter Calvocoressi, *The Secret Ultra*, New York 1981.

6. Gerard Piel, *Science in the Cause of Man*, New York 1962.

7. *In The Battle of France, 1940* (London 1958), Colonel Adolphe Goutard notes: 'Another result of that 'methodic war' concept was the 'bureaucratization' of command. From 1914-1918 onwards, the organization of all these plans of fire, of the deployment of *matériel*, of the setting up of these operations following 'strictly measured orders' of thirty and forty pages needed plethoric staffs which inundated the army in the field with tons of paper.' (p.23.)

8. Churchill, for example, did not give priority to mass production of a British jet plane when it was technically possible. This error of judgement might have prolonged the war for many months since the Third Reich, which had started to produce such planes in large quantities, could have acquired an advantage in the air at the beginning of 1945. Germany actually had a small advantage at the end of 1944, but it was squandered by Hitler's ill-conceived Ardennes offensive. The case of the turbo-jet plane is a good example of reckless risk-taking on each side neutralizing both – the result of too much power being concentrated in too few hands.

9. Eisenhower is supposed to have adopted the position that he would not read any file which was not summarized on one typewritten page and that anything which could not be thus summarized was not worth reading.

10. Zhukov writes in his memoirs: 'Stalin's merit [during the war] consisted in recognising immediately in a correct way experts' recommendations, in complementing, developing and generalising them – in the form of instructions, directives, rules – and transmitting them without delay to the leaders of the army in the field.' (vol. 1, p.360.)

11. Vannevar Bush, *Modern Arms and Free Men*, London 1950.

12. Benoist-Mechin, vol.2, pp. 258-9.

13. Peter Wyden asserts that some of the physicists working at Los Alamos considered themselves 'scientist-slaves'. Ignorance, excessive secrecy, lack of debate in 'high places' dominated this sad picture. 'In 1947, the project's top medical men

wrote a report saying their estimates about the tolerable radiation levels had been wrong guesses and that report was only discovered by accident in 1983 . . . . Although some US scientists still insist that the combined radiation deaths in Hiroshima and Nagasaki were limited to 1,000 or 2,000 people, American medical teams have determined that at least 20,000 (possible twice as many) sustained significant radiation damage. . . . In 1945, the top scientists at Los Alamos had a passionate debate about whether to recommend a demonstration of the bomb rather than use it in the war and Oppenheimer did not even report that debate to the White House before the decision was made to drop the bomb on Japan.' *Day One _ Before Hiroshima and After*, New York 1984.

14. In his farewell speech to his collaborators on the Manhattan Project on 2 November 1945, Robert Oppenheimer stated that since science's 'good purpose', born from the Renaissance, was to conquer 'the greatest possible power in order to control the world', the A-bomb was its 'inevitable product'. (A. Kimball Smith and Charles Weiner (eds.), Robert Oppenheimer, *Letters and Recollections.*) Oppenheimer's argument is a perfect *non-sequitur*. The only inevitable product of the endeavour to conquer nature is the knowledge of how to release atomic energy. Its use for destructive purposes is not inevitable: it is a product of a given social order (better: disorder), of a given form of social organization. This social organization results from the temporary inability of humankind rationally to control (conquer) *social* processes. It is because the social world – which is a part of the natural world – is itself *insufficiently* conquered that the atom bomb was produced – not because there was too much knowledge.

15. Robert E. Sherwood, p.153.

Chapter 9

1. Ilya Ehrenburg, vol. 3, p.8 of German edition. Alexander Werth confirms this measure, trying to apologise for it. (Werth, p.181).

2. The French poets Aragon and Eluard expressed this ideology most graphically in their often moving patriotic resistance compositions see, e.g., *La Rose et le Réséda*, where it is said that when the house is on fire only madmen pursue old quarrels. The class struggle as a 'quarrel' is a very revealing formula indeed!

3. Previous US military expansion in Mexico was not of an imperialist nature, at least not in the scientific sense of the term. But it obviously had a colonialist dimension and therefore harboured an aspect of ethnic (racialist) superiority. US imperialism's conquest of the Philippines at the turn of the century resulted in mass crimes against humanity, which were covered up by racism of a much cruder type.

4. Admiral Halsey is publically quoted to have said of the Japanes armed forces: 'We are drowning and burning the bestial apes all over the Pacific, and it is just as much pleasure to burn them as to drown them.' The US Army and Navy publicly displayed another of his sayings: 'Kill Japs, kill Japs, kill more Japs.' (Quoted in Richard J. Barnet, *Roots of War*, London 1973, p.46.) Halsey is supposed to have told a Washington journalists' dinner party: 'I hate Japs. I'm telling you men that if I met a pregnant Japanese woman, I'd kick her in the belly'. (*Politics*, August 1945, p.2.) 'We must hate with every fibre of our being; Lieutenant General Lesley J. McNair declared in a radio broadcast to the troops in November 1942. (Quoted in Barnet, ibid.)

5. 'Marxism cannot be reconciled with nationalism, be it even of the 'most just', 'purest', most refined and civilised brand.' Lenin, *Collected Works* vol. 20, p.34.

6. 'In many instances, the local 'boss' or his henchman achieved local recognition in this way [by supressing all criticism of the existing regime], and submission to them thus became unavoidable, because they could easily deny food, fuel and other necessities to a recalcitrant individual or family. Often the block association heads became petty tyrants and the position they held was resented . . . . In the urban centres in particular, the *tonarigumi* (ten-household-group) often created more friction than neighbourliness and there was a good deal of hostility against the system.' Kurt Steiner, *Local Government in Japan*, Stanford 1965, p.60. See also Guillain, pp.215-18.

7. Typical of Hitler's basically bourgeois ideology was his refusal in 1943 to extend the drafting into industry launched by Goebbels' 'total war' appeal to upper-class women. This was not *'standesgemäss*, (corresponding to rank), he bluntly stated. The best indicator of the capitalist nature of the Third Reich was the steep increase in profits which, for corporations alone, rose from 3 billion RM in 1933 to 14 billion RM in 1942-43 (gross profits). In the electrical and electrical equipment industry, net profits rose from 100 million RM in 1933 to 481 million RM in 1939, 594 million RM in 1940 and 645 million RM in 1941. Eichholtz, vol. 2, p.566.

8. Aristotle's sophisms on slavery in the first book of the *Politics* contain the same rationalizations. 'Natural' slaves are supposed to be 'naturally' inferior to their masters and devoid of the capacity for rational reasoning. The slave can have some form of virtue – contrary to pure animals, he has a soul – but his virtue consists in accepting submission to his master. Such rationalization belied horrendous crimes against humanity.

9. Another horrible precedent was the mass murder of prisoners of war and slaves (often women) by the Roman ruling class in public spectacles. The so-called gladiators were often forced to kill each other, a cruelty even the Nazis did not generalize.

10. When 'dissident' Soviet authors like Alexander Zinoviev and others now state that the Soviet authorities have actually succeeded in creating a new type of human being, *'homo sovieticus*', devoid of critical thought and reaction – a clear rationaliz- ation of their own inability to attract mass support in the USSR and an obvious nonsense – we have an ugly premonition that this is a first step towards justifying all kinds of barbaric treatment of these human beings, in the first place denying them full human and democratic rights.

11. Already, on 21 September 1939, Heydrich, second-in-command of the SS, stated that the 'primitive Poles' had to be incorporated into the labour process as migrant labourers, whereas the middle layers – intellectuals and other leading elements – had to be liquidated. (Ludolf Herbst, p.123.)

12. On recent sources on this action, see Gotz Aly *et al.*, *Aussenderung un Tod*, Berlin 1985.

13. Hitler publicly stated in his speech to the Reichstag of 30 January 1939: ' . . . if international finance Jewry inside and outside Europe succeeds in precipitating the peoples into war once more, the result will not be the bolshevisation of the earth, and thereby the victory of Jewry, but the destruction of the Jewish race in Europe'. In 1943, Goebbels used these same words in an editorial for his weekly *Das Reich*, adding: 'This is now happening'.

14. Trotsky predicted the physical extermination of the European Jews in his appeal of 22 December 1938 to American Jews, reprinted in the *Fourth International*, December 1945.

15. Heinrich Himmler, *Geheimreden 1933 bis 1945 und andere Ansprachen*, Munich 1974.
16. Report in the April 1945 *Bulletin of the Society for the Prevention of World War Three*, reproduced in *Politics*, May 1945, p.134.
17. J.C.G. Röhl and N. Sombart (eds.), *Kaiser Wilhelm II: New Interpretations*, Cambridge 1984.
18. The Nazi Minister of Justice (sic!) Thierack actually used the formula 'destruction through labour' (*Vernichtung durch Arbeit*) in one of his letters. Official documents indicate that 15,500 concentration camp inmates working for the SS firm *Deutsche Ausrüsstungswerke* performed forty million hours of work in 1943. In this time they produced goods valued at 23.2 million RM, for which they received 'consumption' totalling 13 Pfennigs an hour. (*Deutschland im 2. Weltkrieg*, vol. 4, pp. 415, 417, Berlin 1944.) Even that figures seems exagerated; other sources indicate a 'consumption' of 50 Pfennigs a day, 5 Pfennigs an hour! According to Herman Rauschning, before the war Hitler had already stated categorically: 'We have a duty to depopulate . . . whole tribes will have to be eliminated from Russia.' No less clear was his intention to create a 'modern class of slaves which must receive the benefit of illiteracy'. (*Gespräche mit Hitler*, p.124). As early as July 1941, the SS professor Mayer-Hetling actually worked out the notorious *Generalplan Ost*, which projected the 'freeing' of Russian soil to settle five million 'Germanic' people.
19. In fact, at the same time as the Auschwitz gas chambers and crematorium were working at full speed SS *Obergruppenleiter* Muller wrote: 'Every potential labourer (*Arbeitskraft*) counts!' Transport of concentration camp inmates, including Jews to specific factories and underground workshops was organized on a mass scale. Orders were given to kill immediately only those unable to work as unskilled labourers of average productivity. See the summary of the official Nazi documents in *Deutschland im 2. Weltkrieg*, Berlin 1982, vol.3, pp. 245-50.
20. Lev Kopelev, *No Jail for Thought*, London 1979, pp. 102-14.
21. Leopold Trepper, *Le Grand Jeu*, Paris 1975.

Chapter 10

1. Plan *Weiss*, to invade Poland on 1 September 1939, dates from 3 April of that year. On 23 May Hitler told his Chiefs of Staff that 'Danzig is not the subject of dispute at all. It is a question of expanding our living space in the East . . . . There will be war. Poland will be attacked at the first opportunity.' See the handwritten notes on this speech by Hitler's adjutant, Lieutenant-Colonel Schmundt, which were found among German papers captured by the Western allies. A provocative occupation of radio station Gleiwity and similar commando raids organized by the SS took place on 30-31 August, before the Polish government could even answer Hitler's ultimatum. So much for A.J.P. Taylor's assertion that Hitler was in no way set upon a war with Poland in the summer of 1939.
2. J.A.S. Grenville, *The Major International Treaties, 1914-1973*, London 1974, p. 349. Hitler and Stalin were fascinated by each other, as is revealed by many remarks up until the middle of 1944. A preliminary study of their relationship has been made by Sven Alard, *Stalin and Hitler*, Bern 1974. On 26 August 1942, Hitler said this of Stalin: 'I have a book about Stalin. It must be said that he is a colossal figure, an ascetic giant who, with iron fist, has bonded together the land of giants . . . freeing from all limits 200 million human beings, iron, manganese, nickel, oil. At the top, a

man who said: do you think the loss of thirteen million too much for a great idea?' *Monologe im Fuhrerhauptquartier 1941-44*, p.366.

3. On 10 September 1939 Molotov told von der Schulenburg, the German Ambassador to Moscow, that the Soviet government was surprised by the speed of the German military success in Poland. 'The Red Army, he said, had counted on several weeks, which now have been reduced to a few days.' 'Nazi-Soviet Relations 1939-42', in *Documents from the Archives of the German Foreign Office, Department of State*, Washington 1948, p.91.

4. The prevailing opinion in Stalinist circles at the time was that Stalin, not Hitler, had gained most from the Hitler-Stalin pact. Edgar Snow, for example, reported in January 1940 that 'Hitler was now in Stalin's pocket', and asserted that 'here [in Eastern Asia], as in Europe, Stalin holds the balance of power'. (Edgar Snow, 'Will Stalin Sell Out China?'; in P.E. Moseley (ed.), *The Soviet Union 1922-1962: A Foreign Affairs Reader*' New York 1963, pp. 155-6.) Trotsky was much nearer the mark when he wrote that as a result of the pact Stalin had become a prisoner of Hitler's strategic decisions.

5. No purely military explanation can be given for the fact that 90 fully armed units with 10,000 pieces of artillery and 2,500 tanks did not attack a weak German screen of a dozen divisions holding the Siegfried Line at the beginning of September 1939. According to the German Lieutenant-General Westphal, 'such an attack, launched before any considerable elements of the German army could be brought across from Poland, would almost certainly have carried the French to the Rhine with little trouble, and might well have seen them across the river.' (*The Fatal Decisions*, p.15.) The only possible explanation lies in deficient ideological, political and social leadership: outmoded military doctrine; total lack of self-confidence; fear of Hitler; fear of anti-militarist sentiments inside the French army; fear of revolution in Germany in case of the Third Reich's collapse; etc.. J.B. Duroselle points out that Gamelin had no real immediate offensive plan during 1939, despite the promises made to Poland, and that he could only hope that the front could be stabilised in Poland – a highly implausible prospect.

6. Different sources give the strength of the *Luftwaffe* in the West on the eve of the May 1940 offensive at around 3,000 planes, against which the French air force could marshal 1,300 and the RAF 1,000. (These figures do not include RAF reserves kept for the defence of Britain and the important French reserves in North Africa and the Middle East.) See Goutard, *op cit.*.

7. In a preface to a book by General Chauvineau (*Une invasion, est-elle possible?*, Paris 1939), Pétain wrote: 'Undoubtedly, there are ways of breaking down a hail of automatic gun-fire – namely, tanks and heavy artillery. But they are in short supply, my friends, and it takes a long time to move them into position. The shortage of such equipment holds back the offensive fronts, and their cumbersome nature enables the defenders to move up reserves, with an ease proportional to the narrowness of the offensive front.' In contrast to the German army, the French were certainly slow in putting their armour in line to attack in 1940.

8. General Gamelin, the Allied Commander-in-Chief, did not even have a direct two-way radio link to his field commanders nor a system of telephone lines to several of the army's headquarters. His instructions to General Georges, the commander of the North-Western front, for example, were sent by a daily messenger. (Deighton, *op.cit.*)

9. Despite information on heavy German concentrations in the Ardennes, indicating that the blow might be directed at the Centre and not the Northern front, the French stuck to their initial plans. There is no general agreement, however, among

the historians about exactly how much the French command knew of the *Panzer* movements. For contrasting views see William L. Shirer, *The Collapse of the Third Republic*, London 1972, and Len Deighton, *Blitzkrieg*.

10. Why did Hitler stop his armoured columns fifteen miles short of Dunkirk, thereby enabling the reembarkation of the British Expeditionary Force of 190,000 men and 139,000 French soldiers? Some argue that it was due to a political calculation – London had to be given a chance to save face for a negotiated settlement; others that Goering persuaded him that the *Luftwaffe* could mop up the BEF prior to reembarkation, whilst the *Panzers* had to be saved for a final onslaught on the French army. But in fact, it seems the decision was essentially technical; most of the armoured cars were in bad shape and had to be repaired.

11. The British aircraft industry easily replaced the airplanes lost throughout August and in the early part of September 1940. This confirms that Britain was still a formidable industrial power: in 1941 its aircraft production even surpassed Germany's.

12. Some Soviet authors deny the importance of the Battle of Britain and argue that only inconclusive aerial skirmishes took place over the British Isles in the summer of 1940; see for example, Pavel Jiline, *Ambitions et méprises du Troisième Reich*, Moscow 1972, pp.82-4. Solid German evidence about Operation Sea Lion and the key role attributed to the destruction of the RAF prior to the invasion of Britain makes this thesis untenable. Maisky, in his *Memoirs*, tells quite a different story.

13. Roosevelt calmly cabled Churchill on 1 May 1941: 'If additional withdrawals became necessary (in the Eastern Mediterranean, including North Africa and the Near East), they will all be part of the plan which at this stage of the war shortens British lines, greatly extends the Axis lines, and compels the enemy to expend great quantities of men and equipment.' (*Churchill and Roosevelt: The Complete Correspondence*, vo.1, p.179.) Roosevelt's attitude in part reflected wartime US self-sufficiency in oil.

14. On the terrible losses suffered by German paratroopers and glider formations over the Hague on 10 May 1940, see E.H. Brongers, *De Slag om de Residentie 1940*, Baarn 1968. In Crete, 6,500 of the 22,000 paratroopers committed were lost – the highest percentage of killed and wounded on the German side in any single battle of WWII, not excluding Stalingrad.

Chapter 11

1. On the different measures through which German industry and banks forced European capitalists to abandon all or part of their property, see Dietrich Eichholz, pp. 160-91. For the systematic appropriation of Soviet economic wealth by German monopolies, see ibid., pp. 460-90.

2. Germany used 2,740 airplanes for the invasion of the USSR. The Red Army had over 8,000 – of which, however, only 1,800 were modern craft. (Gruchmann, pp. 226-27). On the devastating effects of the *Luftwaffe* attack on the Red Army's airfields, see Erickson, pp. 113-14.

3. According to official German statistics, the German forces had also lost 1,812 tanks, 76,500 armoured cars, 3,838 airplanes, 2,700 guns, 16,000 machine guns and 86,000 horses by 1 November 1941. After the Battle of Moscow, the losses almost doubled, except in the category of airplanes. Eichholz, vo.2, p.42.

4. For the rapid re-building of Soviet field strength, see Erickson, p.251.

5. Halder wrote in his diary on 3 July 1941: 'It is no exaggeration to say that the campaign against Russia has been won in fourteen days.' The Ribbentrop statement is reported in Galeazzo Ciano, *Diario 1937-43*, Milan 1980, p.526.

6. R.E. Sherwood, pp. 303-04.

7. Hitler would later state: 'When I started Operation Barbarossa, I opened the door into a dark, unseen room'. It was his stark under-estimation of the economic potential and social cohesion of Soviet society, his belief in the 'bankrupcy of Bolshevism', in particular, which caused the surprise.

8. After adumbrating the statistics of the great material losses suffered by the Soviet Union after the German occupation of most of its European area, Erickson refers to the human dimension of the initial military defeat: 'The tally of almost three million prisoners of war in German hands and of the Red Army's strength falling to its lowest point in the whole war was lamentable proof of a persistent and ignorant profligacy with these once enormous armies and an almost soulless indifference to their fate.' (p.222.)

9. During WWII the USSR never recovered its pre-war industrial output, as is shown by the following table:

Soviet Output in Millions of Tons

	1940	1941	1942	1943	1944
pig iron	14.9	13.8	4.8	5.6	7.3
steel	18.3	17.9	8.1	8.5	10.9
coal	165.9	151.4	75.5	93.1	121.5
electrical power (billion of Kw)	48.3		29.1	32.3	39.2
grain	95.6	56.4	26.6	29.6	48.8
sugar beet	18.0	2.0	2.2	1.3	4.1
potatoes	76.1	26.6	23.6	35.0	54.8
milk and dairy products	6.5	5.3	2.9	2.4	2.7

(taken from Soviet sources by the East German publication *Deutschland im Zweiteu Weltkwig*, vol. 3, p. 467.)

10. In early October Sorge informed Stalin that the Japanese had irrevocably committed themselves to moving 'southwards' against the British and the Americans, allowing him to reduce the Soviet strength in the Far East by transferring some ten divisions, 1,000 tanks and 1,000 airplanes to the west.

11. Hitler and Mussolini jointly declared war on the USA and thereby provided the American administration with a necessary and valuable reason in the nation's eyes for the USA involving itself in the European conflict.

12. Hiroyuki Agawa, *Yamamoto, Chef de Guerre malgré lui*, Paris 1982, pp. 221, 231, 267 *et al.*

13. This was probably the result of insufficient intelligence regarding the size and composition of the US fleet. The suggestion that the Japanese Navy walked into a trap set by Roosevelt appears improbable in the light of the available evidence.

14. On 11 September 1941 the US Joint Chiefs of Staff submitted to Roosevelt a document signed by General Marshall and Admiral Stark which stated: 'Should Germany be successful in conquering all of Europe [i.e. in defeating Russia], she

might then wish to establish peace with the United States for several years for the purpose of organising her gains, restoring her economic situation, and increasing her military establishment, with a view to the eventual conquest of South America and the military defeat of the United States.' R.E. Sherwood, p.411.

15. *Churchill and Roosevelt: The Complete Correspondence*, vol.1, pp. 49-50.

16. At the start of the war Harry Truman, the future US President, formulated his view of American strategy with customary bluntness: 'If we see that Germany is winning the war, we ought to help Russia, and if Russia is winning, we ought to help Germany, and in that way kill as many as possible.' (Quoted in Barton J. Bernstein, 'Confrontation in Eastern Europe' in Thomas G. Paterson (ed.), p.93.)

17. The reputation of the British Army sank to its lowest in the summer of 1942. The loss of Benghazi in January and Rommel's successes in May and June, combined with defeat at the hands of the Japanese in the Far East, cast an all-pervasive gloom over Britain's leaders. In the United States there was 'a growing feeling that the British are absolutely incapable of exercising command or using equipment', which encouraged the opinion that the alliance with them should be scaled down and attention be switched to the Far East. (Christopher Thorne, pp. 132-34.) No wonder that Churchill ordered the church bells to be rung to celebrate the victory at El Alamein.

Chapter 12

1. At the Casablanca conference in January 1943, the British discovered that 'while their American colleagues were quite prepared to expound their plans for the Pacific theatre, they resolutely refused to discuss them. They were settled and not open to debate: the British had no *locus standi* in the matter'. Michael Howard, *Grand Strategy*, London 1972, vol.4, p. 243 (Quoted in Thorne, p.165.)

2. This was the time when American hostility to British-French-Dutch regulation of production and distribution of rubber, tin and oil was placing a serious question mark over the future relationship of the two sides of the Atlantic. This is not surprising given that the US derived ninety per cent of her crude rubber and seventy-five per cent of her tin from Malaya and the Dutch East Indies.

3. *New York Times* of 12 December 1941: The United States is 'the natural leader of the democratic forces'; *Chicago Tribune* of 10 January 1942: 'If there is to be a partnership between the United States and Great Britain we are, by every right, the controlling partner. We can get along without them.' Morgenthau: 'The United States, when the war is over, is going to settle . . . what kind of Europe it is going to be . . . Who is going to pay for it? We are going to pay for it. The English are going to be busted.'; Stimson: if the war is to be won it 'must be won on the morale and the psychology and courage of the American forces and leaders'; etc. etc.. (Quoted in Thorne, p.138.)

4. Thorne, pp.384-93.

5. *The Chicago Tribune* proclaimed on its front page: 'We are going back to Baatan!'. National hysteria following the expulsion of MacArthur's forces from the Philippines led to the arrest of thousands of Japanese Americans living on the West Coast and their internment in concentration camps.

6. 'In one of its vital aspects, the Pacific war of 1941 to 1945 was a racial war, and needs to be seen as such within a perspective of a hundred years or more. This is not to say that the immediate causes of conflict were essentially racial ones . . . . The skin colour of those involved was not a matter of primary significance. And yet, in its

wider setting, the war between Japan and the West did bring sharply into focus tensions of a racial nature that had long existed, with that aspect achieving much greater prominence once the battle had been joined. Time and time again . . . it was the threat to Western, white prestige that troubled those in power in Washington and London.' (Thorne, p.7.)

7. Storry, *A History of Modern Japan*, p.215. Halliday pp. 43, 47.

8. David H. James, *The Rise and Fall of the Japanese Empire*, London 1951, pp. 211-12.

9. Halliday, p.143.

10. See J.S. Furnivall (ed.), *Thakin Nu, Burma under the Japanese,*, London 1954.

11. On 25 January 1942, rather unwillingly, Thailand declared war on Britain and the United States. While USA ignored this declaration, Britain responded in kind, thus raising American suspicions of possible British territorial ambitions vis-à-vis Thailand, which were partially justified.

12. *The Second World War*, vol. 12, London 1964, p.85.

13. For an account of Cripps's mission to India, set in the context of the war as seen from London, see Addison, pp. 201-05.

14. The Congress leadership was strongly anti-Axis. It wanted Britain to win the war and it wanted to defend India by arming the population, a line which the British administration naturally resisted.

15. The Indian National Army never exceeded 50,000 soldiers, mostly recruited among the POWs taken by the Japanese at Singapore. It was mainly involved in skirmishes on the Burma-Indian frontier. Some of its cadres were later incorporated into the Indian Army.

16. Jawaharlal Nehru, *The Discovery of India*, London 1960, p.463.

17. Ibid., pp. 474-75.

18. Ibid., pp. 507-12. British sources give the lower figures of one and a half million, in itself high enough.

19. Attlee wrote in a memorandum to his Cabinet colleagues: 'India has been profoundly affected by the changed relationship between Europeans and Asiatics which began with the defeat of Russia by Japan at the beginning of the century. . . . The reverses which we and the Americans are sustaining from the Japanese at the present time will continue the process. . . . The fact that we are now accepting Chinese aid in our war against the Axis Powers and are necessarily driven to a belated recognition of China as an equal and of Chinese as fellow fighters for civilisation against barbarism makes the Indian ask why he, too, cannot be a master in his own house.' (Quoted in Thorne, p. 157.)

20. One British response was to set up in December 1942 a high-level inter-departmental committee, comprising officials from the Foreign Office, Dominions Office, Colonial Office, India Office and Ministry of Information to 'study the state of American feelings about the British Empire' and to make 'recommendations concerning the best methods of stimulating favourable and moderating hostile feelings with a view of securing a general sentiment sympathetic to the maintenance of the British imperial system and to recognition of the Empire as a suitable partner with the USA in world affairs.' Thorne, p.222.

21. Sherwood, pp. 498, 528; David Fraser, pp. 222-24; Lidell Hart, pp. 399-403.

22. Thorne, p.163.

23. Japan's anxiety that Germany was getting bogged down in Russia, and was therefore unable to pursue what Tokyo saw as the priority war against USA, was transmitted to the German naval attaché in Tokyo after the battle of Tunis in a warning that the loss of the Mediterranean would decisively strengthen Anglo-

American position in the Middle East and Burma, thereby destroying any hope of a negotiated peace with the Americans. *Deutschland in Zweitem Weltkrieg*, vol.3, p.449.

24. Erickson, pp. 337-38.

25. In August 1942, Beria and his 'boys' were sent to the Northern Caucasus and the Volga delta to prevent the incipient revolt of the highland nationalities: the Chechens, Ingushi, the Crimean Tartars, the Karachai, the Balkars, the Kalmyks and the Volga Germans were subsequently to pay a monstrous price for the Red Army's failings that summer.

26. At that time, distrusting his officers, Stalin had appointed political commissars, drawn largely from the NKVD, to supervise the field commanders and to punish the 'culprits' for the initial wave of defeats. As ever, Stalin's propensity for correcting his own errors of judgement by harsh punishment of subordinates and a search for scapegoats only added to the tragedy. Erickson, p. 175.

Chapter 13

1. The concept of 'total war' was originally elaborated by General Ludendorff in a book of the same title (Munich, 1935). Above all he stressed the necessity for a political leadership committed to – in fact, subordinate to – the war, and of ensuring moral and ideological stability on the home front. For Ludendorff, this was clearly one of the lessons of the 1914-18 war. General Ludwig Beck, former Chief of Staff of the *Wehrmacht*, and future head of the military conspiracy against Hitler on 20 July 1944, criticised Ludendorff's concept in a confidential speech delivered to a close circle of friends in June 1942 (later published in Ludwig Beck, *Studien*, Stuttgart 1955). Beck accused Ludendorff of reversing Clausewitz's relation between war and politics: a subordination of the latter to the former would lead to escalating violence for the sake of violence, making all negotiation and compromise between states impossible. The relevance of this critique to Germany's situation in the mid-1940s is obvious.

2. Darlan, Vichy's nominal representative in North Africa, was a committed collaborator with the Nazis – if anything more so than Laval. He signed an agreement with the Americans on 22 November 1942 according to which he would switch sides (i.e. support the Allied cause) in return for the Allies respecting his authority in North Africa and equipping his military forces. Benoist-Méchin, vol. 1, pp. 116-124; Durosell, pp. 286-7; Kolko, p. 66. Stalin approved the rehabilitation of Darlan. Maisky, p. 801; *Churchill and Roosevelt: The Complete Correspondence*, vol. 2, p. 51.

3. The Darlan and Giraud regimes were neo-fascist in character and rested upon an alliance of *colons* and local bankers and industrialists. Anti-semitic and brutally repressive of all but right-wing tendencies, Giraud's rule was unacceptable to all anti-Nazi and anti-fascist forces. Kolko, p.67.

4. 'The part that the Communists were playing in the resistance, as well as my own intention that their forces be incorporated with those of the nation at least for the duration of the war, led me to the decision to include two in the government. Since the end of August, the 'party', foreseeing this, had willingly promised the co-operation of several members. But, at the last moment, all kinds of setbacks kept those whom I invited to join the Committee of Liberation from giving me a positive

answer. . . . In reality, two viewpoints divided the delegation. The extremists, following André Marty, wanted the party to make no alliances and to prepare, in the midst of the struggle against the enemy, to seize power by direct revolutionary action. The tacticious wanted to infiltrate the state by collaborating with others, first of all with me. The originator of this strategy was Maurice Thorez . . . ' De Gaulle, *War Memoirs. Unity 1942-1944*, London 1959, pp. 154-55.

5. Though the untrained American troops had suffered a tactical defeat at Kasserine, the German army got itself trapped at Tunis with the loss of 300,000 soldiers, 200,000 of whom were taken prisoner. Von Tippleskirch, *Geschichte des 2. Weltriegs*, p.306.

6. Despite his success at El Alamein, Montgomery never succeeded in destroying the bulk of Rommel's forces which effected a relatively orderly retreat into Tunisia. Their fate was sealed, however, when Hitler refused Rommel's request for a rapid and surprise embarkation, a North African equivalent of Dunkirk.

7. *Istoriya Velikoi Otechestvennoi voiny Sovetskogo Soyza 1941-1945*, vol. 3, Moscow 1960, p.26. (Quoted by Erickson, p. 563).

8. V.I. Chuikov, *Nachalo puti*, (Quoted by Erickson, p.409.)

9. Von Trippelskirch, pp. 292-93.

10. Marshal Chuikov, *Stalingrad: la Bataille du Siècle*, Moscow 1982, p.14.

11. Von Manstein's own account (*Verlorene Siege*) exaggerates his role and importance in the sequence of events.

12. Chuikov, p.344. That the initial plan did indeed have the reconquest of Rostov as its main objective is confirmed by Churchill; see *Churchill and Roosevelt: The Complete Correspondence*, vol.2, p.39.

13. Gehlen's secret service transmitted a note on 12 November 1942, exactly one week before the Red Army's offensive at Stalingrad, in which an imminent attack against the 3rd Rumanian Army was predicted, but the Soviet forces were considered to be still too weak to launch an offensive on a broader front. (*Kriegstagesbuch des OKW*, vol.4, pp.1306-7.)

14. There exists an ample literature on the Battle of Midway. See, for example, Gordon W. Prange, *Miracle at Midway*, London 1983.

15. *The Japanese War Machine*, pp.171-72.

16. John Toland, *The Rising Sun*, pp. 131-142.

17. The Japanese Colonel Tsuji, who pressed for the reconquest of Guadalcanal is supposed to have said: 'I merit a thousand deaths.' Toland, p.151.

Chapter 14

1. The increasing importance of partisan activity behind the German lines in Russia throughout the operations of 1943-1944 should be emphasized. According to Paul Carell (*Verbrannte Erde*, Ulstein 1945, p.431), on the eve of the decisive Battle of Minsk, which started on June 22 1944, Soviet partisans interrupted the railway connections between the Dnieper and the area to the West of Minsk with 10,500 explosions. All telephone lines along the rail network were cut; the whole communications system of *Heeresgrupee Mitte* (Army Group Centre) was paralysed for nearly forty-eight hours; virtually all bridges were blown up.

2. Major-General F.W. von Mellenthin, *Panzer Battles*, London 1977, p.431.

3. *Kriegstagebuch des Oberkommandos der Wehrmacht*, vol. 6, pp. 798-99, 814-15, and especially 829-35.

4. The King and Badoglio immediately dramatized the 'Bolshevik danger' in

order to extract favourable armistice conditions from the Western Allies: 'The fascists have destroyed the middle classes. The Reds have massively come on to the streets in Milan and Turin. The King, and the patriots which group themselves around him, are the only force left to prevent rampant Bolsheviks from taking over,' Badoglio's envoy, Marchese d'Ajeta told the British Ambassador Campbell at Lisbon. (*Churchill and Roosevelt: The Complete Correspondence*, vol.2, p.380.)

5. On the whole sordid affair, see Ivan Palermo, *Storia di un armistizio*, Milano 1967.

6. The bungling of an excellent opportunity to conquer Rome immediately after the landing at Anzio on 22 January 1944, was a repetition.

7. By no means was this an intervention designed to make Italy 'communist'. On the contrary, when the Italian masses – and even a large part of American public opinion – demanded dismissal of the monarchy and Badoglio, Stalin came to their aid by sending an Ambassador to the Badoglio regime. (*Churchill and Roosevelt: The Complete Correspondence*, vol.3, p.42.) Togliatti was sent back to Italy to put a brake on the more radical wing of the CP and the more radical aspirations of the Italian masses. (See Paolo Spriano, *Storia del Partito Comunista Italiano*, vol. V, Torino 1975, pp. 54, 120-24.) Togliatti even entered the Badoglio government.

8. One should add that the Italian armistice, which excluded the Soviet Union from any political representation in the military government arrangements on the grounds that the Russian army was not actually present, became an important precedent for analogous exclusion of the Anglo-American allies from similar arrangements in Rumania, Bulgaria and Hungary, occupied only by the Red Army.

9. These are the statistics given by John Erickson, *The Road to Berlin*, pp. 97-121. Marshall Babadjanian gives slightly lower tank figures for the Red Army (in *La Bataille de Koursk*, Louis Perroud ed. Moscow 1975, p.138.)

10. Von Mellenthin (pp. 262-263) indicates that there was a strong difference of opinion on the advisability of the whole *Operation Citadel* between von Manstein, who proposed it, and Guderian, who opposed it from the start. Hitler wavered, taking an intermediate position. His hesitations, refusal to commit sufficient reserves and decision to withdraw forces to oppose the landing in Sicily, are quoted by Manstein as reasons for the final failure of the operations. (*Verloren Siege*, pp. 504-06.)

11. It is interesting to note that the Battle of Kursk provides negative confirmation of the importance of surprise in attempts at massive breakthroughs by armoured forces. The Soviet High Command was well aware of the time and place at which Operation Citadel would occur, thanks to information received from its master-spy Rossler, operating out of Switzerland, who had access to the *Oberkommando der Wehrmacht* on a daily basis. The failure of the disastrous Stalin-Timoshenko offensive in Kharkov in May 1942 resulted from a similar lack of surprise, the *Fremde Heere Ost* having 'turned' a Soviet commissar, Mishinkshkii.

12. Erickson, *The Road to Berlin*, pp. 137-45.

13. In a letter sent to Stalin on 20 June 1943 Churchill stated: 'Already we are holding in the west and south of Europe the larger part of the German air forces and our superiority will increase continually. Out of a first-line operational strength of between 4,800 and 4,900 aircraft, Germany according to our information has today on the Russian front some 2,000, compared with some 2,500 this time last year. We are also ruining a large part of the cities and municipal centres of Germany, which may well have a decisive effect by sapping German resistance on all fronts.' (*Churchill and Roosevelt: The Complete Correspondence*, vol. 2, p.267).

14. In the last months of 1944 the Politz plant produced up to three-quarters of the

200

German output of aircraft fuel was destroyed on 19 January 1945 and all gasoline production was stopped. Reserves were down to 12,000 t., while current needs were 40,000 t. a month. The situation was similar for gasoline used by motor vehicles. *Kriegstagebuch des OKW,*, Vol. 8, pp. 1317-1319.

15. *The Effects of Strategic Bombing on the German War Economy*, Overall Economic Effects Division, United States Strategic Bombing urvey, Washington D.C., p.2.

16. *Deutschland im 2. Weltkrieg*, Berlin, 1984, p. 140.

17. It is significant that carpet bombing of towns like Hamburg, Cologne, Munich, Essen and Frankfurt was largely concentrated on working-class districts. Bourgeois residential areas were generally spared. Rumour has it that direct contacts in Lisbon between German and US agents were partially responsible for these options.

18. As has already been indicated in chapter 3, these fears had a basis in reality. The conspirators of 20 July 1944 wanted to establish a military dictatorship in Germany – with a rigid state of siege and a strict prohibition on strikes and even the distribution of leaflets – for the same reason. (See *Spiegelbild einer Verschwörung* pp. 61, 70, *et al.*) A memorandum by Stauffenberg stated categorically: 'Bolshevik policy towards the Reich is favoured by the fact that similarities in the political and economic edifice exist together with an obviously different social structure. Moreover, the socialist working class, the radicalized German youth, and the presence of twelve million foreign workers in the Reich created a truly fertile soil.' (Ibid., p.34.)

19. Dick Wilson, *When Tigers Fight*, London 1982, pp. 227-30. Stillwell's second Burmese offensive, while tactically successful, dangerously depleted Chinese potential in Central China and led to Chiang Kai-shek's forces suffering great defeats in 1944.

20. The Pacific War Research Society, *The Day Man Lost*, Tokyo 1981, p. 47, ... Gluchmann, *Der . . . Welkreig*, pp. 405,09.

21. MacArthur considered Leyte Gulf to be the decisive turning-point of the war in the Pacific, but admitted that the Imperial Navy had come within an inch of destroying the American beachhead when Admiral Kurito prematurely withdrew his fleet. (*Reminiscences*, pp. 248, 255-57, 263-65.)

Chapter 15

1. Kesselring's military plans were aided by advance knowledge that the Italian ruling class was preparing a reversal of alliances as well as by the American commanders' hesitation and ineptitude following the landing at Salerno. Even before Mussolini's downfall, the *Wehrmachführungsstab* had prepared the *Alarich* and *Konstantin* plans which implied an occupation of Italy and Italian-held territories by the German Army.

2. In actuality, the surrender of German troops in Italy did not lead to their immediate dispersal or departure, since the Allies intended that they should hold the fort against any takeover by the Resistance until their own arrival. The German army was therefore ordered to stay put, to 'maintain in operation all public utility and essential civil services' and, with the aid of the CLNAI, provide for 'the general maintenance of law and order'. ('Instrument of Local Surrender of German and Other Forces Under Command or Control of the German Commander-in-Chief Southwest', Appendix A, in Modern Military Records Division, National Archives, Alexandria, Va. USA, quoted in Kolko, p. 385.)

3. On the superiority of German weapons in Normandy, see Max Hastings,

Overlord, New York 1984, pp. 186-95.

4. Rommel understood that time would be on the Allies' side if they were permitted to establish sufficiently deep beachheads to allow troops, tanks and armour
to concentrate on the spot. Von Rundstedt, on the other hand, was correct in
thinking that the Allies would take some time to disentangle themselves from the
initial problems – a period in which smaller counter-moves could be planned with
great efficiency. Hastings, pp. 283-86; Kurt von Tippelskirsch, *Geschichte des
zweiten Weltkriegs*, Bonn 1951, pp. 435-36.

5. Quoted in Liddel Hart, pp. 583-84.

6. Ibid., pp. 283-86; David Frazer, pp. 438-46; Geoffrey Powel, *The Devil's
Birthday*, London 1984. For the German version of events, see *Kriegstagesbuch des
Oberkommandos der Wehrmacht*, vol.7, pp. 391-93.

7. Warlimont, *Inside Hitler's Headquarters*, pp. 487-88. (Quoted in Kolko, p.371.)

8. Churchill wrote to Roosevelt on 28 June 1944: 'General Wilson . . . General
Alexander . . . and Field-Marshal Smuts . . . put before us the prospect of an
attack eastward across the Adriatic . . . and General Wilson conceived it possible
that, on this plan, he and General Alexander could have possession of Trieste by the
end of September.'

9. Erickson, *The Road to Berlin*, pp. 289-90. In the preceding passage the author
recounts Stalin's cynical cat-and-mouse game with the *Armija Krajowa* and the
Mikolayczik government. The leader of the uprising has given his own version of it
in T. Bor-Komorovski, *Histoire d'une armée sécrète*, Paris 1952. After years of
slander, official Polish and Soviet historiography has now largely rehabilitated the
Warsaw uprising and its participants.

10. Erickson, p.514.

11. Ibid., p. 426.

12. General Gavin, On to Berlin, New York 1979, pp. 310-11.

13. Ibid 312. the author gives a twenty-three page summary of the dispute which
arose in SHAEF over whether or not to advance on Berlin.

14. Quoted in Thorne, p. 593.

15. R. Heiferman, in *The Japanese War Machine*, pp. 195-207.

16. Roosevelt always made clear his aversion to becoming involved militarily to any
great extent on the Asian mainland: 'fighting on the mainland of China we must
leave to the Russians'. Stimson told Marshal that he 'did not think the country
would stand for' the despatch of large numbers of troops to China. (Thorne, p.523.)
R.E. Sherwood confirms this: 'MacArthur's calculations were based on the assumption that the Russians would contain the great bulk of the Japanese forces on the
Asiatic mainland . . . the entry of the Soviet Union . . . into the Japanese war by
midsummer . . . could mean the saving of countless American lives.' (Sherwood,
p.86.) In the Far East, as in Europe, the final settlement was essentially a Soviet-
American affair. See also Stettinius, *Roosevelt and the Russians*, London 1950.

17. Stettinius, *Roosevelt and the Russians*; Forrestal Diaries, pp. 55, 74, 78-9.

18. Truman's *Memoirs*, vol. 1, Garden City 1955, pp. 439-44. The division of the
country for purposes of military occupation only was discussed at Yalta and
Potsdam: the December 1945 Moscow conference decided on a four-power trustee-
ship 'to prepare Korea for independence within five years'. For the complex
conflicts leading up to the political and social division of the country in 1948-49, see,
inter alia, McNair and Lach, pp. 622-31.

19. 'Byrnes had already told me that the weapon might be so powerful as to be
potentially capable of wiping out entire cities and killing people on an unprecedented scale. And he added that it was his belief the bomb might well put us in a

position to dictate our own terms at the end of the war.' Truman, p.87.

20. 'Most historians now agree, in retrospect, with the conclusion of the US Strategic Bombing Survey: namely that Japanese would have surrendered without the use of atomic bomb and without invasion. . . . In the middle of June (1945) . . . six members of the Japanese Supreme War Council authorised Foreign Minister Togo to approach the Soviet Union 'with a view to terminate the war if possible by September'. At this time the Emperor himself became personally involved in the efforts . . . '. Gar Alperowitz, 'The Use of the Atomic Bomb' in Thomas G. Patersen (ed.), p.55.

21. On the alternative possibilities of using the A-bomb in a purely demonstrative way, see Peter Wyden, *Day One*. On military diehards, see the compilation by the Pacific Research Society published in Japan in 1965 and translated into English under the title, *Japan's Longest Day*, New York 1972.

22. MacArthur, pp. 300-01.

23. *The Day Man Lost*, p.87.

Chapter 16

1. Other Nazi leaders, *Wehrmacht* chiefs, and the 20 July 1944 conspirators all had a more realistic estimate of the military outcome than Hitler. Generals Olbricht and Stülpnagel stated in mid-June 1944 that given Allied superiority in the West, their breakthrough to Paris within six weeks was unavoidable – which is precisely what happened. They also said that if there was no rapid capitulation, the Russian army would arrive on German soil, and Germany was in danger of being occupied and broken up. Hans-Adolf Jacobsen (ed.), *Spiegelbild einer Verschwörung*, Stuttgart 1984, pp. 136, 98 *passim*. (This volume contains the minutes of the interrogations of the July conspirators.)

2. In the spring of 1944 Goebbels himself proposed to Hitler that peace be made with Stalin, on the basis of Rumania, Bulgaria, Greece, Finland, the Baltic republics and Poland east of Poznan reverting to the Soviet sphere of influence. Hitler did not react. Dr. Rudolf Semmler, *Goebbels*, Amsterdam n.d., pp. 135-37. The Japanese and Mussolini also advocated peace with the USSR in 1943. (*Deutschland im zweiten Weltkrieg*, vol. 3, pp. 454-55, 423.)

3. Robert E. Sherwood, p.710.

4. Vojtech Mastny, *Russia's Road to the Cold War*, New York 1979, pp. 133-39.

5. The devious game played by Western Allies with the German surrender is described by Kolko, pp. 382-88. Erickson is less than accurate on this point.

6. Diane Shaver Clemens, *Yalta*, Oxford 1970.

7. Ludolf Herbst, pp. 21, 437, 352 *passim*. Ohlendorf had been a commander of one of the SS *Einsatzgruppen* in Russia charged with mass killing of Jews, Communists, partisans, etc. He was executed by the Allies as a war criminal in 1946.

8. Herbst, pp. 458-59.

9. David Frazer, p.451.

10. The Soviet *diktat* occurred despite the very real contribution of the Rumanian army to the final onslaught on Hungary and Austria in which 600,000 Rumanian soldiers participated and in which 120,000 of them died. In exchange Rumania was allowed to recover Transylvania.

11. In 1938 Eastern Europe (excluding the Soviet Union) produced only eight per cent of Europe's total industrial output, and of this small share a third was due to

Czechoslovakia. Rothschild, p. 15.

12. For Soviet and British attempts to get a foot in the door by diplomatic means, see *Forrestal Diaries*, New York 1951, p.68 *passim*, Also Thorne, pp. 655-56.

13. Talking to the US Ambassador Harriman in June 1944, Stalin agreed that Chiang Kai-Shek was the only man who could hold China together. 'He reaffirmed his opinion that Chaing Kai-Shek was the best man under the circumstances, and must therefore be supported . . . He said that the United States should and could take the leadership in this field (China), for neither Great Britain nor the Soviet Union could. We should, he suggested, bring Chaing Kai-Shek more fully under our influence . . . ' Herbert Feis, *The China Triangle*, New York 1967, pp. 140-41.

14. On the conflict in Iran, see Bruce R. Kuniholen, *The Origins of the Cold War in the Near East*, Princeton 1980. Not only was there a *de facto* occupation of Iran in 1941 by Soviet and British troops, but also sordid attempts by the Kremlin to extract oil concessions from a weak and disarmed Iranian government. On the other hand, there seems to have been a genuine attempt by them to instal a 'people's democracry' in Tabris in 1945-46 – an attempt which was abandoned when Truman intervened with direct military threats.

15. On the independent shop-steward and workers' council activities in East Germany and Czechoslovakia, see Benno Sare, *La classe ouvrière d'Allemagne orientale*, and Jiri Kosta, *Abriss der Sozialökonomischen Entwicklung der Tchechoslovakei 1945-1977*, Frankfurt 1978, pp. 43-4.

16. Some of these developments flowed from the huge Japanese victories of 1941-42, which inflicted crushing blows to the prestige of Western imperialism among the Asian masses – something from which it never recovered. This greatly increased the masses' self-confidence and spurred on the post-war uprisings, some of which were deliberately prepared for by sectors of the Japanese warlords. Jon Halliday (*op cit.*, especially pp. 324-30) provides a good summary, with a large and useful bibliography. He nevertheless overstates the case when he asserts a basic difference between the attitudes of Japanese and Western imperialism towards the Asian masses. This judgement seriously underestimates the degree of Japanese racism towards non-Japanese Asian peoples (to begin with, the Koreans and the Chinese – but by no means only them) and the terrible plunder and hardship imposed by Japanese occupation in all occupied territories, including Indonesia and Burma, where their initial arrival had been greeted with popular support. This support was invariably lost as a result of the harsh exploitation they imposed, political propaganda and promises notwithstanding.

Chapter 17

1. For a long time Communist authors condemned the Marshall Plan as detrimental to the European (capitalist) economy. A tacit revision of this thesis is now underway. Thus the Belgian CP's ex-MP Nagels stresses in *Un contre-projet pour l'Europe* (Bruxelles 1979) that the Marshall Plan was of crucial importance in relaunching the capitalist economy in Western Europe.

2. *The Time for Decision*, Cleveland 1944, p.332. See David Horowitz, *From Yalta to Vietnam: American Foreign Policy in the Cold War*, New York 1965. Welles, however, qualified this statment by insisting on 'non-interference in the internal affairs of the European countries'. This constituted a totally self-contradictory combination. In fact 'the inter-American system' Welles gave as an example precisely implied constant and oppressive 'interference' in the 'internal affairs' of Latin

American countries. The same obviously applied to the axiom that the East European governments should be 'cooperative and well-disposed' to the USSR.

3. It was at the Moscow meeting with Stalin in October 1944 that Churchill pencilled his famous notes dividing up the Balkans and Eastern Europe into spheres of influence. It worked as follows: Rumania: 90% USSR, 10% Britain; Bulgaria: 75% USSR, 25% Britain; Greece: 10% USSR, 90% Britain; Czechoslovakia, Hungary and Yugoslavia: 50% USSR, 50% Britain. These percentages were subsequently changed in tortuous sessions between Eden and Molotov. Churchill, *The Second World War*, vol.6, London 1954, p.227.

4. Admiral Leahy's reflections on the emergency meeting held at the White House to prepare for discussions with Molotov who arrived in Washington on 22 April 1945. Truman was unusually blunt at the subsequent meeting with Molotov, who then complained: 'I have never been talked to like that in my life.' Yergin, p.83.

5. Bulgaria unlike Hungary or Rumania, never sent its troops into the Soviet Union but employed them for occupation of the neighbouring states. The Red Army simply walked into Bulgaria; not a shot was exchanged between Soviet and Bulgarian units.

6. According to Alanbrooke's diary, Churchill told him: 'We now had something in our hands which would redress the balance with the Russians. The secret of this explosive and the power to use it would completely alter the diplomatic equilibrium which was adrift since the defeat of Germany.' (Quoted in Yergin, p.120.)

7. Ibid., p.117. At Potsdam, Churchill was replaced by Attlee, the new Prime Minister, and Eden by Bevin – without any change in the political direction of the conference. 'Only the English, with their fantastic capacity for empiricism, could possibly have admitted a man like Attlee to the Socialist ranks', the French Foreign Minister Bidault subsequently wrote.

8. The Treasury finally had its way against the Foreign Office on the question of Greece. Thanks to bad weather and the fuel crisis that winter, the British finally decided to 'put an end to our endless dribble of British taxpayers' money to the Greeks'. It was their intention 'to present the matter (of Greece) in Washington in such a manner as to incite the Americans to assume responsibility'. (Yergin, p.280.) And this was indeed what happened: 'The Americans took fright lest Russia should overrun the whole of the Balkans and the Eastern Mediterranean. The Treasury officials told me afterwards that they never thought that the effect would be so quick and so volcanic.' (Dalton, quoted by Yergin, pp.280-81.)

9. Quoted in ibid., p.281.

10. Ibid.

11. Ibid., p.283.

12. *The Observer*, 3 April 1944.

13. The Soviet Union's demand for reparations must be set against the background of Hitler's 'scorched earth' policy in Belorussia and the Ukraine. In three typical *Wehrmacht* orders (21 December 1941, 30 August 1943, 7 September 1943) it was stated that all villages were to be burnt, regardless of the consequences for the inhabitants; all food and agricultural tools taken away; all the fields destroyed; all food production made impossible; and all industrial, handicraft and transportation equipment removed. Paul Carell, *Verbrannte Erde*, pp. 463-65, 293-95.

14. The US Ambassador to Moscow, Harriman, cabled the State Department in January 1945 that the Soviet Union placed 'high importance' on a substantial post-war credit as a basis for the development of Soviet-American relations. 'From his (V.M. Molotov's) statement, I sensed an implication that the development of our friendly relations would depend upon a generous credit.' A formal request for a

six billion dollars credit was made on 3 January 1945. But on 23 April Truman told Molotov explicitly in Washington that economic aid would depend on a satisfactory settlement of the Polish question. (Thomas G. Paterson, 'Foreign Aid as a Diplomatic Weapon', in *op. cit.* (ed.), pp. 69, 70, 72.)

15. It is of course shocking – and reflects Bevin's historical responsibility – that the same party which in Britain stood for nationalization of coal and steel, resisted their nationalization in the Ruhr, even though the owners had been among the main financial supporters of the Nazis and had profited heavily from their policy of plundering Europe and importing forced labour on a massive scale into Germany.

16. The KPD received ten per cent of the popular vote in the regional elections in West Germany in 1946-7. It had three hundred thousand members and held important positions throughout the country in local unions and among the shop stewards.

17. The German working class in both Eastern and Western zones of occupation was strongly in favour of suppressing private property in the means of production. In the spring of 1946 a referendum was held in Soviet-occupied Saxony and American-occupied Hessen on the question of nationalization of basic industries. 77.7% in the former and 72% in the latter voted in favour of expropriating the capitalists. Commenting on Stalin's desire to see German heavy industry dismantled, Isaac Deutscher wrote: 'He could not have been unaware that his scheme, as chimerical as ruthless, if it had been carried out, would have entailed the dispersal of the German working class, the main, if not the only, social force to which communism could have appealed and whose support it might have enlisted'. (Deutscher, *Stalin*, Harmondsworth 1982, p.523.) Stalin's whole strategy towards Europe, was of course, premised on deep distrust, especially of the German working class.

18. In April 1945 Stalin told Tito and Djilas in Moscow: 'This war is not as in the past; whoever occupies a territory also imposes on it his own social system. Everyone imposes his own system as far as his army has power to do so.' (Djilas, *Conversations with Stalin*, Harmondsworth 1963, p.90.) Trotsky had written as early as 1939: 'As I am writing these lines the question of the territories occupied by the Red Army still remains obscure. . . . It is more than likely that in the territories scheduled to become a part of the USSR, the Moscow government will carry though the expropriation of the large landowners and statification of the means of production. This variant is most probable not because the bureaucracy remains true to the socialist program, but because it is neither desirous nor capable of sharing the power, and privileges the latter entails, with the old ruling classes in the occupied territories.' ('The USSR in War', 25 September 1939, in Leon Trotsky, *In Defence of Marxism*, New York 1942, p.18.)

19. According to Jacques Hannak, in Austria Renner, who was installed as President, and under whom a coalition government was set up with CP participation as soon as the Red Army entered Vienna, actually succeeded in fooling Stalin. Stalin thought that he had a blackmailer's hold on the old social-democratic leader. The fact that Renner had publicly called for support for the *Anschluss* during the 1938 referendum possibly played a role in this wager. But Renner correctly judged that the Austrian masses were not interested in his behaviour of seven years ago, but would judge him by the way he defended Austria's independence against the Soviet occupation forces here and now. This is what happened. At first, Renner accepted a Communist as Minister of the Interior in the coalition government. But when the CP suffered a crushing defeat in the elections of 25 November 1945, the Communist was replaced by the social-democratic Helmer, who easily prevented a CP take-over

in connection with the strike wave of 1947. (Jacques Hannak, *Kark Renner und seine Zeit*, Wien 1965, pp. 669-87.) It is interesting to note that in their systematic opposition to coalition governments with Communist participation in Eastern and Central Europe, the British and American imperialists strongly protested the creation of the Renner provisional government by the Soviets, only to revise their judgement afterwards. It is true that 'afterwards' they had their own armed forces in Austria.

20. Robert E. Sherwood, pp. 400-01, 710, 713, 715-16 *et al*.

21. Several Soviet authors – as well as some authors in the West – tend to exagerate this matter. In fact, Hitler had first withdrawn crack divisions from the Eastern front to make the Ardennes offensive possible. All available evidence confirms that the offensive had already ended – in the first place because of a lack of fuel for the German tanks – and the Americans had already gone over to a counter-offensive, before the Red Army attacked the Oder front or before any German divisions were withdrawn from the Western to the Eastern front.

22. The difference made by the American troops in Europe is well illustrated by the crisis over Trieste in mid-May 1945. When the Yugoslav partisan army tried to extend its occupation of that zone, Truman asked Eisenhower through General Marshall to send three divisions to the Brenner Pass or above Trieste. Marshall answered that Eisenhower was ready to send five divisions. Truman asked Admiral King to have the US Navy steam into the Adriatic. General Arnold told Truman that several air force squadrons were ready to move at a moment's notice. Truman cabled all this to Stalin, and the crisis was solved. Truman, *Memoirs*, vol.1, pp. 249-50.

23. Attlee's intervention against MacArthur's plan to use the atom bomb in Korea after the massive defeat of the US forces at the hands of the Chinese People's Liberation Army was probably one of the key factors preventing its legitimation after Hiroshima and Nagasaki.

Chapter 18

1. On this subject, see Ernest Mandel, *Late Capitalism*, London 1976 and *The Long Waves of Capitalist Development*, Cambridge 1981.

2. It should not be forgotten that throughout the 1930s many European countries' industrial production indexes or their average real wages stood below the 1913 level.

3. During the bombing of Indochina by the US air force in 1964-73, three times as much destructive power was unleashed as during the whole of World War II in both Europe and Asia and during the Korean War: 7.5 million tons of bombs, including 400,000 tons of napalm.

4. According to Amnesty International, torture is today regularly practised (i.e. institutionalised) in more than fifty countries.

5. Joseph Schumpeter, *Zur Soziologie der Imperialismen* (1919) published in English in 1951 under the title *Imperialism and Social Classes*.

6. See, for example, *The Road to Serfdom* (1944).

7. This was of course rendered inevitable by the irreparable damage done by the Second World War to the finances, merchant marine and navy of British imperialism. In a very telling document, (cited in Howard, *Grand Strategy*, pp. 632-36), British authorities stated in March 1943 that 'while the United Nations shipping position is improving and likely to continue doing so, the British import position is becoming steadily worse'. In 1937, Great Britain imported nearly five million tons a

month. This figure dropped to two and a half million tons at the end of 1940 and the beginning of 1941, to two million tons in the summer of 1942, and to one and a quarter million tons between November 1942 and February 1943. In 1941 stocks of food and raw materials other than oil had been built up to four million tons above minimum safety level. In April 1943, they were one million tons below that 'bedrock minimum'. As for the financial situation, it was even worse. British foreign holdings had practically been liquidated. Its dollar balances were below $ one billion.

8. E. Mandel, *The Second Slump*, 3rd edition, London 1986.

9. On the post-war strike wave in the USA, see Jeremy Brecker, *Strike*, San Francisco 1972.

10. The liquidation of the British Empire in India offers striking confirmation of Plekhanov's application of historial materialism to the question of the role of individual in history. He asserts that when the historical need (class interest) for a certain type of personality arises, events will produce it – in fact, will produce several of them. To handle the withdrawal from India as smoothly as possible, British imperialism had at its disposal not only a 'left Labour Lord', scion of a noble family and friend of Nehru and Gandhi – Sir Stafford Cripps – but also a scion of the royal family itself, Lord Mountbatten. David Cannadine summarizes his role quite adequately: 'His progressive views, his experience East of Suez, and his close links with the king-emperor himself, made him the ideal man for ending British rule in India in 1947 . . . . When he was born, Queen Victoria was on the throne, the British Empire was the largest the world had ever known, and the pound was worth not only twenty shillings but also five dollars. When he died, Mrs. Thatcher was at 10 Downing Street, the British Navy was but a shadow of its old self, the British Empire had disintegrated into the Commonwealth, and the pound was worth less than two dollars'.

Index

(Battles in *italic*.)